The New World Order Threatens America and the World

Frank de Varona

ALEXANDRIA LIBRARY PUBLISHING HOUSE

MIAMI

The picture on the cover is the main building and the headquarters of the Bank for International Settlements. It is an 18-story circular skyscraper that arises over city of Basel, Switzerland. The building was constructed in 1977 and is called the Tower of Basel.

The building is completely air-conditioned and self-contained. It has a nuclear bomb shelter in the basement, a private hospital, and some 20 miles of subterranean archives. From the top floor of the Tower of Base there is a panoramic view of Germany, France, and Switzerland.

The Bank for International Settlements is the central bank of the central banks of 60 nations. Similar to the Federal Reserve Bank, central banks of the world are mostly private banking cartels that dominate and control their governments. It is for this reason that the writer chose the picture of the Bank for International Settlements as representing the New World Order.

www.alexlib.com

info@alexlib.com - 305-469-6797

To the memory of my parents,
Norma Cubría de León and
Jorge Luis de Varona Ortiz,
to my brother Jorge and to my sister Norma
and to the two most important
women in my life,
my wife, Haydée, and my daughter, Irene,
to her husband Mark and to my grandson,
Daniel Francisco.
May God grant all of them the privilege
to live in a free, prosperous, and democratic
United States

Table of Contents

About the Author

Frank de Varona is an educator, historian, journalist, and internationally known expert on politics, economics, foreign affairs, and national security issues. He was an Associate Professor in the Curriculum and Instruction Department, College of Education, at Florida International University (FIU) from 1997 to 2004. During his seven years at FIU, he taught many graduate and undergraduate courses and supervised social studies student teachers in secondary schools.

Frank de Varona was born in Camagüey, Cuba in 1943 but his ties to the United States are very strong. One of his ancestors, Vasco Porcallo de Figueroa, came as Lieutenant Governor of La Florida and Lieutenant General of the expedition of Hernando De Soto in 1539. Later, his ancestor, the Spanish conquistador, returned to Cuba. His son went on with De Soto's army and explored ten Southern states. Unlike Hernando De Soto, he survived the expedition and returned to his father in Cuba.

Professor de Varona's great aunt, Mercedes Cubria, came to live in the United States at the age of six. She joined the Women Army Corps (WACs) during World War II as a second lieutenant. Mercedes Cubria served in the Army with distinction during the Second World War, the Korean War, and the Cold War as an intelligence officer. She retired from the Army as a highly decorated Lieutenant Colonel.

At the age of 17, Frank de Varona participated in the Bay of Pigs invasion in 1961 along with his brother Jorge and several cousins in an effort to eradicate communism in Cuba. After the defeat, the 1,220 captured freedom fighters from the Assault Brigade 2506, who fought bravely against tens of thousands enemy soldiers, were sentenced to a 30-year prison term and served two years. All the captured prisoners of the Brigade 2506 were tortured, denied sufficient food and medicine, and had no access to medical doctors or dentists while in prison. Frank de Varona contracted dysentery and hepatitis, along with other prisoners, from drinking polluted water with dead rats in it at the Castillo del Príncipe prison in Havana. The last seven months of imprisonment for Frank de Varona and his brother Jorge were sent to the Isle of Pines prison. They were placed in a small room with 214 other prisoners without soap, toilet paper, toothpaste and fed rotten food. When Frank de Varona came back to Miami as a result of the negotiations between the Kennedy administration and the Cuban bloody regime, he had lost 60 pounds.

Frank (Francisco) de Varona and his brother Jorge appeared in the communist newspaper *Hoy* on May 3, 1961. The article said that the two brothers were the sons of the landowner (cattle rancher) Jorge Luis de Varona and that everyone should denounce any crime committed by these landowners' mercenaries. By that time, all the properties, cattle, homes, bank accounts, cars, etc. had been confiscated from their parents and they were very poor.

When Frank de Varona returned to the United States, he continued his education and received a Bachelor's degree in political science and economics and a certificate in Latin American Studies from the University of Florida in 1966. He earned a Master's degree in social studies at the University of Miami in 1969 and a Specialist in Education degree in educational administration and supervision at the University of Florida in 1976. He completed additional graduate work at the University of Florida, Florida International University, and Boston University.

From April to August 1966 and during the summer of 1968, Mr. de Varona worked as an escort interpreter for the U.S. State Department. In this position, he traveled with Latin American professionals from many fields throughout the United States. One of the visitor participants, Jorge Sánchez Méndez, became Minister of Industry and Vice President of Costa Rica.

Republican presidential candidate Senator Bob Dole talked with Frank de Varona in Orlando, Florida.

Professor de Varona had a distinguished 37-year career in the Miami-Dade County Public Schools (M-DCPS) as a social studies teacher; intergroup relations specialist; assistant principal; coordinator of adult education; principal of an adult education center, middle school, and senior high school; region director for personnel and labor relations; region superintendent; associate superintendent responsible for the pre-kindergarten through 12th grade, adult, and vocational curriculum and for the direct supervision of alternative, magnet, community, and adult and vocational schools, public radio and television, and student services; and interim deputy superintendent of schools for federal programs, equal education opportunity, food service, and transportation.

Secretary of Education Shirley Hufsteader and Florida Commissioner of Education Ralph Turlington visited Miami Edison Senior High School and Principal Frank de Varona showed them around in 1980.

President Carter and Congressman Claude Pepper visited Miami Edison High School in 1980. They appeared in the photo with Principal Frank de Varona and his Assistant Principal Harold Lannon.

Professor de Varona retired from M-DCPS, the fourth largest school district in the United States, in February 2012. On February 2013, Mr. de Varona returned to work as a part-time adult education coordinator with M-DCPS and retired for the last time in February 2014. Upon his retirement, he continued his career as a journalist and writer in Miami, Florida, where he lives with his family.

Professor de Varona has written 24 books and published many articles in magazines and books in the United States and Spain. His book *Latino Literacy: A Complete Guide to Our Hispanic History and Culture* (Henry Holt & Company, 1996) received outstanding national reviews. Congresswoman Ileana Ros-Lehtinen wrote the preface of the book.

Frank de Varona's other books are *Hispanics in U.S. History, Volume I* (1989), *Hispanics in U.S. History, Volume II* (1989), *Bernardo de Gálvez* (1990), *Simón Bolívar* (1992), *Benito Juárez* (1992), *Miguel Hidalgo y Costilla* (1993), *Hispanic Presence in the United States* (1993), *Perspectives: Authentic Voices of Latinos* (1995), *Florida Government Lessons* (1996), *World History: The Human Odyssey* (Bilingual Supplement) (1997), *Florida Resource Book* (1997), *Multicultural Guide to Dade County* (1997), *Florida Government and Economics Resource Book* (1998), *Simón Bolívar: The Liberator* (2003), *Florida: History, Geography, Government, and Economics* (2005), and *Presencia Hispana en los Estados Unidos Quinto Centenario* (2013).

Professor de Varona is the only individual in the nation who has written six books on the Obama administration. Three of those books are in Spanish: ¿Obama o McCain? (2008), *El Verdadero Obama: Sus conexiones marxistas, socialistas y radicales* (2010), and ¿Obama o

Romney? (2012). The other three books are *America in Decline* (2014), *Obama, Hillary Clinton and Radical Islam* (2016), *Russia, China, and their Allies Threaten America* (2016). Professor de Varona wrote the current book *The New World Order Threatens America and the World* (2017).

Professor de Varona has worked as a contributing writer and/or editorial consultant for over 18 different publishers. In this capacity, he has reviewed over 70 world history, world geography, U.S. history, civics, government, economics, Spanish, language arts, and elementary textbooks as well as biographies.

Professor Frank de Varona was awarded on November 15, 2015 the Grand Cross of the Knight of the National Brotherhood of the Monarchy of Spain in Seville, Spain. In the picture he appears with his wife Dr. Haydée Prado de Varona, a clinical psychologist.

King Juan Carlos I of Spain awarded Professor de Varona the Cross of the Royal Order of Isabel La Católica with the rank of Encomienda in 1994. He was awarded the Grand Cross of the Knight of the National Brotherhood of the Monarchy of Spain in 2015. Professor de Varona received the Byzantine Imperial Order of Constantine the Great with the rank of Commander in 1991. These awards were given to him for his many books and articles regarding the Hispanic contributions to the United States and his work to include these contributions in U.S. textbooks.

Frank de Varona wrote several articles and biographies as well as summarized documents for the CD-ROM *The Hispanic American Experience* produced by Primary Source Media. He was also a consultant for the Spanish language arts program of Jostens Corporation and for the software program of U.S. history of Davidson and Associates.

Professor de Varona has written curriculum programs for school districts and conducted workshops for teachers and school administrators in Miami-Dade, Broward, and Palm Beach Counties in Florida. He has also conducted workshops in the Alexandria, Virginia, and New York City Public Schools. He has served as consultant in Spain, Dominican Republic, and Honduras. The Agency for International Development asked Professor de Varona to assist Honduras in the developmental and establishment of middle school curriculum programs.

As a journalist, Professor de Varona has written many articles on political, economics, national security, foreign affairs, Hispanic presence and contributions to the United States, and historical and educational issues for the following newspapers: *Diario Las Américas, La Voz de Miami Beach, El Nuevo Herald,* and *El 20 de Mayo* (from Los Angeles). He has written over 400 political and historical articles for the following electronic magazines or websites: *Gaspar Lugareño, Emilio Ichikawa, Neoliberalismo, La Nueva Nación, El Nuevo Acción, Baracutey Cubano, Bear Witness Central, and LibertadUSA.* He has written articles for the following magazines: *El Camagüeyano Libre, Girón (Bay of Pigs Veteran Association), Hispania, and Ideal.*

Frank de Varona has produced four television documentaries for *Channel 17* in Miami, Florida. He was producer, director, and interviewer for a one-hour weekly program in *Channel 14* in Miami from 1990 to 1992. Professor de Varona had a radio program in *La Poderosa* and *Cadena Azul* radio stations from 2007 to 2008 and for several months in 2013 and 2016. During the last four years, Professor de Varona is being interviewed once or twice a week by journalist Mariano González Solis at the *Estación del Pueblo,* a radio station in Orlando, Florida on current political, economic, and social events in the United States and the world. Professor de Varona appears frequently on numerous local, national, and international television and radio programs, including *C Span,* the *Voice of Americas, radio and TV Marti,* and *FoxNews in Spanish, America Teve* television station in Spanish. He is a frequent contributor to *NTN 24 Television* with headquarters in Bogotá, Colombia which is seen in Latin America and the United States.

Professor de Varona has conducted workshops at various colleges and universities and at national conferences, such as National Association of Bilingual Educators (NABE), Teachers of English for Speakers of Other Languages (TESOL), National Council for the Social Studies

(NCSS), Florida Council for the Social Studies (FCSS), and Dade County Council for the Social Studies (DCCSS). Professor de Varona has been invited as a speaker during the Hispanic Heritage Month celebrations by the Department of Labor, Nuclear Regulatory Commission, Internal Revenue Service, Drug Enforcement Administration, and Naval Observatory as well many school districts and universities across America.

Frank de Varona served as vice president, secretary, and treasurer of the Governor's Hispanic Affairs Commission. He appears in the middle on the first row and behind him is Governor Bob Graham.

Professor Frank de Varona (second from the left) served as a consumer member of the Florida Board of Dentistry. He was appointed by Governor Bob Graham.

While active in state, regional and national organizations, professor de Varona was appointed to various state commissions by governors. He served as vice president, secretary, and treasurer of the Governor's Hispanic Affairs Commission, Governor's Commission on a Free Cuba, Florida Humanities Council, Florida Historical Markers Commission, Florida Cuban Heritage Trail, Florida Historical Preservation Board Commission, Board of Dentistry (consumer member), and the International Education Commission.

Secretary of Education Lamar Alexander appointed Professor de Varona to the U.S. Department of Education National Council on Educational Statistics Advisory Committee under the administration of President George H.W. Bush. He also served on the Advisory Board of the U.S. Department of Educational Southeastern Educational Improvement Laboratory.

In 1980, Republican Presidential candidate Ronald Reagan and his wife, Nancy Reagan placed a wreath at the Bay of Pig Monument in the Little Havana neighborhood of the city of Miami, Florida. Five veterans of the Assault Brigade 2506, including Frank de Varona, were selected to greet the future president.

After the ceremony Presidential candidate Ronald Reagan and his wife, Nancy Reagan, went to the Centro Vasco Restaurant in Little Havana. The future president held a press conference and Frank de Varona and the four other veterans of the Assault Brigade 2506 were invited.

To Frank de Varona
With best wishes,
Ronald Reagan

President Ronald Reagan and Secretary of Education Bell met with Hispanic educators, including the author, in the Roosevelt Conference room next to the Oval Office in the White House in 1983. Sitting next to Frank de Varona is Dr. Lauro Cavazos, who was at the time president of a university in Texas. Later, President Reagan appointed Dr. Lauro Cavazos Secretary of Education, becoming the first Hispanic appointed to a Cabinet position in history.

Professor de Varona was invited to the White House on three occasions during the presidency of Ronald Reagan. Professor de Varona also met with Vice President George H.W. Bush in the White House when, as an officer of the Florida Hispanic Affairs Commission, he visited Washington, D.C. to lobby Congress on behalf of Contra military aid.

To Frank De Varona
With best wishes,
George Bush

Vice President George H.W. Bush met with Frank de Varona (second from left) and the members of the Florida Hispanic Affairs Commission in the White House.

Professor de Varona is the South Florida Director of *Bear Witness Central* and *LibertadUSA*. He is an advisor and a member of the International Assembly of the Cuban Patriotic Council, Vice President of the Partido Ortodoxo del Pueblo, Chairman of the Keep Government Accountable Coalition, and Vice Chairman of the Republican Party Conservative Coalition. He was elected in 2016 as representative of District 25 to the Republican Party Executive Committee of Miami-Dade County for a four-year term.

Republican 2016 Presidential Candidate, Senator Marco Rubio, with Frank de Varona and his wife, Dr. Haydée Prado de Varona, at a breakfast in West Miami in December 2015. After withdrawing from the presidential race, Senator Rubio was reelected to the U.S. Senate.

Treasurer Catalina Vasquez Vilalpando, who served in that position from 1989 to 1993, dedicated a dollar the author.

During the visit of then Republican presidential candidate Donald Trump to the Bay of Pigs Museum in Little Havana, Frank de Varona was invited by the Trump Campaign to present him with the insignia of the Assault Brigade 2506 together with the president of the Bay of Pigs Veteran Association and another brigade member.

Professor de Varona has organized various events in Miami-Dade County in support of President Donald J. Trump. In March 2017, a national rally was convoked to counter the numerous violent protests being organized by radicals across America. Over 3,000 participated in the March Rally held at Miami's Tropical Park in support of the president. He has also participated in various events in support of President Trump and his agenda. Many of the West Dade Trump Victory Office volunteers recruited by Professor de Varona participated in these rallies and events in support of President Trump. Professor de Varona keeps in contact with the White House Political Affairs Office to coordinate events such as the visits to Miami of the president and the vice president and ways to support President Trump's America First Agenda.

Cuban Patriotic Council member and Trump campaign volunteer Magali Alfaro appears in this picture with Frank de Varona and another volunteer during a march in support of President Donald J. Trump in Miami.

Frank de Varona appears in this picture with his daughter Irene and grandson Danny at the West Dade Trump Victory Office where he served as Office Manager during the presidential campaign along with 200 volunteers that he recruited. The photo was taken by Haydée Prado de Varona.

A group of Trump West Dade Office volunteers (from left to right Irene de Varona, George Garces, Lucy de Varona, Ana Maria Lamar, Frank de Varona, and his frequent visitor, grandson Danny Linares de Varona. The photo was taken by Haydée Prado de Varona.

Frank de Varona greeted Florida's Governor Rick Scott at the Cuban Diaspora Museum in Miami during a celebration of Cuban and Venezuelan freedom fighters. The photo was taken by Haydée Prado.

To: Frank De Varona,

Melania and I are grateful for your loyal support and steadfast commitment to the Republican National Committee. Working together we can achieve our positive vision to Make America Great Again. Warmest Regards,

This is a picture of President Donald J. Trump and his wife, the beautiful and sophisticated First Lady Melania Trump, on Inauguration Day on January 20, 2017.

In this picture appears Roger Stone, a friend of President Donald J. Trump, with Frank de Varona during his book presentation, *The Making of the President 2016*, in Miami, Florida. Stone was invited by the Republican Women of Miami Club on May 22, 2017. Roger Stone told Frank de Varona that he is married to a daughter of a veteran of the Bay of Pigs invasion. He was very friendly and answered all questions with honesty.

Acknowledgments

In this book, like the 23 others that I have written previously, my wife, Dr. Haydée Prado de Varona, has helped me immensely by writing and editing parts of the manuscript. Without her valuable work and support, this book would have never been written. I am also deeply grateful for her patience and understanding during the many long hours and weekends that I have spent working and researching the topics included in this book. I am forever indebted to her as in 2011, she donated me, with immense love, one of her kidneys. Thanks to her, I did not have to receive dialysis. My health has improved immensely due to her most generous gift of life.

My thanks go to my friend, Rolando Perez, president and founder of *Bear Witness Central*, a patriot organization that defends freedom and liberty in the United States of America and throughout the world. Mr. Perez, a successful businessman, lives in Jacksonville, Florida. My appreciation go to Mr. Perez's late beautiful and kind wife, Maria Julia, who worked hard for *Bear Witness Central* and supported her husband in all of his endevours .

Mr. Perez has created this great organization that has two websites. One website is in English, *bwcentral.org*, and the other one is in Spanish, *www.libertadusa.com*. Rolando Perez has published all the articles that I have written in English and Spanish in these websites over many years. Moreover, he has enhanced my articles by incorporating beautiful pictures and in some cases even videos.

Rolando Perez appointed me Director of *Bear Witness Central* in South Florida. Thanks to these websites, this book, as well as others, was written since Mr. Perez initially published all my articles in these websites. The website *bwcentral.org* is one of the most important websites in the nation. It publishes the work of many well-known writers who describe and analyze important events in our nation and the world. The website includes a multitude of videos and political cartoons. This website has received up to 60,000 hits in one day. The other website, *www.libertadusa.com*, is one of the most popular websites in Spanish in the United States and Latin America.

I am also very grateful to Dr. Juan Torres, a successful physician, who lives with his wife and two children in Orlando, Florida. He is the Director of *Bear Witness Central* in central Florida and works closely with Rolando Perez and with me.

Dr. Torres has introduced me to many patriots and leaders of various conservative, religious, and Tea Party organizations in the nation, who are extremely concerned with what is happening in our beloved country since 2008. I have participated with Dr. Torres, Mr. Perez, and other directors in numerous national conferences.

I called Dr. Torres "Mr. Network" for his active participation in many organizations throughout the nation and for his effectiveness in working with a multitude of leaders of conservative and religious organizations. He is frequently invited to speak all over the nation. Dr. Torres founded one of the earliest Hispanic Tea Parties in the nation, the Latin American Tea Party. When Dr. Torres met Rolando Perez, he decided to join forces with him in *Bear Witness Central.*

I am honored of working with Alex Newman, also Director of *Bear Witness Central,* who is the author of books and the foreign correspondent of the excellent magazine *New American.* I am also honored of having been working with Armando Escalante, who is the Director of *Bear Witness Central* in the Greater Daytona, Florida area, and Nevin Gussack, Director of *Bear Witness Central* in Palm Beach County.

Mr. Gussack has helped me with computer issues and exchanged ideas with me frequently. Mr. Newman and Mr. Escalante have presented with me at numerous Bear Witness conferences in many cities. I am also grateful to Aldo Tuero Rosales of *El Nuevo Acción* and Lorenzo del Toro of *Ideal* magazine, who have published many of my articles.

I am very appreciative to Eduardo Macaya for helping me establishing a John Birch Society Chapter in Miami. Mr. Macaya, a Viet Nam War Veteran and a founding member of the Cuban Patriotic Council, is the Miami Chapter leader. My thanks go to Wayne Morrow, coordinator of the John Birch Society in Florida, for his constant assistance to our Miami Chapter. I was very happy to have met the CEO of the John Birch Society Arthur Thompson and his Vice President Martin Ohlson in my house over breakfast. Both of them encouraged me to establish a Chapter in Miami.

I am also very grateful to the late Dr. Horacio Aguirre, former owner of the Spanish newspaper *Diario Las Américas,* and his daughter, Helen Aguirre de Ferrer, for publishing many of my articles in this newspaper since 1973. Likewise, I am very appreciative to Antonio Purriños, the owner of the Spanish newspaper *La Voz de Miami Beach,* who has published many of my articles in his newspaper.

My appreciation also goes to Jorge Rodriguez, president and owner of two Spanish radio stations in Miami, La Poderosa 670 AM and Cadena Azul 1550, who offer me the opportunity to have a weekly 90-minute program from 2008 to 2009. In 2013 and 2016, I was invited to participate in a series of programs regarding the Hispanic heritage of America. While I had the radio program, I was able to cover the 2008 presidential campaign, which led me to write a book in Spanish entitled ¿Obama o McCain? (2008).

From that time until today, my research on Barack Obama and his destructive administration has never stopped. Numerous employees of those two radio stations, including the late Ruby Feria, Roger Vivas, Ariane González Brizuela, Enrique Encinosa, and Sergio Rioseco, have interviewed me countless times regarding domestic and international issues. My thanks go to Mariano González Solis who interviews me twice a week in La Estación del Pueblo Radio Station in Orlando, Florida. My deep appreciation for all his technical support goes to Alex Garcia.

My appreciation to Maricela Aranegui, owner of the Aranegui Institute, and her manager Niurka Quiñones, for carrying of my books at their bookstore and inviting me to give conferences. Lastly, my thanks to Kiko Arocha, book publisher who has helped me with many of my books.

I am the only one responsible for any errors that may appear on this book.

Introduction

"I sincerely believe, with you, that banking establishments are more dangerous than standing armies." Thomas Jefferson wrote in a letter to John Adams.

"A conspiracy is nothing but a secret agreement of a number of men for the pursuance of policies which they dare not admit in public." Mark Twain.

"The real truth of the matter is, as you and I know, that a financial element in the large centers has owned the government ever since the days of Andrew Jackson." President Franklin D. Roosevelt

"The real rulers in Washington are invisible, and exercise power from behind the scenes." Supreme Court Justice Felix Frankfurter.

"World events do not occur by accident: They are made to happen, whether it is to do with national issues or commerce; and most of them are staged and managed by those who hold the purse strings." Former British the Defense Minister Denis Healy.

"The word Establishment is a general term for the power elite international finance, business, the professions and government, largely from the Northeast, who wield most of the power regardless who is in the White House. Most people are unaware of the existence of this legitimate Mafia." Edith Kermit Roosevelt, granddaughter of President Teddy Roosevelt.

This is the reverse side of the Great Seal of the United States from 1776.

The Latin phrase "Novus Ordo Seclorum" that has appeared on the reverse side of the Great Seal since 1782 and on the back of the U.S. one-dollar bill since 1935 translates to "New Order of the Ages" but many Latin scholars say that the best translation is the New World Order.

The New World Order

The term New World Order, for an increasingly number of people, refers to the existence of a very powerful secretive elite with a global agenda that wants to establish a one-world government under the United Nations. Under this system, a global ruling organization would supplant all individual national governments for the betterment of the world. All countries would give up their wealth, constitution, laws, armed forces, currency, liberty, freedoms, and sovereignty. No country would be allowed to own guns and each country´s armed forces would be abolished. The wealth of the rich nations would be distributed to poor nations.

Senator Jesse Helms, Republican Senator from North Carolina.

Senator Jesse Helms was born on October 18, 1921 and died on July 4, 2008. He was a national leader in the conservative movement. Jesse Helms was elected five times as a Republican Senator from North Carolina. As chairman of the Senate Foreign Relations Committee from 1995 to 2001, Senator Helms was very influential in foreign policy.

Senator Helms was very aware of the danger of the New World Order. On December 15, 1987, he spoke from the Senate floor and stated the following:

"This campaign against the American people, against the traditional American culture and values, is systematic psychological warfare. It is orchestrated by a vast array of interests comprising not only the Eastern establishment but also the radical left. Among this group, we find the Department of State, the Department of Commerce, money center banks and multinational corporations, the media, the educational establishment, the entertainment industry, and the large tax-exempt foundations."

"Mr. President, a careful examination of what is happening behind the scenes reveals that all of these interests are working to create what some referred to as a New World Order. Private organizations such as the Council on Foreign Relations, the Royal Institute of International Affairs, the Trilateral Commission, the Dartmouth Conference, the Aspen Institute for Humanistic Studies, the Atlantic Institute, and the Bilderberg Group serve to disseminate and to coordinate the plans for this so-called New World Order in powerful business, financial, academic, and official circles..."

"The influence of establishment Insiders over our foreign policy has become a fact of life in our time. This pervasive influence runs contrary to the real long-term national security of our nation. It is an influence which, if unchecked, could ultimately subvert our constitutional order."

Another conservative Republican Senator, Barry M. Goldwater, agreed with the views expressed by Senator Jesse Helms. Senator Goldwater was also aware of the danger of all these organizations founded by globalists.

Barry M. Goldwater, Republican Senator from Arizona, denounced the Trilateral Commission.

Barry M. Goldwater was born on January 2, 1909 and died on May 29, 1998. He was elected five times as a Republican Senator from Arizona. In 1964, the Republican Party selected him at its presidential candidate but he lost to Lyndon Johnson, who ran for reelection. Senator Goldwater has been credited for the resurgence of the conservative as well as the libertarian political movement in the 1960s. Senator Goldwater wrote the book *With No Apologies* in 1979. Senator Goldwater expressed his disappointment to Henry Kissinger, a powerful leader of the New World Order, regarding President Richard Nixon's failure to reduce the size of the federal government, cut spending, abolish nonproductive programs, and minimize the harm of overregulation on businesses.

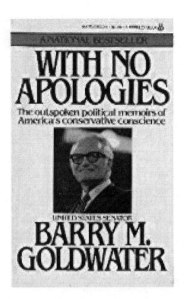

Senator Goldwater wrote the book *With No Apologies* in 1979.

Senator Goldwater wrote on his book the following: "The Trilateral Commission founded by David Rockefeller is the newest international cabal. It is intended to be the vehicle for multinational consolidation of the commercial and banking interests by seizing control of the political government of the United States. What the Trilaterals truly intend is the creation of a worldwide economic power superior to the political governments of nation-states involved… As managers and creators of the system, they would rule the future."

Hillary Clinton was the presidential candidate selected by the globalist elite at two Bilderberg meetings to accelerate the road to a planetary government in which the United Nations would have complete control of America. In essence, America would be subjugated to the United Nations and lose its sovereignty. Fortunately, Donald J Trump was elected president on November 8, 2016.

This new planetary arrangement under the club of dictators that is the corrupt United Nations would be a diabolical socialist/Marxist society. The middle class would slowly disappear. The entire world would be divided into a society of masters and slaves or rulers and servants, such as in communist Cuba and North Korea. There would be one monetary system, one religion, one currency, and one economy in the world.

Traveling would be restricted, except for the rulers. Education, healthcare, the media, courts, energy, retirement and other social benefits, income, housing, transportation, and communication would be <u>controlled by the masters of the one-world government</u>. The population growth would be controlled, as it is being controlled in China.

Individuals would be told what to eat, what amount of energy to use, where to live and the size of your dwelling, and where to work. Private property would be abolished. There would be one religion and all constitutions and laws from all nations would be abolished.

Many people think that this evil New World Order is a conspiracy theory that has no validity whatsoever and that it is a figment of the imagination of some crazy alarmist writers. They ridicule those who believe in the diabolical New World Order and often refer to them as demented individuals. However, there are many writers, including this author, who believe that <u>a very powerful elite has been working for many years</u> to establish a <u>socialist one-world government</u>.

When Secretary of State Hillary Clinton testified before the Senate Foreign Relations Committee on May 24, 2012 in favor of the approval of the Law of the Sea Treaty, she made fun of the critics who were against the approval of this misguided treaty. Secretary Clinton made the following statement: "Of course, that means that black helicopters are on their way." She was referring to the Army of the United Nations that uses black helicopters and was ridiculing those who believe that President Barack Obama is pushing the United States toward the United Nations-dominated one-world government.

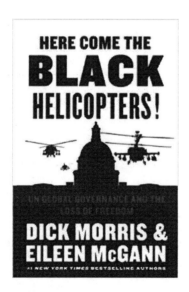

Dick Morris and Eileen McGann wrote an excellent book in 2012 describing the New World Order titled *Here Come the Black Helicopters! United Nations Global Governance and the Loss of Freedom.*

Hillary Clinton, who wrote a dissertation on Saul Alinsky in college and was his friend until his death, was aware that Alinsky said that using ridicule was a very effective weapon in attacking opponents. Another disciple of Alinsky, former president Obama, used ridicule to attack those who disagreed with his radical policies.

Amazon described this book as follows: "Morris and McGann exposed the most potent threat to date to our cherished way of life: the brazen and treacherous Liberal plan to circumvent our democratic processes by putting ultimate governing power in the hands of unaccountable international organizations. Filled with shocking, incontrovertible evidence as well as a concrete action plan, *Here Come the Black Helicopters!* is an essential read that will open the public's eyes to the catastrophe that will surely occur if we allow our misguided politicians to hand the reins of government over to a devious and frighteningly inept United Nations."

Morris and McGann explained that there is a growing threat to the freedom and autonomy of America as a nation. Bureaucrats in the United Nations and their globalist allies in the United States are determined to take away America's national sovereignty.

They call it "global governance." Global governance is nothing less than a power grab by the United Nations and the globalist elite to take away America's wealth and technology and redistribute them to less successful countries in the world.

These individuals want to take away "our ability to self-govern and, instead, impose an international rule of law that is designed to operate against our national interest, violate our democratic ideals and history, and make us subservient to the radical socialist policies of the United Nations and its agencies." This is global governance that is anti-American and anti-freedom.

Many articles have been written on the atrocities committed by the U.N. Army around the world. America should never allow this U.N Army or police to be on its soil.

The president and Congress should never allow any U.N. official from any of its many agencies to interfere with the policies and internal affairs of the United States. This is why many members of Congress and organizations, such as the John Birch Society, have recommended that the United States quit the corrupt dictators' club that is the United Nations.

Socialist British writer H. G. Wells, a member of the Fabian society.

Socialist British writer H. G. Wells, a member of the Fabian society, explained that Western capitalism and Eastern communism would merge into a world government and that sovereign nations would end. He predicted that when this occurs, many would die fighting against this New World Order.

Many head of states, such as President Woodrow Wilson and Prime Minister Winston Churchill, used the term New World Order to explain a new period of history with dramatic changes after World War I and World War II. They saw this new period in history as an opportunity to implement proposals for global governance to address worldwide problems in a new collective effort.

The Soviet Union dictator Nikita Khrushchev served as Premier from 1953 to 1964.

After World War II, many people were concerned regarding the danger of a one-world government dominated by the Soviet Union and international communism. Those who were alive in the 1950s remember what the leader of the Soviet Union, Nikita Khrushchev, said at the

United Nations. The Soviet Union dictator stated the following: "Your grandchildren will live under Communism. You Americans will not accept Communism outright, but we will keep feeding you small doses of Socialism. You will finally wake up to find that you already have Communism. We will not have to fight you. We will so weaken your economy, until you fall into our hands." We also remember Khrushchev banging his shoe on the table at the United Nations and screaming "we will bury you," referring to the capitalist countries.

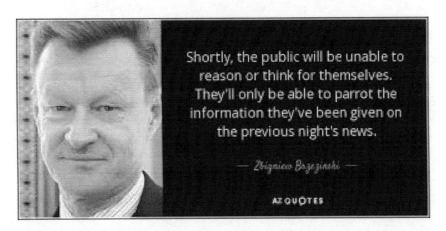

Shortly, the public will be unable to reason or think for themselves. They'll only be able to parrot the information they've been given on the previous night's news.

— Zbigniew Brzezinski —

AZ QUOTES

Zbigniew Brzezinski was one of the founders of the Trilateral Commission together with the late David Rockefeller.

Zbigniew Brzezinski, former National Security Adviser to President Jimmy Carter, was one of the founders of the Trilateral Commission together with the late David Rockefeller. On May 26, 2017, Brzezinski died at the age of 89. His daughter Mika is a host for the radical left channel *MSNBC*.

Brzezinski stated the following at the 1995 State of the World Forum: "We cannot leap into a world government through one quick step, but rather via progressive regionalization." Now there are 27 nations in the European Union. The United States, Canada, and Mexico created the North American Free Trade Association (NAFTA). Many other Asian, African, and Latin American nations have created various regional associations or groupings.

On June 23, 2016, to the dismay of the globalists the people of Great Britain voted by 51.9% to leave the European Union. There are many who are totally opposed of the European Union and its unelected bureaucrats who dictate from Brussels what they need to do.

The nations of the European Union have lost their sovereignty, currency, and many of the elements that make them an independent country. There is an immense backlash in Western Europe to abandon the European Union.

President George H. W. Bush is part of the globalist elite who wants a one word government. During the 2016 presidential election President George H. W. Bush and his son, President George W. Bush, supported Hillary Clinton since she was the candidate backed by the Bilderberg Group. There were other Never Trump Republicans in Congress who did not vote for the Republican presidential candidate. Among them was Republican Congresswoman Ileana Ros Lehtinen who announced she would vote for Jeb Bush by writing his name on the ballot. Republican Congressman Carlos Curbelo also announced that he would not vote for Donald J. Trump. Both Representatives are from South Florida.

On September 11, 1990, President George H. W. Bush gave a speech to a joint session of Congress, which he called "Toward a New World Order." The president stated the following: "In the words of Winston Churchill, a world order in which the principles of justice and fair play....The weak against the strong... A world where the United Nations, freed from cold war stalemate, is poised to fulfill the historic vision of its founders…" What vision of its founders was President Bush talking about? Was it a united one-world government?

Former President Bill Clinton, former Prime Minister Gordon Brown of Great Britain, former Secretary of State Henry Kissinger, and more recently former President Barack Obama and former Vice President Joe Biden have also used the term New World Order. On April 5, 2013, Biden stated that his administration´s "affirmative task would be to create a New World Order."

Secretary of State Henry Kissinger is shown in this picture with Zhou Enlai and Mao Zedong,

Secretary of State Henry Kissinger met with Mao Zedong who was the bloody dictator of the People's Republic of China who murdered millions of Chinese. During the Korean War, Mao Zedong sent a million Chinese soldiers to fight against American soldiers and other United Nations soldiers without a declaration of war. It was Kissinger who negotiated rapprochement with China. He is a part of the globalist elite and always attends the meetings of the Bilderberg Group. A few years after that the United States corporations began investing in China and giving American technology that has helped that enemy nation become a superpower.

Talk show host Sean Hannity stated in his *FoxNews* Channel program that "conspiracy theorists were right regarding the existence of a New World Order." Glenn Beck has also discussed the emerging threat of a one-world government. Many books have been written regarding the desire of secret societies to control the world. Some of these books go back to the age of the Enlightenment and the Illuminati.

Conclusion

Americans are facing an enormous threat to their individual freedoms and democratic way of life by the very wealthy members of globalist elite and their many powerful organizations. The threat of a one-world government is real and is being pushed by some globalists in the Democratic Party and Republican Party, high officials in federal government, and their allies in the corporate world.

This book may surprise many but every chapter is well documented and alarming. However, with God's help Americans and citizens of other nations can fight the diabolical globalists who want to enslave all of us. It is very important to share the information presented in this book by with as many people as possible.

Chapter 1

The Illuminati and the House of Rothschild

Adam Weishaupt (1748-1830) was founder of the Order of the Illuminati in Bavaria.

The Order of the Illuminati (which means the enlightened ones) was a secret society founded by university professor Adam Weishaupt on May 1, 1776 in Bavaria, Germany. Weishaupt was raised by Jesuit priests and became a professor of canon law at the University of Ingolstadt. He later despised the Jesuits and the church and became anti-Catholic. The movement of the Illuminati consisted of people who were anti-religious and believed in liberalism, republicanism, free thought, and secularism. Its objective was to free the world from the church in Rome. The movement expanded and gained several thousand members in several European countries.

Adam Weishaupt in his Illuminati Manifesto for World Revolution stated the following: "A cover is always necessary. In concealment lies a great part of our strength. Hence, we must always hide ourselves under the name of another society." The very powerful Bilderberg Group has always used concealment and secrecy in all of its meetings to keep Americans and Europeans from knowing what the globalists are planning to do.

Over the following years, the Order of the Illuminati grew considerably in numbers. By 1782, the order had 600 members. They included important individuals of Bavarian public life, such as Baron Adolph von Knigge and the banker Meyer Amschel Rothschild, founder of the Rothschild banking dynasty who provided funding for this secret society. The Illuminati membership expanded and included noblemen, politicians, doctors, lawyers, and jurists, as well as intellectuals and some leading writers such as Johann Wolfgang von Goethe. By the end of 1784, the Illuminati had from 2,000 to 3,000 members.

Meyer Amschel Rothschild, the founder of the Rothschild banking dynasty.

Meyer Amschel Rothschild, the founder of the Rothschild banking dynasty, was a prominent Illuminati who contributed money to the secret society. He sent his sons to Great Britain, Austria, France, and Naples to expand his banks. One of his sons remained in Frankfurt. Meyer Rothschild said the following: "Let me issue and control the nation's money and I care not who write its laws."

Another of Meyer Rothschild's sons, Anselm, headed the Frankfurt branch. Nathan went to London and eventually became the most successful of the Rothschild sons. Salomon was sent to Vienna and ran the Austrian branch of the firm.

Another son of Meyer Amschel Rothschild, Carl, moved to Naples and became court banker to the Bourbon kingdom. The other son, James, went to Paris and established a powerful bank. The Rothschilds were involved in the first bank of the United States, which was abolished by President Andrew Jackson in 1836.

Several excellent books have been written about the House of Rothschild. Below are two of them:

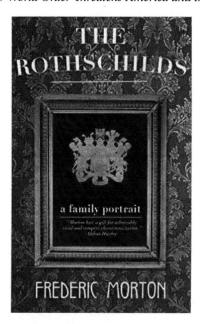

Frederick Morton wrote *The Rothschilds A Family Portrait* in 1962.

Frederick Morton wrote *The Rothschilds A Family Portrait* in 1962. The book has been updated since that time. Amazon describes this book as follows: "No family in the past two centuries has been as constantly at the center of Europe's great events, has featured such varied and spectacular personalities, and has had anything close to the wealth of the Rothschilds. To this day they remain one of the most powerful and wealthy families in the world."

"In Frederic Morton's classic tale, the family is finely painted on the page and brought vividly to life. Here you'll meet Meyer, long-time adviser to Germany's princes, who broke through the barriers of a Frankfurt ghetto and placed his family on the road to wealth and power; Lord Alfred, who maintained a private train, private orchestra (which he conducted), and private circus (of which he was ringmaster); Baron Philippe, whose rarefied vintages bear labels that were created by great artists, among them Picasso, Dali, and Haring; and Kathleen Nica Rothschild de Koenigswarter, the "jazz baroness," in whose arms Charlie Parker died."

"The family itself has been at the center of some of the most crucial moments in history: the defeat of Napoleon at Waterloo, the development of the Suez Canal, the introduction of Jews in the House of Lords. Through it all, the Rothschild name has continued to represent the family ideal, and no author has so nimbly captured the eccentric brilliance of blood as Frederic Morton".

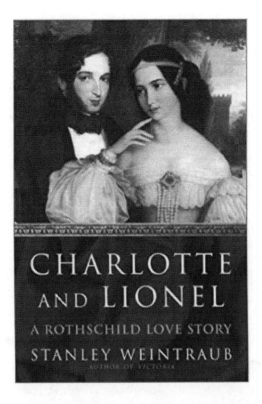

Stanley Weintraub wrote *Charlotte and Lionel A Rothschild Love Story* in 2003.

Stanley Weintraub wrote *Charlotte and Lionel A Rothschild Love Story* in 2003. Amazon described this book as follows: "Charlotte was young and beautiful. Lionel, almost ten years older, was rich and her cousin. Theirs was an arranged betrothal joining two branches of Europe's most powerful banking firm. It seemed an unlikely love match, and even their wedding had to survive catastrophe. Yet their marriage lasted through tragedies and triumphs. Charlotte became one of the grand chatelaines of the Victorian era; Lionel, England's leading financier, persevered through years of bigotry to become the first of his faith to be seated in Parliament. In *Charlotte and Lionel,* acclaimed biographer Stanley Weintraub, using full access to the Rothschild family archives, tells the story of their stunning and surprising love for each other, opening a fascinating window into a memorable age."

"Together, Charlotte and Lionel de Rothschild challenged and redefined their place in Victorian society. At her celebrated salons, England's leading politicians and policy makers met and shared opinions. Disraeli regularly argued politics with adversaries; Gladstone discussed religion with Charlotte; "Tom Thumb" (with P. T. Barnum) entertained; artists and writers and aristocrats mingled. Refusing to swear a Christian oath, Lionel was elected to Parliament half a dozen times before he could take his seat. After a decade-long battle, the House of Commons changed its rules, enabling Lionel and future Jewish or non-Christian members to serve."

"Lionel (and, behind the scenes, Charlotte) influenced events worldwide, helping to fund relief to a starving Ireland, aiding persecuted Jews in Eastern Europe and the Middle East, brokering the purchase of the Suez Canal, and arranging for France's postwar reparations to Germany. Yet despite the distractions of their power, glamour, and wealth, and problems of health for which money could buy no solutions, they remained intensely devoted to each other and their family. Although Charlotte lost a daughter, then her beloved husband, and had to come back herself from severe illness, she remained unbroken. *Charlotte and Lionel* presents the evocative tale of one of the least known yet most touching love stories from the glamorous decades of Victorian England."

As time went on, the Rothschild family became the owners of the central banks of Germany, Great Britain, Austria, France, and Naples. In 1817, the Rothschild sons were made noblemen by the Austrian emperor. Today, the descendants of Meyer Amschel Rothschild run a financial empire that covers the world with branches in Europe, Australia, the United States, Canada, Mexico, Rio de Janeiro, Tokyo, Hong Kong, and Singapore. Many of them are members of the New World Order globalist organizations.

The Rothschild family became extremely wealthy during the 19th Century by financing nations to fight each other. Professor Stuart Crane stated the following:

"If you will look back at every war in Europe during the 19th Century, you will see that they always ended with the establishment of a balance of power. With every reshuffling there was a balance of power in a new grouping around the House of Rothschild in England, France, or Austria. They grouped nations so that if any king got out of line a war would break out and the war would be decided by which way the financing when. Researching the debt positions of the warring nations would usually indicate who was to be punished."

Gary Allen explained in his book, *None Dare Call It Conspiracy,* that the House of Rothschild and other international bankers were very close to many governments and lent enormous sums of money to many nations. Thus, the term "international bankers" is given to these cosmopolitan and international bankers. Allen pointed out that one major reason for the omission of the role of international bankers in political history is the fact that the Rothschilds were of Jewish origin. Anti-semites have portrayed the entire conspiracy as being Jewish. However, this is not true as all other insiders were Anglo-Saxons Protestants, such as J. P. Morgan and the Rockefellers.

Gary Allen wrote a bestseller book, *None Dare Call It Conspiracy*, which was published in 1971

Gary Allen wrote a bestseller book, *None Dare Call It Conspiracy*, which was published in 1971. Congressman John G. Schmitz wrote an introduction of Gary Allen's book and stated the following:

"This book is a primer for anyone who wishes to understand the basic workings of the global network of Insiders that is determined to wield power over all of mankind in the coming New World Order. The story you are about to read is true. The names have not been changed to protect the guilty. This book may have the effect of changing your life. After reading this book, you will never look at national and world events in the same way again."

"*None Dare Call It Conspiracy* will be a very controversial book. At first it will receive little publicity and those whose plans are exposed in it will try to kill it by the silent treatment. For reasons that become obvious as you read this book, it will not be reviewed in all the proper places or be available on your local book stand. However, there is nothing these people can do to stop a grass roots book distributing system."

"Eventually it will be necessary for the people and organizations named in this book to try to blunt its effect by attacking it or the author. They have a tremendous vested interest in keeping you from discovering what they are doing. And they have the big guns of the mass media at their disposal to fire the barrages at *None Dare Call It Conspiracy*. By sheer volume, the experts will try to ridicule you out of investigating for yourself as to whether or not the information in this book is true They will ignore the fact that the author about to conjecture. They will find a typographical error or ague some point that is open to debate. If necessary they will lie in order to protect themselves by smearing this book. I believe those who pooh-pooh the information herein because psychologically many people would prefer to believe we are because we all like to ignore bad news. We do so at our own peril."

Allen wrote that the Rothschilds were very active in the United States. During the American Civil War, the Union or the North was financed by the Rothschilds through the American agent, August Belmont. The Confederacy or the South was financed through the Erlangers, who were relatives of the Rothschilds.

Wars have enriched these international bankers beyond anyone's imagination. By lending enormous amounts of money to nations, the international bankers became creditors of these governments. These loans allowed the bankers to monopolize the rulers of nations as well as to control the policies of governments.

Eventually, these international bankers owned the central banks of various European nations. The international bankers were able to issue money and direct the credit policies of governments. Another term that is used for these bankers and other members of the New World Order is "Insiders."

An observer pointed out that "once the government is in debt to the bankers, it is at their mercy." For example, if these international bankers, who controlled the central banks of many nations, were to refuse to renew treasury bills, it would provoke a catastrophic economic situation.

Conclusion

The New World Order is real and the House of Rothschilds remains very powerful.

Chapter 2

The Illuminati are expelled from Bavaria

Baron von Knigge played a very important role in the organization and expansion of the Order of the Illuminati. As a former Freemason, he was in favor of adopting rites similar to Masons. Members of the Illuminati were given a symbolic secret name taken from antiquity. For example, Weishaupt was given the name of Spartacus and Baron Knigge was called Philo.

The membership levels also became a complex hierarchy. There were a total of 13 degrees of initiation, divided into three classes. The first culminated in the degree of illuminatus minor, the second illuminatus dirigens, and the third was that of king. In 1784, the Order of Illuminati was disbanded by Charles, Elector of Bavaria, because he felt that this secret society was conspiring to destroy his government and the Catholic Church. Weishaupt and his followers fled Bavaria and the Illuminati went underground. Some writers have speculated that the Illuminati survived and still exist today.

Arthur R. Thompson wrote a book titled *To the Victor Go the Myths & Monuments: The History of the First 100 Years of the War Against God and the Constitution, 1776-1876, and Its Modern Impact* in 2016.

Arthur R. Thompson wrote a book titled *To the Victor Go the Myths & Monuments: The History of the First 100 Years of the War Against God and the Constitution, 1776-1876, and Its Modern Impact* in 2016. The book has 492 pages. Thompson is the CEO of the John Birch Society. He devoted over 40 years researching information to write this remarkable book.

Arthur R. Thompson and the vice president of the John Birch Society, Marty Olson, came from Wisconsin to visit this writer at his home and discussed the book *To the Victor Go the Myths &*

Monument. Thompson dedicated his outstanding book to this writer, who in turn gave each of the two visitors three of his books dealing with the Obama and Hillary Clinton administration.

This writer agreed to establish a John Birch Society Miami Chapter. Vietnam veteran and member of the Cuban Patriotic Council Eduardo Macaya accepted the Leader position of the Miami Chapter and this writer became the secretary. Wayne Morrow, the coordinator of the John Birch Society in Florida, was of immense help and met with Macaya and this writer on numerous occasions.

On June 20, 2016, James Thornton wrote a review of *To the Victor Go the Myths & Monument,* which was published on the *New American website.* Below is his review:

"*To the Victor Go the Myths & Monuments* is a historical overview of the first 100 years of our country's existence, as well as being much, much more. The author explains that those who study history soon discover that history books do not always contain the entire story, which often happens because of space constraints or because an author is unaware of certain facts."

"History can also be restricted to selected portions of the true story because of an author's bias, his agenda, or because he is serving the agenda of others. A history in which facts are deliberately ignored or in which the author creates "facts" distorts the true picture of past events. Such distortions, built up over time, can have deadly effects on a people and on nations. As George Orwell (whom the author quotes on the title page) put it many years ago, "The most effective way to destroy a people is to deny and obliterate their own understanding of their history.""

"If, in addition to distortions of the historical record, one adds another factor — the intentional dumbing down of a people — then the disintegration of a country can be accomplished even more quickly. I refer here to the modern phenomenon of large numbers of high-school or even college graduates who are unable to find the Pacific Ocean on an unlabelled map of the world, or to arrange major events or historical personages in chronological order (i.e., that Washington lived before the Civil War and that John F. Kennedy was president a century after that conflict)."

"Even the ability to use and understand the English language has fallen on hard times. The vocabulary of the average young person has dwindled alarmingly; a diminishing vocabulary means a diminishing ability to understand the lessons of history or to grasp today's crucial issues. Thus, one can see why control of education has long been a major objective to those desiring revolutionary changes in America."

"Another component that assists in distorting the past in order to shape the future is the control of the publication and distribution of books, especially history books. Of course, there are independent publishers, but their books do not usually receive the promotion and publicity given to establishment publishers, such as favourable reviews in major newspapers and magazines. As the author points out, books such as *None Dare Call It Treason* and *None Dare Call It* were bestsellers; neither received serious notice in the mass media. "*Conspiracy*, sold six to 12 million copies each in the 1960s and 1970s."

"*To the Victor Go the Myths & Monuments* by the John Birch Society (the parent organization of *The New American*) CEO Arthur R. Thompson is both very broad and very detailed in its scope. Since space does not allow an examination here of all of the periods covered, I will concentrate on two important ones: the decades after American independence and the period leading to the Civil War. In the decades following independence, conspirators and radicals wished to propel our country in the direction followed by the revolutionary regime in France, with its bloody extermination of opponents and potential opponents, and its highly centralized government."

"The author writes: The American War for Independence produced a country that in many respects was the opposite of what would be produced by the French Revolution. It became a struggle between two opposing forces, good and evil, manifested in their governments, and as a result a struggle over the New World geography and people that the New and the Old World governments would govern."

"Our American Revolution did not aim at the destruction of the social system of Colonial America. It aimed simply at guaranteeing that Americans (who at that time were overwhelmingly English) would enjoy all of the rights of other Englishmen. Because of the intransigence of the British government at that time, that guarantee could only come about through independence. The French Revolution, by way of contrast, aimed at the systematic dismantling of traditional France, the destruction of its social system, and the extirpation of religion."

"Those who have studied that period in depth know that the French Revolution was the product of the machinations of a group known as the Illuminati, the members of which opposed Christianity and Christian government, which they sought to replace with a godless despotism. People of the same mentality, mostly agents of the French revolutionary government, worked to accomplish similar objectives in America, using inflammatory rhetoric to try to incite rebellion and chaos. They were particularly hostile toward President Washington and the new Constitution since the president was conservative in outlook, opposing any radicalism, and the Constitution was an instrument of governance that upheld both liberty, on the one hand, and a stable conservatism, on the other."

"Placing limits on government power, the Constitution was especially detested by the radicals. Through secret societies controlled by or heavily influenced by French agents, it was hoped that a mass insurrection could be fomented. As in revolutionary France, an explosion of mob violence could bring radicals to power. As the book notes, that nearly happened during the administration of John Adams."

"In short, the activities of revolutionary France and its supporters in the newly independent America were much the same as the activities of the USSR and its supporters in America in the 20th century — to subvert and overthrow the legitimate government of the United States and to replace it with a revolutionary dictatorship. The conspirators failed then, but they did not give up."

"During the first half of the 19th century, the issue seized upon by the enemies of our Constitutional Republic was slavery. Their strategy was as old as warfare itself: "divide and conquer." The author writes, The English abolished slavery peacefully in 1833 and provided £20 million plus an apprenticeship for ex-slaves — a great deal cheaper than waging war. And they did not have to kill two-thirds of a million men-at-arms and untold numbers of civilians to accomplish the end of slavery, as the Conspiracy did in America."

"Extremists in the North, who were often socialists in outlook and therefore not only opposed private ownership of slaves but private ownership of property as well, made incendiary speeches and published diatribes against the South and its people. In 1859, the infamous John Brown launched a raid on a military armoury in Harpers Ferry, Virginia (now in West Virginia), hoping to arm slaves after inciting a mass slave insurrection. Brown was captured, convicted of treason against the State of Virginia, and hanged. That, however, served to inflame passions further. For Northern abolitionists, Brown was a martyr whose death won many new adherents to their cause. In the South, thoughts of a slave insurrection sent shivers of horror through the entire populace and created boundless resentment, even hatred, of the North. To rabid abolitionists all Southerners were evil and the whole of their society was deserving of obliteration. To Southerners, it seemed like the whole of the North not only was against them, but sought their annihilation."

"Only a small percentage of the Southern population were slave owners, so it was not the defense of slavery that motivated Southerners — it was that they were fiercely independent and therefore resented being pushed around by outsiders. So it was that firebrands on both sides, often with connections to Conspiracy-directed organizations or unknowingly manipulated by such organizations, fanned the flames of war. Many abolitionists argued for the disunion of the South from the other states before the war, yet once the war was under way, they became fanatical unionists, screaming for blood."

"With the election of Abraham Lincoln in 1860, the fuse was ignited, and at the end of the bloodiest war in our history, the Conspiracy achieved its goals: The South was devastated, its social system largely overturned; state sovereignty was greatly weakened; and the process toward ever-greater centralization under the federal government was set in motion."

"Arthur R. Thompson's book is superb, indeed a "must read." Some of the particulars about certain important figures and events in America's history will astonish readers. Very often, while reviewing events during the country's first 100 years, he brings out analogous events from our own time, so better to illustrate the similarities of the dangers experienced then and now. Moving back and forth from the past to the present and then back again shows that threats to the liberty and independence of our land are nothing new. Almost from the beginning, America represented a magnificent prize much coveted by the representatives of evil. And just as they will not relent, so too must patriotic Americans be relentless in repelling their intrigues and deception."

"Most importantly, the author affirms that the situation is far from hopeless. Through persistence, organization, and coordinated effort, we can be victorious, thereby assuring the blessings of liberty for ourselves and for our progeny."

Arthur R. Thompson stated in his book the following:

"America was founded by people who wanted an independent country based on principles that ultimately led to the formation of the Constitution that insures the independence of the American people, limits government power, and protects God-given rights. Europe, on the other hand, has had a history of men who have usurped the rights of the people for centuries. The only real change in Europe has been which personalities and organizations controlled the people."

"This was the main reason that America was settled: To move out of that atmosphere and form something new in the history of man which became known as liberty. America served as an example to the rest of the world that the common man could rule himself with very limited control from government and prosper as individuals and as a country. There were those who could not allow this to happen if they meant to rule."

"*To the Victor Go the Myths and Monuments* is the story of a group of people from Europe who banded together to subvert American liberty, government, and religious system. It started within a group of men during the Enlightenment, then the Bavarian Illuminati, Revolutionary France, and German intellectuals and how they infiltrated into all aspects of our society, working to slowly change our American system into a system that they could control. This was to be accomplished by managed ignorance of our history." How they were able to subvert our schools, the publishing of history, the use of volatile issues, capture and even form our political parties in order to accomplish their purpose is the story of this book. It is not simply the story; it exposes those who were involved. You will find that not all of your heroes were really heroes. It will not be a dull read. History can be interesting, if told in a manner that opens your eyes to the real world."

He explained that the goals of the Illuminati were:

1. The destruction of Christianity.

2. The destruction of nations as such in favor of universal internationalism.

3. The discouragement of patriotism and substitution of the cry for universal brotherhood.

4. The abolition of family ties and marriage by means of systematic corruption.

5. The suppression of the rights of inheritance and property.

Thompson said that the aims of the Illuminati could be summarized as follows: "The overthrow of all government, the destruction of all religion, the abolition of private property, the death of individualism and family, the deification of sensuality, the repudiation of marriage, the state control of children, and the establishment of a world government." This description sounds very much of the goals of communism.

Thompson pointed out that in a report of the California State Investigative Committee on Education in 1953, it was stated the following: "The so-called modern communism is apparently the same hypocritical and deadly world conspiracy to destroy civilization that was founded by the secret order of the illuminati in Bavaria on May 1, 1776 and that race its whorey (ruthless or vulgar) head in our colonies here and at the critical before the adoption of our federal Constitution".

Conclusion

In the decades following American independence, conspirators and radicals tried to propel the United States in the direction followed by the revolutionary regime in France, with its bloody extermination of opponents and potential opponents, and its highly centralized government. The American Revolution did not want the destruction of the social system of Colonial America. It wanted simply to guarantee that Americans would enjoy all of the rights of other Englishmen. The French Revolution, by way of contrast, aimed at the systematic dismantling of traditional France, the destruction of its social system, and the extirpation of religion.

The Illuminatis were present in America during the American Revolution and beyond. The goals of the Illuminatis are very similar to the goals of communists.

Chapter 3

The Illuminatis in France and Germany
and their influence in America

Arthur R. Thompson said that the Illuminatis were involved in the Age of Reason with famous writers such as Voltaire, who wanted to destroy Christianity and inject atheism in its place. He pointed out that the planners behind the French Revolution and the Reign of Terror were Illuminatis and these individuals had a profound influence on American society. In France, they adopted other names such as Jacobin Club.

This was Seal of the Jacobin Club from 1789 to 1792.

After 1792, the Society of the Friends of the Constitution (in French, *Société des amis de la Constitution*) was renamed Society of the Jacobins, Friends of Freedom and Equality (in French, *Société des Jacobins, amis de la liberté et de l'égalité*), commonly known as the Jacobin Club or simply the Jacobins.

As explained in *Wikipedia*, this radical group was the most influential political club during the French Revolution. The Jacobin Club grew into a large nationwide republican movement with a membership estimated at a half million or more. The Jacobin Club was heterogeneous and included both prominent parliamentary factions of the early 1790s, the radical Mountain, and the more moderate Girondins.

From 1792 to 1793, the Girondins dominated the Jacobin Club and led the country. Believing that revolutionary France would not be accepted by its neighboring countries, they called for an aggressive foreign policy and declared war on Austria and Prussia. The Girondins were the dominant faction when the Jacobins overthrew the monarchy and created the republic. When the Republic failed to deliver the unrealistic gains that had been expected, they lost popularity.

The Girondins sought to curb fanatical revolutionary violence and were therefore accused by the Mountain of being royalist sympathizers. The National Guard eventually switched its support from the Girondins to the Mountains, allowing the Mountains to stage a coup d'etat.

In May 1793, led by Maximilien de Robespierre, the leaders of the Mountain faction succeeded in sidelining the Girondin faction. The Mountain faction controlled the government until July 1794. Their time in government was characterized by radically progressive legislation imposed with very high levels of political violence.

Maximilien de Robespierre

Maximilien de Robespierre is best known for his role in the French Revolution's Reign of Terror. During this short period thousands were executed. The Reign of Terror ended a few months later with Robespierre's arrest and execution in July 1794

In June 1793, they approved the Constitution of Year 1, which introduced universal male suffrage for the first time in history. In September 1793, twenty-one prominent Girondins were guillotined, beginning the Reign of Terror. In October, during the Reign of Terror, the new constitution was ratified in a referendum in which most eligible voters avoided participating in. The Mountains executed tens of thousands opponents nationwide in an effort to suppress the Vendée insurrection and the Federalist insurrections and to prevent any other insurrections during the War of the First Coalition.

Comte de Mirabeau, a prominent Illuminati.

Prominent Illuminati, the Comte de Mirabeau, was an associate of Benjamin Franklin. In addition to his place in the French National Assembly, Mirabeau also served as a member of the Jacobin Club until his death in 1791. Mirabeau invited the Illuminist leader Christian Bode to bring the program of Illuminatis to France. Another Illuminati, Nicholas Bonneville, was a close friend of Thomas Paine and the Illuminati Marquis de Lafayette had many friends among the leaders of the American Revolution.

Marquis de Lafayette

Arthur Thompson wrote in his book that there were many Jacobin Clubs formed in America. The first one was organized in Philadelphia in 1792, which was then the capital of the Thirteen States that made up America. Approximately 42 Jacobin clubs were founded, all of them in support of revolutionary France. The formation of these clubs showed the influence of the Illuminatis in early America. Many Illuminatis, after being expelled from Bavaria, moved to other parts of Germany. The University of Göttingen in Germany had many professors who were members of the Illuminati.

George Bancroft

Many prominent Americans studied at the University of Göttingen. Among these individuals were George Bancroft, who became founder of Harvard University's Round Hill School, Secretary of the Navy, and president of the American Historical Society.

Jean-Jacques Rousseau

During the period of the French Revolution, Jean-Jacques Rousseau was the most popular of the "philosophers" among the members of the Jacobin Club. According to Thompson, the Round Hill was a boarding school which embraced the Enlightenment. Its curriculum was based on the teachings of Jean-Jacques Rousseau and the Illuminati Johann Heinrich Pestalozzi from Switzerland. Other Illuminatis were Ralph Waldo Emerson, the famous writer who became the leader of the death of God movement; and J.P. Morgan, the famous business-man. Thompson said that there were many industrialists who financed socialist and terrorist causes. Among these individuals were Robert Owen, the Scottish industrialist who promoted communism in Europe and the Americas; Andrew Carnegie, the steel magnate; and business tycoon Cornelius Vanderbilt.

J.P. Morgan was born in 1837 and died in 1913.

J.P. Morgan became a prominent banker, who studied in England and Germany, was the agent of the English Rothschilds in America. His son helped the Bolsheviks to come to power in the Soviet Union.

In Germany, the Illuminati used the name Thule Society. In our nation, an offshoot of this German secret society became Skull and Bones, the fraternity at Yale University in which three U.S. presidents and other powerful individuals were members.

Conclusion

The Illuminatis were involved in the Age of Reason with famous writers such as Voltaire, who wanted to destroy Christianity. They were the planners behind the French Revolution and the Reign of Terror and these individuals had a profound influence on American society. In France, they adopted other names such as Jacobin Club.

Many Illuminatis, after being expelled from Bavaria, moved to other parts of Germany. The University of Göttingen in Germany had many professors who were members of the Illuminati. Many Americans studied at that German university and became Illuminaties.

Today, some writers are convinced that the Illuminatis are present in powerful organizations in our nation, such as the Council on Foreign Relations and the Trilateral Commission; and in the Bilderberg Group in Europe. All three organizations want to establish a New World Order.

Chapter 4

The Order of Skull and Bones

The logo of the Order of Skull and Bones

Antony Sutton, a British-born author of 26 books and an economist who died in 2002, wrote a book titled *America's Secret Establishment: An Introduction to the Order of Skull and Bones* (1986). Sutton explained in his book that Bones, as the secret Yale University in New Haven, Connecticut organization order is also known, is "America's secret establishment." The society's alumni organization, the Russell Trust Association, owns the society's real estate and oversees the organization. The society is known informally as "Bones" and members are known as "Bonesmen".

Some writers argue that Bones is an offshoot of the secret German university group called the Thule Society. This German society had a fascist philosophy and many of its members founded the Nazi Party.

The Order of Skull and Bones was founded in 1832 at Yale University by William Russell and Alphonso Taft. William Russell was attending a German university when he became in contact with members of the secret Thule Society and received permission to form a branch of the German society in our nation. William Russell went on to become a military general and state legislator. Alphonso Taft became the United States Attorney General, Secretary of War, and ambassador to Russia and Austria-Hungary. He was also the father of President William Howard Taft.

Since 1879, Skull and Bones selects new members among students every spring as part of Yale University's "Tap Day". Since the society's inclusion of women in the early 1990s, Skull and Bones selects fifteen men and women of the junior class to join the society. Skull and Bones "taps" those viewed by them as campus leaders and other notable figures for its membership.

President William Howard Taft

William Howard Taft was born on September 15, 1857 and died on March 8, 1930. Taft was the son of Alphonso Taft, who was co-founder of Skull and Bones. He served as president from 1909 to 1913. He also served as Chief Justice from 1921 to 1930. He is the only individuals who has held both offices.

William Howard Taft was elected president in 1908, with the assistance of President Theodore Roosevelt. President Taft opposed the creation of a central bank operated by a banking cartel. The Insiders supported former president Teddy Roosevelt as a third-party candidate to divide the Republican vote and elect the progressive Woodrow Wilson in 1912. President Wilson had agreed to allow the American and European banking cartel to create the central Federal Reserve Bank.

The members of Skull and Bones come from wealthy and powerful East Coast families. Three United States presidents have belonged to this secret society. These presidents are William

Howard Taft; George H. W. Bush; and his son, George W. Bush. Senator Prescott Bush was a member of Skull and Bones and was the father of President George H. W. Bush. Bonesmen are rich and powerful individuals in government, banking, commerce, and industry.

Former presidential candidate and former Secretary of State John Kerry is a member of Bones as well as approximately 30 members of the United States Senate and the House of Representatives. Other prominent alumni have been Supreme Court Justices Morrison R. Waite and Potter Stewart; CIA official James Jesus Angleton; Secretary of War Henry Stimson; Secretary of Defense Robert A. Lovett; Governor of Massachusetts William B. Washburn; Henry Luce, founder and publisher of *Time, Life, Fortune,* and *Sports Illustrated* magazines; Senator Stephen A. Schwarzman; Austan Goolsbee, founder of Blackstone Group; Harold Stanley, co-founder of Morgan Stanley; and Frederick W. Smith, founder of FedEx.

In 2004, during the U.S. presidential election, both the Democratic and Republican nominees were Bonesmen. President George W. Bush wrote in his autobiography, "In my senior year I joined Skull and Bones, a secret society; so secret, I can't say anything more." When former Presidential candidate John Kerry was asked what it meant that he and Bush were both Bonesmen, he said, "Not much, because it's a secret."

The Skull and Bones building at Yale University is known as the "Tomb."

The Skull and Bones owns Deer Island, which is on the St. Lawrence River. The 40 acres retreat is intended to give Bonesmen an opportunity to "get together and rekindle old friendships."

Conclusion

There is no question that Skull and Bones members are extremely powerful and influential in the United States and abroad. Many Bonesmen have served or are serving in the Council on Foreign Relations, the Trilateral Commission, and the Bilderberg Group, organizations that are the invisible government in the United States and most of the world.

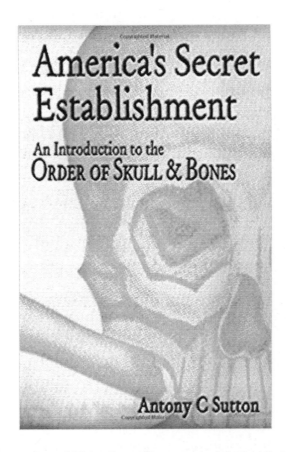

Antony Sutton, a British-born author of 26 books and an economist who died in 2002, wrote a book titled *America's Secret Establishment: An Introduction to the Order of Skull and Bones* (1986).

Chapter 5

The Round Table and the Fabian Society

In 1877, British-born Cecil Rhodes wrote his first will at the age of 23 and expressed his desire to finance a secret society to annex the British Empire to the United States. The group was called the Society of the Elect. In 1890, Rhodes said that his secret society's goal was to "gradually absorb the wealth of the world." He created the Rhodes scholarship, which had the British statesmen Alfred Milner as one of its trustees. Bright British, American, and German students with leadership potential over the years have received scholarships to the University of Oxford. Cecil Rhodes became a very wealthy and powerful South African businessman and invested in gold and diamond mines. Rhodes created the nation of <u>Rhodesia,</u> which was named after him. The name of this African nation was changed to <u>Zimbabwe.</u>

Cecil Rhodes

Professor Carroll Quigley, who was a mentor to a Georgetown University freshman by the name of Bill Clinton, was a noted historian. He died in 1977. He wrote a book called the *Anglo American Establishment* in 1949 that was published posthumously in 1981. One wonders why his book was suppressed for so long. Quigley explained that two Round Table members, Alfred Milner and British official Lionel George Curtis, along with members of the Socialist Fabian Society and a group called the Inquiry, created the Royal Institute of International Affairs (RIIA) in London in 1919. The RIIA is based in the Chatham House.

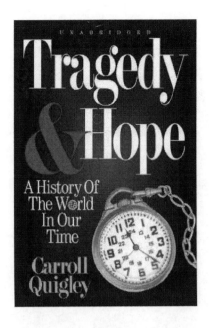

Professor Carroll Quigley wrote the book *Tragedy and Hope* in 1966.

Professor Carroll Quigley wrote the book *Tragedy and Hope* in 1966. He stated the following in his book: "The powers of financial capitalism had another far-reaching aim, nothing less than to create a world system of financial control in private hands able to dominate the political system of each country and the economy of the world as a whole. This system was to be controlled in a feudalistic fashion by central banks of the world acting in concert, by secret agreements arrived at in frequent private meetings and conferences."

Edward House was a Marxist and one of the founders of the Council on Foreign Relations. He worked with President Wilson to establish a world government through the League of Nations.

Colonel Edward House was the "power behind the throne" of President Woodrow Wilson. He was one of the founders of Inquiry, who was President Woodrow Wilson's chief advisor. This powerful presidential advisor would later become one of the founders of the Council on Foreign Relations (CFR) in 1921. Many writers believe that the CFR was created as a branch of the Royal Institute of International Affairs. The Round Table has branches called Institute of International Affairs in Canada, Australia, South Africa, India, and the Netherlands. Lionel Curtis later wrote the book *The Commonwealth of God* in 1938 and promoted the establishment of an imperial federation that would annex the United States.

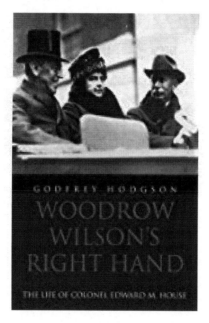

The book *Woodrow Wilson's Right Hand: The Life of Colonel Edward House* (2008) explains the importance of Colonel Edward M. House in twentieth-century American foreign policy. The author of House's biography said that Colonel House served from 1913 to 1919 not only as intimate friend and chief political adviser to President Woodrow Wilson but also as national security adviser and senior diplomat. Even though the relationship between Colonel House and President Wilson ended in a quarrel at the Paris peace conference of 1919—largely because of Mrs. Wilson's hostility to House— for most of the Wilson presidency, House was, indeed, his right hand. As Amazon explained, "House joined Wilson's campaign in 1912 and soon was traveling through Europe as the president's secret agent. He visited Europe repeatedly during World War I and played a major part in drafting Wilson's Fourteen Points and the Covenant of the League of Nations." Colonel House was a globalist who wanted the United States to join the League of Nations, the first major step to create a world government. However, the Senate rejected it.

President Wilson once stated the following: "Mr. House is my second personality. He is my independent self. His thoughts and mine are one. If I were in his place I would do just as he suggested…If anyone thinks he is reflecting my opinion by whatever action he takes, they are welcome to the conclusion." Colonel Edward House proposed the 16th Amendment to the Constitution, which started the income tax, an idea that came from Karl Marx.

The Fabian Society

The Fabian Society was founded in Great Britain on January 4, 1884, as a socialist organization with the objective of advancing the principles of socialism via gradual rather than revolutionary means. At the suggestion of Frank Podmore, the society was named after the Roman general Fabius Maximus, the Delayer. Fabius fought against the Carthaginian army led by Hannibal in a harassment and attrition manner, thus avoiding a head on battle. Similarly, the Fabian Society strives to create a one-world socialist government in a gradual and slow manner in order to avoid a serious confrontation.

A wolf in sheep's clothing was the original coat of arms of the Fabian Society since it wanted to advance socialism secretly and gradually to avoid a serious confrontation.

The society wants to promote greater equality of power and wealth or, in other words, redistribute money from the rich to the poor. The Fabian Society was instrumental in the creation of the British Labor Party. Today, the Fabian Society is one of 15 socialist societies that are affiliated with the Labor Party.

Many prominent intellectuals in Great Britain joined the society. Among these individuals are George Bernard Shaw, H. G. Wells, Bertrand Russell, Ramsey MacDonald, and Virginia Woolf. The important leaders of the Fabian Society were Sidney and Beatrice Webb. This couple wrote numerous books promoting socialism. The Fabians wanted to confiscate land and stop the collection of rent by land owners. Great Britain implemented many socialist programs and almost went bankrupt. Britain became "the sick man of Europe." There were constant strikes and the bosses of unions were governing the nation.

British Prime Minister Margaret Thatcher

It was Prime Minister Margaret Thatcher who saved the country by reducing the size of the government and giving free enterprise room to flourish. Prime Minister Thatcher pushed major labor union reforms, reduced inflation, and cut taxes. She privatized many of the nationalized industries and brought prosperity to her nation. Prime Minister Thatcher worked closely with President Ronald Reagan.

The Fabians were very influential in India. After achieving their independence, Jawaharlal Nehru implemented socialism in India by nationalizing important industries such as steel, telecommunications, mines, and transportation. Property rights were restricted and high taxes were implemented. This economic system was a complete failure and today India has completely abandoned socialism. Several U.S. presidents have appointed Fabian socialists to their administrations.

President Franklin D. Roosevelt

President Franklin D. Roosevelt appointed many Fabian socialists to his administration. He also had several Soviet Union spies in his administration. One of Stalin's spies, Alger Hiss, was one of the founders of the United Nations.

Conclusion

It is quite unfortunate for the world that in spite of the complete failure of the socialist economic model, many countries have implemented it in the past and others are currently using this failed economic model. European nations that have implemented socialist policies such as Greece, Spain, Portugal, Ireland, Italy, and Cyprus are today almost bankrupt. One has to look at Cuba, Venezuela, and North Korea to see the massive poverty that Marxism has brought to these countries. It is very worrisome and sad that powerful organizations want to create a one-world socialist government.

Chapter 6

The Federal Reserve Bank

President Woodrow Wilson official White House portrait

Thomas Woodrow Wilson was born on December 28, 1856 and died on February 3, 1924. He became the 28th President of the United States from 1913 to 1921.

President Woodrow Wilson signed the Federal Reserve Act on December 23, 1913. President Wilson was placed in office by domestic and international bankers in order for them to be allowed to establish a banking cartel which is the Federal Reserve. Later, at the request of Wall Street banks, Wilson betrayed Czar Nicholas II of Russia, America's strong ally during World War I, by issuing a passport to Leon Trotsky and allowing him to leave New York City with 275 other communists. Thus President Wilson committed high treason since once the Alexander Kerensky was overthrown, the Bolsheviks took power and made a peace treaty with the German Empire allowing for tens of thousands of German soldiers to be deployed to the Western Front to kill and wound American, Canadian, British, French and other Allied nations soldiers. During World War I, more than 117,000 Americans died and over 205,000 were wounded during 1917 to 1918 fighting in France.

The Federal Reserve Bank, which is a banking cartel made up of national and international bankers, issues money out of thin air. This private central bank was created on December 23, 1913. The Federal Reserve Act, which was signed by President Woodrow Wilson, was unconstitutional. Article 1, Section 8 of the Constitution clearly states that only Congress has the power to issue or print the currency and determine its value.

There are many books that explain the role of the banking cartel that created the Federal Reserve Bank and assumed control over the finances of the United States and practically of its entire government. The best book on this topic is *The Creature of Jekyll Island: A Second Look at the Federal Reserve,* 5th Edition (2010), which was written by G. Edward Griffin. Jekyll Island, an island off the coast of Georgia, is where the conspirators secretly met in November 1910. This book is about the most blatant scam in history. It accounts for the causes of wars, boom-bust cycles, inflation, depression, and prosperity.

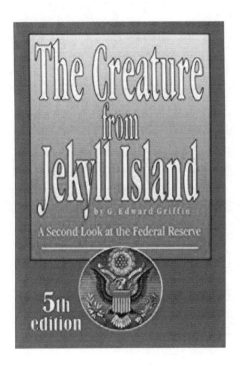

G. Edward Griffin wrote the book *The Creature of Jekyll Island: A Second Look at the Federal Reserve.*

The panic of 1907 was artificially created by J.P. Morgan to justify the creation of the Federal Reserve. J.P. Morgan provoked the panic by spreading a rumor about the insolvency of the Trust Company of America. The United States had a privately-owned central bank from 1816 to 1836.

President Andrew Jackson abolished the first central bank in America. He stated at the time the following: "The bold effort the present bank had made to control the government, the distress it had wantonly produced… are both premonitions of the fate that awaits the American people should they be deluded into a perpetuation of this institution or the establishment of another like it."

After many years, a very small group of domestic and international bankers decided to create a privately-owned central bank. A secret meeting was called by Senator Nelson Aldrich, Republican from Rhode Island and chairman of the Senate Banking Committee. Aldrich's daughter, Abby, married John D. Rockefeller, Jr. Sixty years after the secret meeting, Aldrich's grandson, Nelson Aldrich Rockefeller, became vice president of the United States under President Gerald Ford. Previously, Nelson Rockefeller had served as governor of New York and unsuccessfully ran for the presidential nomination of the Republican Party.

The bankers who secretly met with Senator Aldrich in Jekyll Island

The purpose of the secret meeting in Jekyll Island, Georgia, which Republican Senator Nelson Aldrich initiated, was to create the Federal Reserve Bank. In addition to Senator Aldrich, five other individuals met at the Jekyll Island Club House in 1910. (This writer has been several times to this place in Jekyll Island). These individuals, along with the bankers who they represented, made up approximately 25% of the total wealth of the entire world. As indicated in the book *The Creature from Jekyll Island* (2010), the five individuals were the following:

- Abraham Piatt Andrew, Assistant Secretary of the U.S. Treasury.
- Frank A. Vanderlip, president of the National City Bank of New York, the most powerful of the banks at that time. Vanderlip represented William Rockefeller and the international investment banking house of Kuhn, Loeb & Company.
- Henry P. Davison, senior partner of J.P. Morgan Company.
- Benjamin Strong, head of J.P. Morgan´s Banker Trust Company, who later became the head of the Federal Reserve Bank.
- Paul M. Warburg, a partner in Kuhn, Loeb & Company and a representative of the Rothschild banking dynasty in England and France. He was the brother to Max Warburg, who was head of the Warburg banking consortium in Germany and the Netherlands.

The Creature of Jekyll Island: A Second Look at the Federal Reserve became the number one best seller in Amazon´s category of money and monetary policy. It also ranked 32nd in all non-fiction categories. This book is a classic exposé of the Federal Reserve Bank. It explains the most blatant scam in history. The book has 608 pages and describes how the Federal Reserve Bank is the cause of inflation, depression, prosperity, boom-bust cycles, and wars.

Another important book is the one written by Congressman Ron Paul titled *End the Fed* which was published in 2010. The book became a bestseller in the *New York Times* Best Seller list. Ron Paul, as the title of the book indicates, advocated the abolition of the Federal Reserve System. Congressman Paul argued that "in the post-meltdown world, it is irresponsible, ineffective, and ultimately useless to have a serious economic debate without considering and challenging the role of the Federal Reserve." In *End the Fed*, Congressman Ron Paul used his knowledge on American history, economics, and anecdotes from his own political life to argue that the Fed is both corrupt and unconstitutional. Congressman Paul and his son, Republican Senator Rand Paul, have demanded for years that the Federal Reserve be audited by Congress. However, none of those bills filed by them and others have been enacted into law.

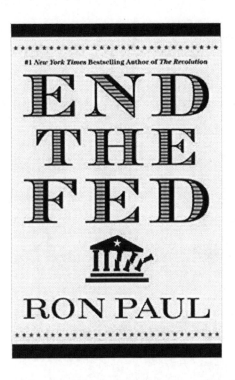

Republican and Libertarian Congressman Ron Paul Republican wrote the book *End the Fed* in 2010.

Congressman Ron Paul stated that the Federal Reserve System is inflating currency today and that these practice threatens to put the United States into an inflationary depression where the United States dollar, which is the reserve currency of the world, would suffer severe devaluation.

Congressman Paul explained how inflation is a hidden tax making warfare much easier to wage. Because people will reject the notion of increasing direct taxes, inflation is then used to help service the overwhelming debts incurred through wars. In turn, the purchasing power of the Americans is diminished, yet most people are unaware of this. According to Ron Paul's theory, this diminution has the strongest impact on individuals with low income since it is a regressive tax. Congressman Paul argues that the Consumer Price Index presently does not include food and energy, yet these are the items on which the majority of the income of poor individuals is spent.

As explained in this chapter by this writer, Congressman Paul stated that most people are not aware that the Fed—created by the Morgans, Rockefellers, and others at a private club off the coast of Georgia—is actually working against their own personal interests. That private millionaire club is, of course, the Jekyll Island Club. Instead of protecting the people, Congressman Paul argued that the Fed now serves as a banking cartel where "the name of the game is bailout"—or otherwise known as privatized profits but socialized losses. Congressman Paul as well as other writers explained the historical links between the creation of central banks and wars, explaining how inflation and devaluations have been used as war-financing tools in the past by many governments from monarchies to democracies.

The four Insiders who met in Jekyll Island

Senator Nelson Aldrich was a Republican from Rhode Island and chairman of the Senate Banking Committee.

Another grandson of Senator Nelson Aldrich was the late David Rockefeller. He was highly involved with the Council on Foreign Relations (founded in 1921) and the Bilderberg Group (founded in 1954). David Rockefeller established the Trilateral Commission in 1973, an organization that Senator Barry Goldwater, the Republican Party presidential candidate for the 1964 election, described as "intended to be the vehicle for multinational consolidation of the commercial and banking interests by seizing control of the political government of the United States."

Paul Moritz Warburg was a traitor since he helped the Bolsheviks come to power in Russia.

Paul Moritz Warburg was born in Hamburg, Germany on August 10, 1868 and died on January 24, 1932. He was one of the conspirators who aimed at taking control over America's economy in the hands of international bankers.

In 1895, Paul Warburg became a partner in his family banking firm M.M. Warburg and Company in Frankfurt, Germany, which was founded by his great grandfather. In 1902, Paul Warburg and his brother Felix moved to New York City. His brother, Max Warburg, who later became a major financier of the Russian Bolshevik Revolution, stayed at home in Frankfurt to run the family bank. M.M. Warburg and Company worked together with the Rothschild's bank in Frankfurt

Paul Warburg was married in that city to Nina J. Loeb, daughter of Solomon Loeb, founder of the New York investment banking firm of Kuhn, Loeb & Co. Paul's brother, Felix Warburg, married Frieda Schiff, daughter of Jacob Schiff, who ran Kuhn, Loeb & Co. Paul Warburg joined his father-in-law's company as a partner overseeing international loans to several governments. He made an annual salary of $500,000, an enormous amount at that time. Paul's brother, Felix Warburg, also worked at the most powerful international banking firm of America, Kuhn, Loeb & Co.

In 1911, Paul Warburg became a naturalized U.S. citizen. The head of Kuhn, Loeb & Co. was Jacob Schiff, who was the father-in-law of his brother Felix and whose family in Frankfurt had ties with the Rothschilds going back a century.

Paul M. Warburg was sworn in as a member of the first Federal Reserve Board on August 10, 1914. He was appointed vice chairman (called "vice governor" before 1935) on August 10, 1916. He resigned from the Board on August 9, 1918. Although Warburg left the Federal Reserve Board in 1918, he continued to serve the Federal Reserve as a member of the Federal Advisory Council from 1921 to 1926.

Warburg was also a director of the Council on Foreign Relations (1921–1932), a trustee of the Institute of Economics (1922–1927), and a trustee of the Brookings Institution after it merged with the Institute of Economics in 1927. Warburg died at his home in New York in 1932. At the time of his death, he was chairman of the Manhattan Company and a director of the Bank of Manhattan Trust Company, Farmers Loan and Trust Company of New York, and First National Bank of Boston.

Benjamin Strong

Benjamin Strong was another American banker who met secretly in Jekyll Island with the Insider conspirators. He was born on December 22, 1872 and died on October 16, 1928. Strong served as Governor of the Federal Reserve Bank of New York for 14 years until his death. Strong exerted great influence over the policies and actions of the entire Federal Reserve System—and indeed over the financial policies of the United States and Europe.

Strong's knowledge of the banking history of the United States, coupled with his intense interest in international affairs, made him a dominant force in U.S. monetary and banking affairs. He was elected president (then called governor) of the Federal Reserve Bank of New York at its first board of directors' meeting on October 5, 1914. He was 41 at the time and served as president of Bankers Trust Company of New York.

Frank A. Vanderlip assisted the Bolsheviks to come to power in Russia. He was a traitor.

Frank A. Vanderlip was born near Aurora, Illinois in 1864 and died in 1937. He served as assistant secretary of the Treasury and handled the sale of $1.4 billion in Spanish-American War bonds. This operation attracted the attention of Wall Street. Vanderlip left the position of assistant secretary of the Treasury to become vice president of National City Bank (today's Citi Bank) in 1901. Vanderlip became a leader in the financing American international trade. In 1909, he was promoted to president of the National City Bank.

Frank A. Vanderlip was a leading banker at the beginning of the 20th Century and worked closely with Senator Nelson Aldrich to develop a proposal for a new central banking system. Many of the provisions of this plan were eventually included in the Federal Reserve Act of 1913.

Henry P. Davison assisted the Bolsheviks to come to power in Russia. He was a traitor.

Henry P. Davison was born in 1867 in Troy, Pennsylvania and died at his home in Long Island, New York in 1922. In 1903, he became one of the founders of the Bankers Trust Company of New York, which became the second largest trust in the country. In 1902, Davison was appointed as vice president of First National Bank. Later, he became a senior partner of the J.P. Morgan Company. Davison was Morgan's right-hand man and he assisted J.P. Morgan & Company in sending several millions in cash to the Bolsheviks. He was a traitor.

The Federal Reserve (The Fed) controls the money supply of America, which allows Insider manipulators to create alternate cycles of boom and bust. This control of the money supply permits the Insiders to earn fabulous amounts of money. However, it also allows the Insiders to control the economy and further centralize the power of the federal government.

Criticisms of the Federal Reserve Bank

The Federal Reserve building is located in Washington, D.C.

The Fed policies influence global economic growth, stock prices, bond yields and exchange rates, including the value of the dollar. The Insiders expanded enormously the money supply during the 1920s and the New York Stock Market soared significantly. When the Insiders of the Fed were ready to contract the money supply or burst the bubble of the New York stock market, they informed their friends to sell their stocks and bonds before the crash and the beginning of the Depression. Later, when the stocks and bonds were at rock bottom, the Insiders and their friends began to buy and became wealthier.

Former Congressman Ron Paul, who served in the House of Representatives Banking Committee and ran for president several times, and his son, Senator Rand Paul, Republican from Kentucky, have repeatedly requested that an independent audit of the Federal Reserve Bank be conducted by the Controller General of the Congress. Ron Paul has called *The Creature from Jekyll Island* a "superb analysis" and has indicated "to be prepared for one heck of a journey through time and mind." Ron Paul agreed with the conclusions of G. Edward Griffin.

The book, *The John Birch Society Agenda*, which was published in January 2012 and revised on May 2017, lists seven reasons for ending the Federal Reserve System. These reasons are the following:

"One, the Fed has institutionalized paper as money without any real value attached to it other than the faith of those who use it.

Two, it is a means to control the economy by the few and was recognized as such by Karl Marx.

Three, the people have no means to find out who owns the Fed and profits from its operation.

Four, the credit of the American people has been used to bring about war and aggrandize a few to wealth beyond imagination.

Five, history has demonstrated that money power has been used to sway the Congress beyond the influence of the people.

Six, there is no question that the Fed, through its extension of credit to the government, is the engine of mass inflation. It has stolen the wealth of the people by diluting the value of the dollar. One significant reason why the Fed's policies have not let to a complete collapse of our nation's economic life is the resiliency of the American businessman to keep the economy as float. Another is the fact that some level of freedom within our economy still exists, even against all odds, to make up for the ongoing destruction of the dollar.

Seven, and most important, the Fed is simply a giant step in the direction of instituting world government. The Fed is one manifestation of this Insider goal. Anyone who thinks that the only problem presented by the Fed is its unconstitutional issuance of money misses a very important point. It is only one of the Marxian planks design to build a world government. There can be little doubt that the Fed is nothing more than one aspect of the Insiders' goal for a New World Order. Elimination of the Fed will go a long way toward the elimination of the structure needed for converting America into a totalitarian branch of a world government... Once a powerful few control the economy, they then control the government, or vice versa."

Currently, the Fed will start slowly shrinking its $4.2 trillion portfolio of mortgage and Treasury bonds purchased during the financial crisis. The Fed is a banking cartel. How these private banks were able to accumulate trillions of dollars?

Conclusion

The creation of the Federal Reserve Bank was an illegal act since the Congress or a president cannot pass a law that violates the Constitution. Sadly, the United States has tolerated this illegal central bank for more than 100 years. Over the years, the Fed has created a massive federal debt and high inflation, which is a hidden tax that confiscates our savings and has illegally, enriched beyond imagination the small banking cartel that owns the Fed.

Chapter 7

The International bankers and capitalists who financed the Bolshevik Revolution in Russia

Jacob Henry Schiff donated millions to Lenin to overthrow Czar Nicholas II. He was a traitor.

Jacob Henry Schiff, whose German name was Jakob Heinrich Schiff, was born on January 10, 1847 in Frankfurt, Germany. His father, Moses Schiff, was a broker for the Rothschilds.

Schiff came to the United States after the Civil War and joined the firm Kuhn, Loeb & Company. Among many other projects, he helped finance the expansion of American railroads and the Japanese military efforts against Tsarist Russia during the Russo-Japanese War.

Schiff also became director of many important corporations, including the National City Bank of New York, Equitable Life Assurance Society, Wells Fargo & Company, and the Union Pacific Railroad. In many of his projects, he was associated with E. H. Harriman. He died on September 25, 1920.

Czar Nicholas II was overthrown with the help of President Woodrow Wilson, many international bankers, and capitalists in the United States who gave enormous financial support to the Bolsheviks, as the communists were then known. All of these individuals committed high treason as Russia was an ally of America during World War I. The communists led by Lenin and Trotsky took Russia out of the war, which freed many German divisions to attack American, British, French, Canadian, and other allied nations troops on the Western Front.

Czar Nicholas II was the last Emperor of Russia. He ruled from November 1, 1894 until his forced abdication on March 15, 1917. Nicholas II and his family were imprisoned. In the spring of 1918, Nicholas II was handed over to the local Ural Soviet. With the approval of the bloody dictator Vladimir Lenin, Czar Nicholas II and his family were eventually assassinated by the Bolsheviks on the night of July 16 and 17, 1918.

Many international bankers and very wealthy capitalists in America were aware that Tsarist Russia was an enormous nation with tremendous potential. The Russian empire covered 8,500,000 square miles. Poland, the three Baltic nations, and Finland were Russian territories. In 1902, Russia produced more than half of the oil of the world and the empire had surpassed the United States as the planet's number one oil producer. Russia was beginning to industrialize. Even though Russia was an ally of America during World War I, the traitors John D. Rockefeller, J.P. Morgan, and their international bankers' friends wanted to overthrow Czar Nicholas II. John D. Rockefeller did not want competition from Russia in oil.

Antony Sutton wrote the book, *Wall Street and the Bolshevik Revolution*, in 1974

Antony Sutton (1925-2002) was a British and American economist, historian, and writer. He wrote the book, *Wall Street and the Bolshevik Revolution*, in 1974. Sutton studied at the universities of London, Göttingen, and California and received his D.Sc. from the University of Southampton. He was an economics professor at California State University, Los Angeles and a research fellow at Stanford University's Hoover Institution from 1968 to 1973.

Antony Sutton explained how John D. Rockefeller and other very rich Americans financed the Bolshevik Revolution. He wrote the following: "Virtually nothing have been written on the close relationship over the past century that the Rockefellers have had with its supposed arch-enemies, the communists. Nevertheless, there has been a continuing, albeit concealed, alliance between international political capitalists and international revolutionary socialists to their mutual benefit."

After the United States entered the war, President Wilson sent Elihu Root, former Secretary of State, on a Special Mission to support the provisional government of Alexander Kerensky. The United States provided a $325 million loan to Kerensky, of which $185 million was distributed.

Daniel Estulin explained the following: "Using Colonel Raymond Robins, head of a Red Cross Mission to Russia, as its emissary, J.P. Morgan & Company sent several million dollars in cash to the Bolsheviks through Henry P. Davison, Morgan's right-hand man."

Estulin explained that the Rockefellers, J.P. Morgan, and the National City Bank founded the American International Corporation in 1915 to coordinate the financial assistance to the communists in Russia. The Chairman of the Board was Frank Vanderlip, former president of the National City Bank, and a member of the group who met in Jekyll Island to conspire in the creation of the banking cartel of the Federal Reserve.

Another organization supporting the Bolsheviks, said Estulin, was the Federal Reserve Bank of New York. This bank was controlled by the five principal banks in New York City. William Laurence Sanders, deputy chairman of the Federal Reserve Bank of New York, wrote to President Wilson, on October 17, 1918, "I am in sympathy with the Soviet form of government as the best suited for the Russian people."

George Foster Peabody, also deputy chairman of the Federal Reserve Bank of New York, who worked with the Rockefellers, said "he supported the Bolshevik form of state monopoly." Another top official of the Federal Reserve Bank of New York, William Boyce Thompson, the then director of the Chase, now Chase Manhattan Bank, stated that "the fullest assistance should be given to the Soviet government in its efforts to organize a volunteer revolutionary army."

Estulin wrote that Leon Trotsky, the other principal leader of the communists in Russia, came with his family and other revolutionaries to New York City on January 13, 1917. Trotsky lived in luxury in America. While in New York, Leon Trotsky received word to return to Russia immediately. With $10,000 for traveling expenses,

Trotsky left on March 26, 1917, on the ship *S.S. Kristianiafjord*, along with 275 communists assisted by Lincoln Steffens, a communist and a John D. Rockefeller's emissary. It appears that John D. Rockefeller himself asked President Wilson for a special passport for Leon Trotsky.

Leon Trotsky was born with the name Lev Davidovich Bronstein in 1879 and died in 1940. He was a Marxist revolutionary, theorist, and Soviet politician. He joined the Bolsheviks just before the 1917 October Revolution, immediately becoming a leader within the Communist Party. Trotsky was removed from power and expelled from the Communist Party. On 20 August 1940, Trotsky was assassinated by Ramón Mercader, a Spanish-born NKVD agent. Mercader, who attacked Trotsky with an ice axe, acted upon instruction from Stalin and was nearly beaten to death by Trotsky's bodyguards, with Mercader spending 20 years in a Mexican prison for murdering Trotsky.

The ship *S.S. Kristianiafjord* stopped in Halifax, Canada on April 13, 1917. Canadian Secret Service and British naval personnel immediately arrested Trotsky. A Canadian cablegram warned that Leon Trotsky was "on his way to take Russia out of the war, which would free many German divisions to attack Canadian troops on the Western Front." Incredibly, another traitor, British Prime Minister Lloyd George, cabled orders to the Canadian Secret Service to free Trotsky. Lloyd George's order was ignored.

Canada's Armed Forces fought bravely during World War I. By the end of the war 625,000 Canadian men and women served with distinction and two-thirds of them in France. More than 60,000 Canadians died and more than 200,000 were wounded in action. The Canadian effort was heroic considering that Canada had eight million citizens at the time. It was for that reason than the Canadian Secret Service did not want to release Leon Trotsky since the Bolshevik revolutionary wanted to take Russia out of the war.

However, another traitor intervened. Mackenzie King, who was a labor expert for John D. Rockefeller, Jr., was able to free Leon Trotsky. King was rewarded with a $30,000-a-year salary as the head of the Rockefeller Foundation Department of Industrial Research, when the average salary in the United States was $500 per year, according to Estulin. Mackenzie King later became Prime Minister of Canada.

Once Lenin and Trotsky succeeded in overthrowing Czar Nicholas II and the Kerensky government that followed in 1918, the headquarters for giving financial support to the communists in the Soviet Union became the building at 120 Broadway on Wall Street. On the top of the building at 120 Broadway on Wall Street was the exclusive Bankers Club. These were the organizers of the World Order. The building at 120 Broadway "not only housed Equitable Life, but also the Federal Reserve Bank of New York, whose directors enthusiastically supported the

Bolsheviks; and the American International Corporation, which has been organized to aid the Soviet Union." The Warburgs sent large sums of money to the communists in the Soviet Union.

Vladimir Ilyich Ulyanov better known as Lenin was the leader of the Bolsheviks in Russia.

Lenin was born in 1870 and died in 1924. He was a Russian communist revolutionary, politician and political theorist. He served as head of government from 1917 to 1924. Under his administration, the Soviet Union became a bloody one-party communist regime. Millions died because Lenin's policies.

Gary Allen has a chapter in his book None Dare Call It Conspiracy explaining how international bankers spent millions to overthrow Czar Nicholas II of Russia and help the communists achieve power in that nation. Allen pointed out that Jacob Schiff, who was the head of the very powerful Jewish banking firm Kuhn, Loeb & Company, spent millions to overthrow Czar

Nicholas II of Russia and more millions to overthrow the government of Alexander Kerensky in order to allow Vladimir Lenin and the communists to take over.

After the February Revolution of 1917, which overthrew the government of Czar Nicholas II, Alexander Kerensky joined the newly formed Russian Provisional Government. On November 7, 1917, his government was overthrown by Vladimir Lenin and the Bolsheviks, which later were called communists in the October Revolution. Russia had a different calendar from the West.

Vladimir Ilyich Ulyanov, better known by the alias Lenin (1870–1924), was a Russian communist revolutionary, who ruled as a dictator in Russia and the Soviet Union when the name was changed. Under his tyrannical regime, the Soviet Union became a one-party nation ruled by the Communist Party.

Millions of people died of famine and mass murders took place under his despotic rule. Thanks to the international bankers who helped Lenin and other Soviet dictators, who came to power later, over 100 million more died as communism expanded to other nations.

Allen said that the financing of the Bolsheviks was done by a syndicate of international bankers, which included, in addition to the Schiff-Warburg clique, the Morgans and the Rockefellers. He wrote that the Morgan organization donated at least $1 million to the communists.

Lord Alfred Milner also provided financial support to the communists in Russia.

Daniel Estulin explained in his book, *The True Story of the Bilderberg Group*, that the Scottish-born steel magnate Andrew Carnegie was also a key supporter of the Bolsheviks. It is very hard to understand why so many bankers and capitalist wanted to overthrow the Russian Czar with the reason being to eliminate completion from a victorious and resurgent Russia after World War I or the Great War as it was called in 1918.

Lord Alfred Milner was born on March 23, 1854 and died on May 13, 1925. He was a wealthy Englishman and a front man for the Rothschilds. He served as paymaster for the international bankers in Petrograd during the Bolshevik Revolution. He was an important financier of the communists and the organizer and the head of a secret organization called the Round Table, a secret organization which was dedicated to bring about a world government where a small group of wealthy financiers would control the planet under a socialist government. Milner was supported by Lord Rothschild of Britain. Milner spent 21 million rubles in financing the Russian Revolution.

Allen explained that Lord Alfred Milner, and Paul, Felix, and Max Warburg represented their respective countries at the Paris Peace Conference at the conclusion of World War I in 1918. These very powerful international bankers, who financed the Bolshevik Revolution, were the same individuals who created the Federal Reserve Bank, which was and still is an international banking cartel.

Allen stated the following: "In the Bolshevik Revolution we have some of the world's richest and most powerful men financing a movement which claims its very existence is based on the concept of stripping of their wealth men like the Rothschilds, Rockefellers, Schiffs, Warburgs, Morgans, Harrimans, and Milners. But obviously these men have no fear of international communism."

"It is only logical to assume that if they financed it and do not fear it, it must be because they control it. Can there be any other explanation that makes sense? Remember that for over 150 years it has been standard operating procedure of the Rothschilds and their allies to control both sides of every conflict. You must have an enemy if you're going to collect from the King…A clique of American financiers not only helped establish communism in Russia, but has striven mightily ever since to keep it alive. Ever since 1918 this clique has been engaged in transferring money and, probably more important, technical information, to the Soviet Union."

The Rockefeller family and communism

The founder of the Rockefeller dynasty was an oil industry business magnate, John D. Rockefeller. He was born on July 8, 1839 and died on May 23, 1937. He was the founder of the Standard Oil Company and considered the richest American of all time.

His wealth continued to grow enormously as the demand for gasoline increased. The *New York Times* estimated after John D. Rockefeller retired from business then he had accumulated close to $1,500,000,000 out of the earnings of the Standard Oil trust and out of his other investments.

John Davison Rockefeller

Rockefeller's wealth was probably the greatest that any private citizen has ever been able to accumulate by his own efforts. "By the time of his death in 1937, Rockefeller's remaining fortune, largely tied up in permanent family trusts, was estimated at $1.4 billion, while America's Gross Domestic Product (GDP) was $92 billion. According to some methods of wealth calculation, Rockefeller's net worth over the last decades of his life would easily place him as the wealthiest known person in recent history. As a percentage of the United States' GDP, no other American fortune past or present would even come close."

Gary Allen's Chapter Six of his book *None Dare Call it Conspiracy* is titled "The Rockefellers and the Reds." He explained that the Rockefeller family has worked with the Rothschilds and their agents since the 1880s. John D. Rockefeller, the founder of the Standard Oil Company, negotiated a rebate on every barrel of oil shipped over the Pennsylvania and Baltimore and Ohio Railroads, which were controlled by Kuhn, Loeb & Company. The rest of the information below is taken from this chapter.

After the Bolshevik Revolution, the Standard Oil of New Jersey bought 50% of the enormous Caucasus oilfields in the Soviet Union even though no private property was allowed to exist. In 1927, the Standard Oil of New York built a refinery in the Soviet Union to help the Bolshevik improve their economy.

The Rockefeller's Chase Bank later merged with the Warburg's Manhattan Bank to form the present Chase Manhattan Bank. The following year the Chase National Bank sold Soviet Union bonds in the United States. Many patriotic organizations denounced the Rockefeller Bank as "a disgrace to America." A loan of $75 million to the communists in the Soviet Union was arranged. The Soviet Union was bankrupt and would have collapsed if it had not been assisted by the Insider international bankers. Without their intervention, communism would have ended. More than a billion people would not have been enslaved by the communists and more than 100 million people all over the world would not have been assassinated!

Sadly, a similar situation is occurring today with the bloody Castro regime in Cuba which is near bankruptcy. Former president Barack Obama, many in Congress from both political parties, and the globalist elite from the Council on Foreign Relations, the Bilderberg Group, and the Trilateral Commission and other allied organizations came to the rescue of the communist regime in the island. Obama recognized Cuba diplomatically in violation of the Helms-Burton Law and began illegally dismantling the commercial embargo. These individuals did not want the communist regime in Cuba to disappear and therefore gave the oppressive regime economic and political concessions in exchange for nothing.

The Rockefeller agent and banker Frank A. Vanderlip, who was the president of the National City Bank of New York, the most powerful of the banks at that time and who also represented the international investment banking house of Kuhn, Loeb & Company, came to the rescue of the Soviet Union. Vanderlip compared Vladimir Lenin to George Washington. He worked together with the Rockefeller public relation agent Ivy Lee to sell the idea that the Bolsheviks were "misunderstood idealists" and "kind benefactors of mankind."

Many years later, *New York Times* reporter, Herbert Matthew, a Council on Foreign Relations member, compared Fidel Castro to George Washington once more. Finally, the Fabian-dominated administration of President Franklin D. Roosevelt recognized the Soviet Union diplomatically. The Rockefeller Chase National Bank established the American-Russian Chamber of Commerce in 1922. The Rockefellers promoted trade with the Soviets and their descendants continue to support communist regimes.

A different view of the Bolshevik Revolution

J.R. Nyquist wrote an article titled "Who was behind the Bolshevik Revolution" which was published in the *WND* website on May 18, 2000. He argued that the books published by Gary Allen and Antony Sutton are not accurate in blaming the Warburgs and Jacob Schiff for helping the Bolsheviks.

Nyquist explained that it was the German Foreign Secretary Arthur Zimmermann who was the chief architect of the communist takeover in Russia. He said that the Kaiser's government provided Lenin 50 million gold marks.

It was true that it was Germany who put Lenin in a sealed train from Switzerland to Sweden. Lenin then crossed into Russia to start the revolution. This writer presents this information but he believes that the books by Allen and Sutton are correct since both of them are respected historians.

During War World II, the bloody dictator Josef Stalin paid tribute to the assistance rendered by the United States to the Soviet Union industry before and during the war. Stalin said that about two thirds of or the large industrial enterprise in the Soviet Union had been built with the help or technical assistance of the United States.

Soviet Union dictator Josef Stalin, President Franklin D. Roosevelt, and British Prime Minister Winston Churchill at the Tehran Conference held on November 1943.

Conclusion

International bankers, and rich capitalists spent millions to overthrow Czar Nicholas II of Russia and helped the communists achieve power in that nation. The financing of the Bolsheviks was done by a syndicate of international bankers, which included, in addition to the Schiff-Warburg clique, the Morgans and the Rockefellers. All of them were traitors and were responsible for over 100 million individuals who have been murdered by communists in the world and tens of millions human beings incarcerated and tortured, including this writer, his brother, many cousins and friends.

While the United States spent billions a year on defense, the Rockefellers and their allies promoted the transfer of technology and increased economic assistance and trade with the communists in the Soviet Union through the Council on Foreign Relations.

Chapter 8

The transfer of technology by the United States to the Soviet Union has continued

Lyndon Baines Johnson

Lyndon Baines Johnson was born on August 27, 1908 and died on January 22, 1973. He was often referred to as LBJ and served as the 36th President of the United States from 1963 to 1969. He became president after the assassination of President John F. Kennedy on November 22, 1963.

The transfer of technology by the United States during the early days to the Soviet Union has continued until today. President Lyndon Baines Johnson, who appointed many members of the Council on Foreign Relations to his administration, traded with the Soviet Union materials that he called non-strategic but that in reality were utilized in wars either directly or indirectly. While American soldiers, sailors, and pilots were dying in the Vietnam War, President Johnson kept selling materials that were killing these Americans.

The procommunist industrialist Cyrus Eaton, who was a secret member of the Council on Foreign Relations and who had started his career as secretary to John D. Rockefeller, promoted trade with the Soviet Union. The Rockefellers and Eaton constructed a $50 million aluminum plant in the Soviet Union even though aluminum is used for jet planes.

Gary Allen wrote the following: "Meanwhile, more than 50,000 Americans have died in Vietnam, many of them killed by weapons which the Rockefellers directly or indirectly supplied to our avowed enemies. Only the technicality of the lack of a formal declaration of war prevents the Rockefellers' trading in the blood of dead Americans from being actionable as treason."

Allen found strange that David Rockefeller, who was at the time president of the Chase Manhattan Bank and Chairman of the Board of the Council on Foreign Relations, took a vacation in the Soviet Union in October 1964. A few days after Rockefeller returned to the United States, Nikita Khrushchev was fired. Allen found the sequence of these events very unusual. He speculated about this visit and asked, "Did David Rockefeller journey to the Soviet Union was to fire an employee?"

Allen wrote the following: "For five decades the communists have based the propaganda on the theme that they were going to destroy the Rockefellers and the other super-rich. Yet we find that for five decades the Rockefellers have been involved in building the strength of the Soviets. We are supposed to believe that those international cartelists do this because they are foolish or greedy. Does this make sense?"

For many years David Rockefeller ran the financial end of the Rockefeller dynasty and Nelson Rockefeller ran the politics. Allen explained that President Richard Nixon was always under the Nelson Rockefeller orbit. When Nixon was elected president in 1968, he hired as Attorney General John Mitchell, who was Nelson Rockefeller's personal lawyer. President Nixon also hired Henry Kissinger, who had been working for the Rockefeller family for many years and who at the time was a paid employee of the Council on Foreign Relations.

Nelson Aldrich Rockefeller

Nelson Aldrich Rockefeller was born on July 8, 1908 and died on January 26, 1979. He served as Vice President under President Gerald Ford from 1974 to 1977. Previously, Rockefeller served as governor of New York.

Secretary of State Hillary Clinton and President Barack Obama transferred major technology to Russia and by doing so seriously endangered the national security of the United States

John David Podesta was born on January 8, 1949.

John Podesta is the former chairman of the 2016 Hillary Clinton presidential campaign. He previously served as chief of staff to President Bill Clinton and counselor to President Barack Obama. Podesta is the chairman of the radical Center for American Progress, which is funded by George Soros.

The Rocci Stucci article explained that Hillary Clinton's campaign chairman, John Podesta, received $35 million from a Putin-connected company to his small company. Podesta violated federal financial law for his failure to disclose his membership in the board of this offshore company. Podesta had a think tank which wrote favorably about the Russian reset while apparently receiving millions from Kremlin-linked Russian oligarchs via an offshore LLC. One of Secretary of State Hillary Clinton's major policy initiatives was the "reset" of the relations with Russia. The reset was one of President Barack Obama's "earliest new foreign policy initiatives," according to the White House. As America's chief diplomat, Secretary Clinton was the central person on this reset, handling a range of issues from arms control to technological cooperation.

On March 25, 2012, President Barack Obama inadvertently was caught speaking on an open microphone in Seoul, South Korea assuring outgoing Russian President Dmitry Medvedev that he was going to have "more flexibility" to deal with issues such as missile defense after his reelection as president. Obama urged Moscow to give him "space" until after the November 2012 election and Medvedev said he would relay the message to incoming Russian president Vladimir Putin.

Obama delivered on that promise by drastically cutting the Pentagon's budget and reducing the number of intercontinental ballistic missiles while Russia improved and built more intercontinental ballistic missiles. Shamefully, Obama, together with Hillary Clinton, transferred technology to Russia that will used by its Armed Forces.

The article said that on July 6, 2009, President Barack Obama went to Moscow and together with Russian President Dmitry Medvedev announced the creation of the U.S.-Russia Bilateral Presidential Commission. The Bilateral Commission's goals where the following: "To improve communication and cooperation between the governments of Russia and the United States. To identify areas of cooperation and pursuing joint projects and actions that strengthens strategic stability, international security, economic well-being, and the development of ties between the Russian and American people." The Bilateral Commission played a very important role in all areas, such as from intellectual property sharing to export licensing to facilitating American investment in Russia and Russian investment in America."

President Obama and Medvedev announced in Moscow that the work of the Bilateral Commission was going to be directed by Secretary of State Hillary Clinton and her counterpart, Russian Foreign Minister Sergei Lavrov. As President Obama explained it, the effort would "be coordinated by Secretary Clinton and Minister Lavrov, and Secretary Clinton would travel to Russia to implement the goals of the Commission."

The Rocci Stucci article stated the following:

"According to leaked U.S. government cables, U.S. State Department officials beginning in 2009 played a substantial role in assisting Russian government entities in accessing U.S. capital and in seeking investments in U.S. high technology companies. Specifically, they worked to support the efforts of the Russian State Investment Fund, Rusnano, to seek investment opportunities in the United States by arranging meetings with U.S. tech firms. They also crafted and delivered joint statements with Russian officials on cooperation on technological matters... In short, no cabinet official in the Obama Administration was more intimately and directly involved in the Russian reset than Hillary Clinton."

"Hillary Clinton and the Obama Administration saw the opportunity for widespread technological cooperation between the U.S. and Russia. During her October 2009 visit to Russia, she noted the country's strength in STEM (science, technology, engineering, mathematics). It is just a treasure trove of potential for the Russian economy. Technological cooperation and investment deals seemed to be the sort of win-win deals President Obama said he sought. But as we will see, the Clintons and close aides appear to have personally benefited from such deals. And these deals also raised serious questions from the FBI, the U.S. Army, and foreign governments that the Russian military was benefiting from them as well."

"A major part of this technological cooperation included Russian plans to create its own version of Silicon Valley. The research facility, on the outskirts Moscow, was dubbed Skolkovo and would be developed with the cooperation and investment of major U.S. tech firms. In 2010, Cisco pledged a cool $1 billion to Skolkovo, and Google and Intel also jumped on board.25 (All three happened to be major Clinton Foundation supporters as well—as we will see, a significant factor for dozens of companies who became involved with Skolkovo.) The idea was simple: match Russian brainpower with U.S. investment dollars and entrepreneurial knowhow to spark technological breakthroughs in a wide variety of areas including energy, communications, sensors, and propulsion systems. Unlike the freewheeling, decentralized, and entrepreneurial culture in California, Skolkovo would have a distinctly different culture. It would be more centralized, and dominated by Russian government officials. Skolkovo was launched as entirely a state project."

"A Skolkovo Foundation was established to manage that effort. Ultimately dozens of U.S. tech firms including Cisco, Google, and Intel would make major financial contributions to the project. Hillary Clinton praised the initiative in a joint statement with Russian Foreign Minister Lavrov. The statement praised American companies like Cisco and Microsoft for "participating in Russia's Skolkovo Innovation Center Project, with over a billion dollars committed.""

"Many of the key figures in the Skolkovo process — on both the Russian and U.S. sides — had major financial ties to the Clintons. During the Russian reset, these figures and entities provided the Clintons with tens of millions of dollars, including contributions to the Clinton Foundation, paid for speeches by Bill Clinton, or investments in small start-up companies with deep Clinton ties."

"Many of those involved in Skolkovo who also donated to the Clinton Foundation have deep ties to the Clintons. For example, John Chambers, the head of Cisco, and member of the Skolkovo Foundation, received the Clinton Global Initiative Citizen's Award from Bill Clinton. Chambers and Cisco gave between $1 to $5 million to the Clinton Foundation. Craig Barrett, former head of Intel Corporation, served on the board of the Skolkovo Foundation and the Clinton Global Initiative. Intel has given between $250,000 and $500,000 to the Clinton Foundation. Those on the Russian side of the Skolkovo research project have also donated to the Clinton Foundation. The man heading up the Skolkovo Foundation in Russia is a controversial figure named Viktor Vekselberg. Described as one oligarch who isn't afraid to get down and dirty, Vekselberg made his billions in the oil and metals sectors. Vekselberg is a Putin confidant and a Clinton Foundation donor via his company, Renova Group."

"The Nuclear Cluster at Skolkovo is committed to enhancing the nuclear capabilities of the Russian state. A major listed beneficiary of this research is Rosatom, the Russian State Nuclear Agency, which manages the country's nuclear arsenal. Rosatom, through its subsidiary ARMZ, purchased a Canadian uranium company called Uranium One in 2010."

The Canadian company Uranium One held 20% of uranium mines in the United States. This Russian purchase damaged the national security and was approved by Secretary of State Hillary Clinton and President Barack Obama. Nine Uranium One shareholders donated more than $145 million to the Clinton Foundation. Some of those donations, including those by Uranium One Chairman Ian Telfer, had not been disclosed by the Clinton Foundation.

National Security implications

The Rocci Stucci article explained the following:

"The serious questions raised by Hillary Clinton's pushing of technology transfer and investments as part of the Russian reset doesn't end with the issues of self-dealing and cronyism. There are serious national security questions that have been raised about both Skolkovo and Rusnano, by the FBI, the U.S. Army, and cyber security experts. Specifically, these experts have argued that the activities of Skolkovo and Russian investment funds like Rusnano are ultimately serving the interests of the Russian military."

"In 2014, the FBI sent letters to a number of firms involved with Skolkovo in what was called an extraordinary warning issued to technology companies. The FBI's Boston Office warned U.S. tech companies that Skolkovo could draw them unwittingly into industrial espionage. The FBI warning singled out the Skolkovo Foundation, with which Hillary Clinton and the State Department had actively encouraged American companies to work. (Memorandums of Understanding signed by American companies to work with Skolkovo were done under the auspices of the State Department). The foundation may be a means for the Russian government to access our nation's sensitive or classified research development facilities and dual-use technologies with military and commercial application, warned Lucia Ziobro, the assistant special agent at the FBI's Boston office. She noted that the Skolkovo Foundation had signed deals with the Russian military contractor OJSC Kamaz, which builds military vehicles for the Russian Armed Forces. The FBI believes the true motives of the Russian partners, who are often funded by their government, is to gain access to classified, sensitive, and emerging technology from the companies, said Ziobro."

"Skolkovo's link to the Russian military-intelligence apparatus is not in dispute. In 2011, when Russian spy Anna Chapman was deported from the U.S. on espionage charges, she returned to Russia and quickly emerged at—of all places—Skolkovo. Chapman was steered to the research center, and the director of Skolkovo suggested she apply for a $1 million research grant for some projects with the Young Guards, a pro-Putin youth group."

"The U.S. Army Foreign Military Studies Program at Fort Leavenworth issued a report in 2013 about the security implications of Skolkovo. The report declared that the purpose of Skolkovo was to serve as a vehicle for worldwide technology transfer to Russia in the areas of information technology, biomedicine, energy, satellite and space technology, and nuclear technology. Of course, technology can have multiple uses—both civilian and military."

"The report noted that the Skolkovo Foundation has, in fact, been involved in defense-related activities since December 2011, when it approved the first weapons-related project—the development of a hypersonic cruise missile engine. The project is a response to the U.S. Department of Defense's Advanced Hypersonic Weapon, part of the Prompt Global Strike program. Sophisticated physical security, consisting of cameras, thermal imaging, and alarms, also suggests that not all of the center's efforts are civilian in nature. Because of the way Skolkovo operates, the government's operation of Skolkovo and investment positions in companies will likely provide its military awareness of and access to technologies."

"The report further noted that Skolkovo is arguably an overt alternative to clandestine industrial espionage—with the additional distinction that it can achieve such a transfer on a much larger scale and more efficiently. In short, the FBI and the U.S. Army have raised serious concerns about these activities serving to subsidize and enhance the military technological capabilities of the Russian government."

"Cyber security experts also expressed deep reservations as early as 2010 that U.S. companies working at Skolkovo may…inadvertently be harming global cyber security. And indeed, Skolkovo happens to be the site of the Russian Security Service (FSB)'s security centers 16 and 18, which are in charge of information warfare for the Russian government. According to *Newsweek*, it is here that the Russian government runs information warfare operations against the Ukrainian government. As Vitaliy Naida, head of the Internal Security (SBU) department for the Ukrainian government told *Newsweek*, It starts with the FSB's security centers 16 and 18, operating out of Skolkovo, Russia. These centers are in charge of information warfare. They send out propaganda, false information via social media. Re-captioned images from Syria, war crimes from Serbia—they're used to radicalize and then recruit Ukrainians."

"According to a study by the Swedish Defense Research Agency, the work of Rusnano will have a hugely beneficial effect on the Russian military: It is possible that the biggest impact of nanotechnology in the short term will be as a driver of the modernization of the Russian Armed

Forces. Indeed, it was Vladimir Putin who made this very point, saying during a 2008 speech during a meeting of the State Council that breakthroughs in nanotechnology and information technology could lead to revolutionary changes in weapons and defense."

"The Russian government sees technologies developed in the civilian sector as dual use, meaning that they have military applications as well. Innovative Russia 2020, the Russian government's innovation policy which was approved in December 2011, stated, Priority will be given to exchange of knowledge and technology between the defense and civil sectors, development of dual-use technology, weapons development, modernization of military material, and improving methods to fight terrorism."

The nation that develops a hypersonic cruise missile first will change the nature of wars. Currently, there is no anti-defensive missile system that could stop a hypersonic missile. Russia and China are far ahead of the United States in the development of such a dangerous weapon.

President Donald J. Trump is being falsely accused by the corrupt and biased mainstream media and Democrats in Congress of collusion with Russia. Yet, it was President Barack Obama and Hillary Clinton who were the two individuals who transferred technology to Russia endangering the national security of the United States.

Where was the corrupt mainstream press then? Why there was no Congressional investigation of this transfer of technology that this writer considers high treason?

The Trump administration blocks the purchase of a firm with sensitive technology by China

Unlike the Obama administration that allowed the purchase of 20% of America's uranium mines by Russia, the purchase of tens of thousands of acres in several states that contained oil and gas by China, and the sale of companies to enemy nations with important technology, the

Trump administration has protected the national security. On September 14, 2017, the United States blocked China's efforts to purchased Lattice Semiconductor Corporation, a firm of advanced computer chips with military applications.

The Congressional Committee on Foreign Investment (CFIUS) ruled against the Lattice purchase. However, in other instances the CFIUS failed to protect the national security especially during the eight years of President Obama. Senate Majority Whip John Cornyn, Republican from Texas, and Congressman Robert Pittenger, Republican from South Carolina, are drafting a bill to overhaul and strengthen the CFIUS. Treasury Secretary Steven Mnuchin has supported the idea to require more scrutiny of purchases coming from nations such as China.

China wants to control the semiconductor industry in the world. The Chinese have encourage technology corporations to place factories and research and development centers, as Boeing, General Electric, General Motors, and others have done, in their country in order to acquire free technology and inventions. American corporations that have established research and development centers in China are required by that communist capitalist regime to share all the technology, new products and inventions. China has also stolen military and industrial secrets from the United States for decades with complete impunity.

The September 16, 2017, *Wall Street Journal* editorial stated the following: "Beijing is extorting U.S. intellectual property. China also obtains trade secrets through computer hacking and old school-spying. An FBI survey in 2015 found that China was responsible for 95% of economic-espionage, with its caseload growing 56% a year.

Conclusion

President Lyndon Johnson, who appointed many members of the Council on Foreign Relations to his administration, traded with the Soviet Union materials that he called non-strategic but that in reality were utilized in wars either directly or indirectly. President Barack Obama and Secretary of State Hillary Clinton have assisted Russia with the major transfer of technology in helping that country to develop a weapon that could destroy the United States.

The Congressional Committee on Foreign Investment needs to be overhaul and strengthen and China's predatory behavior and the stealing of America's military and industrial secrets must end with strong retaliatory response and economic sanctions.

All technology transfers to enemy nations this writer believes are treason!

Chapter 9

The Council on Foreign Relations is the invisible government of the United States

Lionel Curtis

On May 19, 1919, a group of Insiders from the United States and Great Britain led by Colonel Edward M. House, Lionel Curtis, Lord Milner, and other British individuals met at the Majestic Hotel in Paris, France. In 1919, they founded the Royal Institute of International Affairs (RIIA) in London. The British globalist Insiders have always met in the Chatham House. Also present at the meeting were John Foster Dulles and Allen Dulles.

Aung San from Burma leaves the Chatman House.

According to the website of the Chatham House, the Royal Institute of International Affairs is an independent policy institute based in London. Its mission is to help build a sustainably secure, prosperous, and fair world. The website states the following: "In 1919 British and American delegates to the Paris Peace Conference, under the leadership of Lionel Curtis, conceived the idea of an Anglo-American Institute of foreign affairs to study international problems with a view to preventing future wars. In the event, the British Institute of International Affairs was founded separately in London in July 1920." The American delegates developed the Council on Foreign Relations in New York as a sister institute."

"The Chatham House engages governments, the private sector, civil society and its members in open debate and confidential discussion on the most significant developments in international affairs. Each year, the institute runs more than 300 private and public events – conferences, workshops and roundtables – in London and internationally with partners. Our convening power attracts world leaders and the best analysts in their respective fields from across the globe."

Similar to the website of the Council on Foreign Relations, the Royal Institute of International Affairs does not explain that this most powerful organization is the power behind the throne in Great Britain. Both the CFR and the RIIA are led by rich individuals belonging to a globalist elite who are working to establish a planetary government under the United Nations but reporting and following orders from them.

These powerful individuals of the New World Order, after founding the RIIA and the CFR, created similar Institutes of International Affairs in the Great Britain's colonies of Canada, South Africa, Australia, New Zealand, and India. They also created a branch in the United States called the Council of Foreign Relations, which later separated from the Royal Institute of International Affairs

Colonel Edward M. House was the most influential advisor of President Woodrow Wilson, who served from 1913 to 1921. His power was so great that Colonel House became almost co-president during the Wilson administration. Colonel House was one of the founders of the CFR in 1921.

According to Estulin, Colonel House was a Marxist and wanted a one-world government. He supported the creation of the Federal Reserve Bank and the passing of the 16th Amendment of the Constitution, which introduced the graduated income tax. Colonel House wrote the plan for the League of Nations as a way to achieve a world government.

Daniel Estulin wrote *The Bilderberg Group* in 2009.

Daniel Estulin wrote *The Bilderberg Group* (2009). This book has been translated into 48 languages and sold in over 67 countries. Estulin discussed the three powerful organizations, the Council on Foreign Relations (CFR), the Trilateral Commission (TC), and the Bilderberg Group (BG).

The Council on Foreign Relations says it is a think tank. Its website explains the following: "The CFR is dedicated to increasing America´s understanding of the world and contributing ideas to U.S. foreign policies. The Council accomplishes this mainly by promoting constructive close debates and discussions, clarifying world issues, and publishing the *Foreign Affairs* magazine." Other writers describe the CFR as the invisible government of the United States.

From its very beginning, the members of the CFR wanted to form a one-world government with a centralized global financing system. It attracted capitalists, socialists, opportunists, and some idealists. The Rockefeller and the Carnegie foundations financed the organization. All members were sworn to secrecy. Even though top executives from all major newspapers and magazines and later television channels participated in the meetings, no one reported about what took place and what decisions were reached.

Estulin wrote that one of the earliest critics of the CFR was the mayor of New York City, John F. Hylan, who in 1922 stated the following in a speech: "The real menace of our republic is the invisible government, which, like a giant octopus, sprawls its slimy length over our city, state and nation. At the head is a small group of banking houses generally referred to as international bankers. This little coterie of powerful international bankers virtually runs our government for their own selfish ends."

Another fierce critic of the CFR was Senator William Jenner. On February 23, 1954, Senator Jenner stated the following: "Today the path to total dictatorship in the United States can be laid by strictly legal means; unseen and unheard by Congress, the President, or the people... Outwardly we have a Constitutional government. We have operating within our government and political system another government representing another form of government, a bureaucratic elite which believes our Constitution is outmoded and it is sure that it is the winning side...All the strange developments in foreign policy agreements may be traced to this group who are going to make us over to suit their pleasure."

Estulin pointed out that economist and Ambassador John Kenneth Galbraith who was a former member of the CFR said, "Why should businessmen be briefed by government officials on information not available to the general public, especially since it can be financially advantageous?"

Estulin stated the following: "To appreciate the extend of power the Bilderbergers, the Council on Foreign Relations, and Trilateral Commission exercise, it is enough to recall that almost all presidential candidates for both parties have belonged to at least one of these organizations, many of the U.S. congressmen and senators, most major policy-making positions, especially in the field of foreign relations, much of the press, most of the leadership of the CIA, FBI, IRS, and many of the remaining governmental organizations in Washington. CFR members occupy nearly all White House cabinet positions."

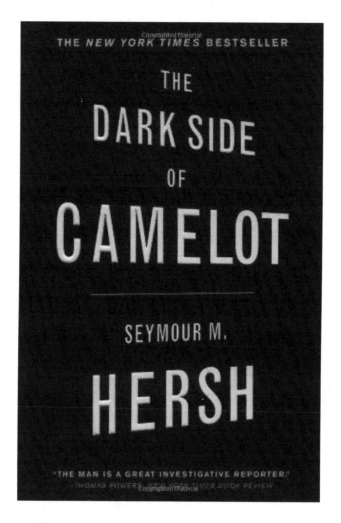

Seymour Hirsch wrote the book *The Dark Side of Camelot* in 1998.

Estulin wrote that most presidents have been members of the CFR. In 1952 and 1956 CFR Dwight D. Eisenhower defeated CFR Adlai Stevenson. In 1960, CFR John F. Kennedy defeated CFR Richard Nixon (The Mafia stole this election from Nixon according to Seymour Hirsch's book *The Dark Side of Camelot*). President Kennedy hired as Secretary of State Dean Rusk, who had worked as president of the Rockefeller Foundation, and 63 other CFR members for the State Department. Thanks to the globalists in the Kennedy administration the members of the Brigade 2506 were defeated at the Bay of Pigs in 1961.

In 1964, Republican Senator Barry Goldwater, who was an anti-globalist nationalist conservative, was defeated by Lyndon B. Johnson. Senator Goldwater defeated Nelson Rockefeller at the Republican Convention. Later Rockefeller and the CFR said that the patriot Senator Goldwater was a "dangerous radical who would abolish Social Security, drop atom bombs on Hanoi, and in general be a reincarnation of the Fascist dictator Mussolini."

In 1968, CFR Richard Nixon defeated CFR Hubert Humphrey. President Nixon hired 115 CFR members at the beginning of his administration. In 1972, CFR Nixon defeated CFR George McGovern. In 1976, CFR Jimmy Carter defeated Gerald Ford. In 1980 non CFR member Ronald Reagan defeated CFR Jimmy Carter. However, Reagan's Vice President was CFR George H.W. Bush. Third Party candidate in 1980 was CFR John Anderson. President Reagan hired 313 CFR members in his administration.

In 1984, President Reagan defeated CFR Walter Mondale. In 1988, CFR George H.W. Bush defeated CFR Michael Dukakis. President George H.W. Bush hired 387 members of CFR, BG, and TC. In 1992, CFR, BG, TC Bill Clinton defeated CFR President George H.W. Bush. Clinton hired almost 100 CFR members in his administration.

In 1996, CFR Clinton defeated CFR Robert Dole. In 2000, non CFR member George W. Bush defeated CFR Al Gore. Like other previous presidents, George W. Bush staffed his administration with CFR members. In 2004, President George W. Bush defeated CFR John Kerry. Both of them belong to the Order of Skull and Bones.

In 2008, non CFR member but selected by the Bilderberg Group Barack Obama defeated CFR John McCain. In 2012, the Bilderberg Group selected President Obama and he defeated Mitt Romney. In 2016, non CFR member Donald J. Trump defeated CFR Hillary Clinton. Although President Trump, who is a patriot and ran as anti-globalist nationalist America First, hired CFR, BG, and TC members in his administration but in lesser numbers than previous presidents.

Estulin pointed out that as presidents of both parties come and go the CFR's power and agenda remain the same. Gary Allen in his book *The Rockefeller File* stated that "While grassroots Democrats and Republicans generally have greatly different views on the economy, political policies, and federal activities, as you climbed the sides of the political pyramid, the two parties become more and more alike."

Donald J. Trump won the 2016 election by running against the establishment of the Democratic and Republican Parties. Many voters were tired of Congressional Republicans not fighting against President Obama's scandals, crimes, and violations of the Constitution.

Estulin said that in April 1974, CFR Richard N. Gardner, former Deputy Assistant Secretary of State, wrote in the CFR journal *Foreign Affairs* the following: "In short, the house of world order will have to be built from the bottom up rather than from the top down…An end run around national sovereignty, eroding it piece by piece, will be accomplish much more than the old fashion assault." James Warburg, son of the traitor Paul Warburg, told the Senate Foreign Relations Committee on February 17, 1950, "We shall have world government whether or not you like it, by conquest or consent."

According to Estulin within a year of the founding of the CFR, the Rockefeller and Carnegie Foundations agreed to finance the agenda of this globalist institution. During most of its existence, the CFR has not been investigated by reporters even though the top executives of the *Washington Post*, the *New York Times*, the *Wall Street Journal, ABC, CBS, NBC, FoxNews, Time, Business Week, Fortune, U.S. News and World Report*, and many other media had belong and presently belong to the CFR. The late Katherine Graham, owner of the establishment Destroy Trump newspaper the *Washington Post*, when asked the lack on investigative reporting of the CFR said, "There are some things the general public does not need to know about us and shouldn't."

The Harold Pratt House is a mansion located on 58 East 68th Street and Park Avenue in New York City. It serves as headquarters for the Council on Foreign Relations. The house was constructed for Harold I. Pratt in the years 1919-1920. The Council on the Foreign Relations moved to Pratt House in April 1945 after it was donated to the CFR by his widow, Harriet Barnes Pratt. She is an heir of the Standard Oil Rockefeller fortune.

There are over 5,000 members that belong to the CFR. However, only a small group of an inner circle is in charge of this organization. Members of the CFR have included the following former U.S. presidents: Herbert Hoover, Dwight D. Eisenhower, John F. Kennedy, Richard M. Nixon, Jimmy Carter, George H. W. Bush, and Bill Clinton. The presidents who do not belong to the CFR, as well as those that do, have named CFR members to the most important cabinet positions (such as the secretaries of State, Defense, and Treasury). All presidents have also appointed CFR members to the Joint Chiefs of Staff, director of intelligence, the CIA, NATO, and important White House positions, such as director of the National Security Council.

The Council of Foreign Relations established another headquarters in Washington, D.C. the building is located at 1777 F Street, NW. Secretary Hillary Clinton once said that it was great the CFR had an office in the nation's capital so she would not have to go to New York to receive its orders. She, of course, made the remarks in jest. However, it is a fact that CFR members have always controlled the Department of State.

The CFR membership is made up of former ambassadors, cabinet officers, bankers, CEOs of multinational corporations, industrialists, high ranking armed force officers, media owners and editors and important reporters, university presidents and key professors, Supreme Court justices, federal judges, think-tank leaders, wealthy Wall Street investors, and entrepreneurs. One very powerful member, who has served as president of the CFR, was the late David Rockefeller. There are several Rockefellers who currently belong to the CFR.

There are three types of memberships in the CFR. Two of them are life time memberships and term memberships. There is also a corporate membership. The CFR describes the corporate membership as follows:

"Founded in 1953 with 25 corporate members, the Corporate Program has since expanded to include more than 140 companies from various industries and regions of the world.

Through CFR's unmatched convening power, the program links private sector leaders with decision-makers from government, media, non-governmental organizations, and academia to discuss issues at the intersection of business and foreign policy."

"Executives at member companies have access to the Council's intellectual capital through briefings with CFR fellows, rapid response conference calls and livestreams, access to *Foreign Affairs* magazine, and hundreds of meetings each year in New York, Washington, DC, and other major cities throughout the United States and around the world."

Benefits of Corporate Membership

"Corporate membership is available at three levels: Founders ($100,000), President's Circle ($60,000), and Affiliates ($30,000)."

"Member companies are offered briefings by in-house experts, a members-only website with CFR resources tailored to the private sector, and roundtables designed specifically for executives. The highlight of the program year is the annual Corporate Conference, which addresses such topics as competitiveness, geopolitical risk, and the global economic outlook."

"Additionally, the program provides professional development opportunities for individuals who have fewer than ten years of experience through its Young Professionals Briefing series and for individuals on a senior management track through its Corporate Leaders Program."

The best book written on the CFR is *The Shadows of Power: The Council on Foreign Relations and the American Decline* (1988) by James Perloff. Perloff wrote that "since its founding in 1921, the Council has been the Establishment's chief link to the U.S. government."

Arthur Schlesinger, Jr., a member of the CFR and author of the book, *A Thousand Days* (1965), who served in the Kennedy administration, said that the Council on Foreign Relation is a "front organization" for "the heart of the American establishment." Writer David Halberstam in his book *The Best and the Brightest* (1972) called the CFR "the Establishment unofficial club."

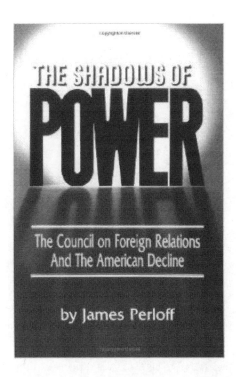

The Shadows of Power: The Council on Foreign Relations And The American Decline (1988) was written by James Perloff.

Perloff wrote that the CFR has two main objectives. The first is the creation of a world government under the single global authority of the United Nations. The ultimate goal is to erase all national identities and boundaries and for the United Nations (U.N.) to rule the planet.

The United States and other nations would lose completely their sovereignty, currency, laws, constitutions, and courts. The wealth of rich nations would be distributed to Third World countries, which are ruled mostly by dictators. In the United States the dollar would be abolished and Americans would pay U.N. taxes.

American industries and businesses would be regulated by the U.N. Environmental Protection Agency. The right to own weapons and private property would be abolished and many other horrible sanctions would be imposed on Americans under this diabolical plan.

The masters would be the powerful individuals who belong to the Council on Foreign Relations (CFR), the Bilderberg Group (BG), and the Trilateral Commission (TC), which would control the United Nations, and the rest of the people of the world would be enslaved. There are 140 multinational companies from various industries and regions of the world that currently belong to the corporate membership of the CFR.

Admiral Chester Ward co-authored with Phyllis Schlafly a book entitled *Kissinger on the Couch* (1975).

Admiral Chester Ward, former judge advocate general of the United States Navy, was a member of the CFR for almost 20 years. He was shocked by what he discovered about this powerful organization. In 1975, Admiral Chester Ward co-authored a book with Phyllis Schlafly entitled *Kissinger on the Couch* (1975).

The authors denounced the CFR by stating the following regarding this organization: "It has a goal of submergence of the United States sovereignty and national independence into an all-powerful one-world government... This lust to surrender the sovereignty and independence of the United States is pervasive throughout most of the membership."

The second goal of the CFR, according to James Perloff, is the advancement of socialism/communism. To support this argument, Perloff wrote that dozens of Marxists and socialists, among them Soviet Leon Trotsky and Premier Nikita Khrushchev and Yugoslavia communist dictator Tito, have published articles in the *Foreign Affairs* journal of the CFR. Perloff pointed out that when Trotsky died, he was praised in the journal of the CFR.

Perloff wrote in his book that there has always existed an affinity between Marxists and the CFR. For example, in 1959, Fidel Castro, Soviet Union Foreign Minister Anastas Mikoyan (who later visited Havana, Cuba), and other communists were invited as guest speakers of the CFR. In subsequent years, other communists were invited, such as Daniel Ortega of Nicaragua, communist revolutionary leader Guillermo Unger of El Salvador, and various officials of the People's Republic of China. John McCloy, who served as chairman of the CFR, was a close friend of the Soviet dictator Nikita Khrushchev and visited the private house of Khrushchev and swam in his pool.

Perloff concluded in his book that the accusations against the Council of Foreign Relations regarding its strives towards a world government and its receptivity to communism are true. Additionally, Perloff stated that the CFR's heavy presence in Washington, D.C. has led to a weakening of the United States as a superpower and the destruction of many of its allies over the years.

A granddaughter of President Theodore Roosevelt, Edith Kermit Roosevelt, described the word Establishment as follows: "It is the power elite international finance, business, the professions and government, largely from the North East, who wield most of the power regardless of who is in the White House. Most people are unaware of the existence of this "legitimate Mafia." Yet the power of the Establishment makes itself felt from the professor who seeks a foundation grant, to the candidate for a cabinet post or State Department job. It affects the nation's policies in almost every area."

James Perloff indicated that the American Establishment is associated with big businesses and the children of these rich families are sent to private schools such as Groton. Upon graduation, they attend Ivy League universities such as Harvard, Yale, Princeton, and Columbia. While these rich youngsters are enrolled in these Ivy League universities, they join exclusive fraternities, such as Skull and Bones in Yale.

The following three United States presidents have been members of this exclusive fraternity at Yale University: William Howard Taft, George Herbert Walker Bush, and his son, George W. Bush. In the 2000 presidential election, George W. Bush and the Democratic candidate Senator John Kerry were both Bonesmen, as member of this powerful and influential fraternity are called.

Bright students are given scholarships as Rhodes scholars and attend Oxford University in Great Britain. One such student was Bill Clinton, although unlike many others, he came from a poor family.

Perloff wrote that upon graduation many of the sons and daughters of the American Establishment pursue a career in Wall Street, perhaps joining an international investment bank such as Chase Manhattan or a prominent brokerage house or law firm. Many others are hired as employees or members of the boards of powerful and influential foundations such as the Rockefeller, Ford, and Carnegie foundations. All others may work at think tanks such as the Brookings Institution, which is a branch of the CFR. These foundations and think tanks are closely aligned with the CFR.

Many of these Establishment individuals serve in Congress and high positions in the federal government, including the presidency. In order to be appointed to the most important cabinet positions in a Republican or Democratic administration, especially to the Department of State, it is a prerequisite to belong to the Council on Foreign Relations. All members were sworn to secrecy. Even though top executives from all major newspapers and magazines and later television channels participated in the meetings, no one reported about what took place and what decisions were reached.

James Perloff wrote the book *Truth is a Lonely Warrior:*
Unmasking the Forces Behind Global Destruction (2013).

James Perloff wrote the book *Truth is a Lonely Warrior: Unmasking the Forces Behind Global Destruction* in 2013. Amazon explained the book as follows: "If you are one of those who senses that something just is not right with the explanations we are given for wars, our dying economy, and other world events, this book may be just right for you. Countless lies have been planted in the corporate-controlled media to benefit the rich and the few; these lies have become fact through the mechanism of frequent repetition. Refuting such lies with credibility requires in-depth analysis."

The webpage of the Council on Foreign Relations

The webpage of the Council on Foreign Relations describes this organization as follows: "The Council on Foreign Relations is a think tank." Its website explains the following: "The CFR is dedicated to increasing America's understanding of the world and contributing ideas to U.S. foreign policies. The Council accomplishes this mainly by promoting constructive close debates and discussions, clarifying world issues, and publishing articles the *Foreign Affairs* magazine."

According to the webpage, the membership of the CFR is described as follows: "Since its founding in 1921, the Council on Foreign Relations (CFR) has grown a membership of over 5,000 of some of the most prominent leaders in the foreign policy arena, including top government officials, renowned scholars, business executives, acclaimed journalists, prominent lawyers, and distinguished nonprofit professionals. The membership is divided almost equally among those living in New York, Washington, DC, and across the country and abroad."

"CFR members enjoy unparalleled access to a nonpartisan forum through which they can engage with and gain insight from experts in international affairs. Members have in-person access to world leaders, senior government officials, members of Congress, and prominent thinkers and practitioners in academia, policy, and business, many of whom are members themselves. Convening nearly one thousand events annually, CFR is dedicated to facilitating an intellectual exchange of ideas through expert panel discussions, symposia, town halls, live streams, and CEO forums exclusively for members. Through exposure to CFR's think tank, publications, briefing materials, and special content on CFR.org and ForeignAffairs.com, members benefit from an expansive collection of unmatched intellectual capital and resources."

"The Council on Foreign Relation is an independent, nonpartisan membership organization, think tank, and publisher. CFR members, including Brian Williams, Fareed Zakaria, Angelina Jolie, Chuck Hagel, and Erin Burnett, explain why the Council on Foreign Relations is an indispensable resource in a complex world."

"The David Rockefeller Studies Program—the CFR's think tank—is composed of more than 70 full-time and adjunct fellows who cover the major regions and deal with significant issues shaping today's international agenda. The program also includes recipients of several one-year fellowships. The Studies Program is organized into more than a dozen program areas and centers that focus on major geographical areas of the world or significant foreign policy issues, including the Maurice R. Greenberg Center for Geo-economics Studies, the Center for Preventive Action, the International Institutions and Global Governance program (here lies the most important program to achieve a world government under the United Nations and other international organizations), the Civil Society, Markets, Democracy initiative, and the Renewing America initiative."

"The bimonthly *Foreign Affairs* journal is widely considered to be the most influential magazine for the analysis and debate of foreign policy and economics. Its website, ForeignAffairs. com, publishes original features on a daily basis and hosts the complete archives going back to 1922."

Independent Task Forces work to reach consensus on how to deal with critical foreign policy challenges

"CFR's website is a trusted, nonpartisan source of timely analysis and context on international events and trends. CFR.org publishes backgrounders, interviews, first-take analysis, expert blogs, and a variety of multimedia offerings that include videos, podcasts, interactive time-lines, and the Emmy-winning Crisis Guide Series."

Unparalleled access in an influential forum

"The convening power of CFR is unparalleled, attracting the most prominent world leaders in government and business. CFR Board Co-Chairs are Carla A. Hills and Robert E. Rubin. Each year, CFR organizes nearly 1,000 events, providing a nonpartisan forum for members to engage with and gain insight from experts in international affairs. Members have in-person access to world leaders, senior government officials, members of Congress, and prominent thinkers and practitioners in academia, policy, and business, many of whom are members themselves."

Resources, intellectual capital, and exchange of ideas

"Member resources include CFR's think tank and its wide array of publications and briefing materials. Study and advisory groups provide venues for experts to critique manuscripts and other content produced by our scholars. Members may participate in nonpartisan Independent Task Forces, which offer comprehensive policy prescriptions for major foreign policy issues facing the U.S. government." The above description appears to be that the CFR is an institution dedicated to the analysis of foreign affairs. It states that the Council is a nonpartisan institution which holds 1,000 events in different cities. But is this true? Nowhere does it say that the powerful members of the CFR are the invisible government of the United States.

Several Hispanics have been appointed to the CFR, among them are Cuban-American Dr. Eduardo Padrón and Nestor T. Carbonell Cortina and other Hispanics such as Maurice H. Ferré, Helen Aguirre Ferré, and Antonio Luis Ferré. Helen Aguirre Ferré is now serving in the Trump White House. Together with other Republican Hispanics in the CFR, she is not a part of the conspiracy of the New World Order. The CFR includes Republicans in its organization to conceal what the principal leaders of the CFR want to do. Only a small group of an inner circle is in charge of this organization and often the powerful members of the circle with a circle take decisions that are not share with all the members of CFR.

The Role of the CFR on the Marshall Plan, the creation of the European Union and the United Nations

George Catlett Marshall, Jr. was born on December 31, 1880 and died on October 16, 1959.

General George Marshall was Chief of Staff of the United States Army under Presidents Franklin D. Roosevelt and Harry S. Truman. He served as Secretary of State and Secretary of Defense under President Truman. British Prime Minister Winston Churchill praised General Marshall for his leadership during World War II that brought victory to the Allies.

Not well known was the failure of both President Franklin D. Roosevelt and Chief of Staff of the United States Army George Marshall to notify Pearl Harbor of the impending Japanese attack. Pulitzer-Prize winner author John Toland wrote *Infamy: Pearl Harbor and Its Aftermath* (1982) explaining that the United States had broken Japan's code used to communicate with its embassies. The Roosevelt administration knew the approximate date that Japan was going to attack Pearl Harbor and did not alert Admiral Husband Kimmel and General Walter C. Short in Hawaii. As a result of this dereliction of duty, criminal negligence, and treason by President Franklin D. Roosevelt and Chief of Staff of the United States Army George Marshall the Japanese sank or heavily damaged 18 ships, destroyed 188 aircrafts, and killed over 2,000 soldiers and sailors.

John Toland wrote the book *Infamy: Pearl Harbor and its Aftermath* in1982.

Infamy is a revealing and controversial account of the events surrounding Pearl Harbor. Toland presents evidence that President Franklin D. Roosevelt and his top advisors knew about the planned Japanese attack but remained silent. The book describes the conspiracy afterwards to cover up the facts and find scapegoats for the greatest disaster in U.S. military history.

General Marshall recommended to President Truman to suspend all U.S. military assistance to our faithful ally General Chiang Kai-shek who was the President of the Nationalists in China. This allowed the mass murderer Mao Zedong, who was supplied weapons by the Soviet Union, to defeat the Nationalists in 1949. The globalists and their friend General Marshall believed that Mao Zedong was an "agrarian reformer" or they repeated the misinformation being propagated by Marxist organizations in America.

Former General and Secretary of State under President Harry Truman, George Marshall, gave speech at Harvard University on June 5, 1947. He proposed a plan to help economically Western European nations to recover from the devastation of World War II. What became later became the Marshall Plan was planned by a study done by CFR in 1946 headed by David Rockefeller and Charles M. Spofford.

Carroll Quigley said that the movement started by the Marshall Plan was designed to unite Western European nations and eventually to create a world government. It led to the Hague Congress for European Union which was signed in April 1948; the Schuman Plan in 1950 to create the Coal and Iron Community; and the Treaty of Rome which came into effect on January 1, 1958.

The Marshall Plan (officially the European Recovery Program), was an American initiative to aid 16 Western Europe, in which the United States gave over $13.3 billion (approximately $130 billion in current dollar value as of June 2016) in economic support to help rebuild Western European economies after the end of World War II. The plan was in operation between 1948 and 1951.

The goals of the United States were to rebuild war-devastated regions, remove trade barriers, modernize industry, make Europe prosperous once more, and prevent the spread of communism. The Marshall Plan required a lessening of interstate barriers, a dropping of many regulations, and encouraged an increase in productivity, labor union membership, as well as the adoption of modern business procedures.

The Marshall Plan came with strings attached. According to Estulin, one objective was "the Americanization of Europe as European political and economic elites became welded to their American counterparts with no significant economic or political development taking place without U.S. approval."

The creation of the United Nations by the CFR

According to *Wikipedia*, "On August 3, 1948, Whittaker Chambers, a former American Communist Party member, testified under subpoena before the House Un-American Activities Committee (HUAC) that Hiss had secretly been a Communist, while in federal service. Called before HUAC, Hiss categorically denied the charge. When Chambers repeated his claim on nationwide radio, Hiss filed a defamation lawsuit against him."

Alger Hiss was born in 1904 and died on 1996.

Alger Hiss was a State Department official and later a United Nation official. Hiss was accused of being a Soviet spy in 1948 and convicted of perjury in connection with this charge in 1950. Before he was tried and convicted, he was involved in the establishment of the United Nations as a State Department official.

Wikipedia explained the following: "During the pretrial discovery process, Chambers produced new evidence indicating that he and Hiss had been involved in espionage, which both men had previously denied under oath to HUAC. A federal grand jury indicted Hiss on two counts of perjury; Chambers admitted to the same offense but, as a cooperating government witness, was never charged. Although Hiss's indictment stemmed from the alleged espionage, he could not be tried for that crime because the statute of limitations had expired. In January 1950, he was found guilty on both counts of perjury and received two concurrent five-year sentences, of which he eventually served three and a half years."

The CFR also planned the United Nations. In January 1943, Secretary of State Cordell Hull created a Steering Committee known as the Informal Agenda Group which was made with CFR members. They worked during the war years to establish the United Nations which today is a dictators' club made of anti-Western, anti-Israel Third World nations.

At the founding conference of the United Nations held in San Francisco more than 40 of the American delegates were members of the CFR. Among them was the Soviet Union spy Alger Hiss, who was selected Secretary General of the conference and assisted in writing the United Nations Charter.

President Harry Truman shakes hands with Soviet spy Alger Hiss in San Francisco.

According to James Perloff, after the Senate ratified the U.N. Charter, Senator Pat McCarran said, "Until my dying day, I will regret voting for the U.N. Charter." John D. Rockefeller, Jr. gave a $8.5 million gift to the United Nations to purchase land in New York City East River for its headquarters. Perloff said that "Since the United Nations' founding, the CFR and its mouthpiece *Foreign Affairs* have consistently lobbied to grant the world body more power and authority."

Conclusion

The Council on Foreign Relations is the power behind the throne and the invisible government in America. Members of the CFR include several former U.S. presidents: Herbert Hoover, Dwight D. Eisenhower, John F. Kennedy, Richard M. Nixon, Jimmy Carter, George H. W. Bush, and Bill Clinton. The presidents, who do not belong to the CFR, as well as those who do, name CFR members to their most important cabinet positions (such as the secretaries of State, Defense, and Treasury). Most presidents have also appointed CFR members to the Joint Chiefs of Staff, the CIA, the FBI, and the NSA.

The Council on Foreign Relations was involved in the creation of the European Union as a first step in the creation of a one-world government. The Bank of International Settlements was also very involved in the creation of the European Union and its currency the Euro.

The Council on Foreign Relations was also heavily involved in the creation of the United Nations. Currently the globalist elite want a one-world government under the United Nations but controlled by the globalists.

Chapter 10

The Council on Foreign Relations and its intervention in the affairs of Cuba

The Council on Foreign Relations has controlled completely the State Department and the officials in the White House who have set the U.S. policy in Cuba. As James Perloff indicated, most of the members of the CFR have sympathized with socialism and Marxism in carrying out the goal of bringing about a one-world government.

The United States has a long history of intervening in the affairs of Cuba since the Spanish Cuban American War of 1898. After the first U.S. military government in Cuba (1898-1902), the U.S. forced the Platt Amendment to be included in the Cuban Constitution of 1901 as a condition to ending the U.S. occupation of Cuba. In 1906, the U.S. intervened a second time and governed the island for a period of three years. However, for this book, the author will concentrate on the period from the administration of President Dwight D Eisenhower to President Donald J. Trump.

Even though the majority of Republicans wanted to select Senator Robert Taft of Ohio, the son of the former president and a strong anti-communist for its candidate for president in the 1952 election, the CFR had a different idea. The CFR drafted General Dwight D. Eisenhower as the presidential candidate of the Republican Party even though the general did not even belong to a party. The members of CFR, who owned the major newspapers and other media, promoted General Eisenhower.

James Perloff explained that during the Republican nominating convention, the Establishment used "dirty tricks", such as changing the rules from selecting delegates from Georgia, Louisiana, and Texas. The delegates who were supporting Senator Taft were replaced by supporters of General Eisenhower. Later, Senator Taft said the following: "First, it was the power of the New York financial interests and a large number of businessmen subject to New York influence, who selected General Eisenhower as a their candidate at least a year ago... Second, four-fifth of the influential newspapers in the country were opposed to me continuously and vociferously and many turn themselves into propaganda sheets for my opponent."

During the election of 1952, both presidential candidates belonged to the CFR. The Democratic presidential candidate was Adlai Stevenson. So once again, the Establishment or the CFR controlled both political parties. Once elected president, Dwight D Eisenhower selected his cabinet from the membership of the CFR. Perloff wrote that in 1953 Congress established the Reece Committee to investigate tax-free foundations. For the first, and probably the last time, the CFR came under official scrutiny.

The conclusion of the Committee was as follows: "In the international field, foundations, and interlock among some of them and certain intermediary organizations, have exercised a strong effect upon our foreign policy and upon public education in things international. This has been accomplished by vast propaganda, by supplying executives and advisers to government and by controlling much research in this area through the power of the purse. The net result of these combine efforts has been to promote internationalism in a particular sense-a form directed toward world government and a derogation of American nationalism."

The Reece Committee report indicated that major foundations "have actively supported attacks upon our social and government system and financed the promotion of socialist and collectivist ideas." The report also indicated that the CFR was "in essence an agency of the United States government" and that its "productions are not objective but are directed overwhelmingly at promoting the globalist concept." The CFR-controlled newspapers and other media attacked the report of the Reece Committee.

Perloff wrote that when the Polish people revolted in June 1956 and later the Hungarians in late October 1956 driving out temporarily the Soviets, the Eisenhower administration refused to support those freedom fighters while Soviets sent their tanks and armed forces and killed thousands. The Soviet rule was bloodily restored in both nations. The United States refused to support these freedom-loving Europeans.

In 1957, the *New York Times* reporter Herbert L. Matthews, who was a member of CFR, made the communist rebel Fidel Castro a hero as he portrayed him as the future George Washington of Cuba. He wrote a series of articles in the *New York Times*, which received front page coverage in Sunday editions. Matthews described the future bloody dictator of Cuba as "a man of ideals with strong ideas of liberty, democracy, and social justice..." Until the articles appeared in the *New York Times*, no one knew Fidel Castro. Therefore, it was Matthews who was responsible for the terrible fate of Cuba.

In 1957, *New York Times* reporter Herbert L. Matthews interviewed Fidel Castro and made him a hero. He portrayed Castro as the future George Washington of Cuba

Just as CFR member George Marshall portrayed Mao as an agrarian reformer and stopped the arms shipment to Chiang Kai-shek in China, the same thing happened in Cuba. The CFR-controlled newspapers began to severely criticize President Fulgencio Batista in Cuba and the U.S. government imposed an embargo on weapons to the Batista government. On December 17, 1958, U.S. Ambassador Earl E.T. Smith was given the order by the State Department to tell Batista to step down. Batista fled Cuba on December 31, 1958. The U.S. State Department could have asked Batista to allow the democratic opposition to win in the presidential elections to be held that year, but they wanted Fidel Castro to take power.

The CFR-controlled State Department was responsible for the coming to power of the worst and most bloody dictator in the history of the Western Hemisphere. Several socialist officials of the State Department misinformed President Eisenhower as to the ideology of Fidel and Raúl Castro and other people such as Ernesto Che Guevara, who were fighting Batista in the mountains. William Wieland and Roy Robotton were responsible for Cuba and Latin America at the State Department. They were members of CFR.

Servando Gonzalez wrote an article titled "Chronology of Treason" in 2008 stating the following: "(1957) Journalist Herbert Matthews (CFR), interviews Fidel Castro in Cuba's Sierra Maestra Mountains. In the interview, published in the *New York Times*, Matthews describes Castro as a Cuban Robin Hood and tropical Simon Bolívar, and a lover of democracy and justice. The

New York Times' Chairman of the Board was Arthur Hay Sulzberger (CFR), and the publisher Orvil Dryfoos (CFR).

(1958) Secretary of State John Foster Dulles (CFR) and CIA director Allen Dulles (CFR), of President Eisenhower's (CFR) administration, betray Cuba's President Fulgencio Batista by confiscating arms he had bought and paid to fight Castro's insurgency. The fact demoralizes the Cuban Army and allows for Castro grabbing power in Cuba.

(1958) While State Department official William Wieland (a protégé of CFR founder Sumner Welles and whose mother married a Venezuelan and changed his name to Guillermo Arturo Montenegro), undermines President Batista's government. The CIA's chief of station in Havana, and the American consul in Santiago de Cuba, provides Castro with plenty of money as well as weapons and ammunition smuggled from the U.S. military base in Guantanamo.

(1958) Following the advice of Secretary of State John Foster Dulles (CFR), and his brother, CIA director Allen Dulles (CFR), President Eisenhower (CFR) sends William Pawley (a close friend of Allen Dulles) to Havana. Pawley informs Batista that the U.S. no longer supports him, and suggests him to surrender power and leave the country."

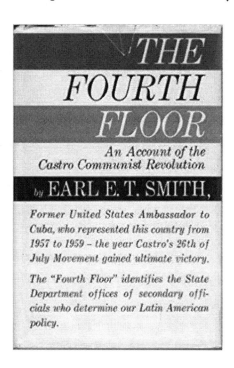

Ambassador Earl E. T. Smith wrote the book *The Fourth Floor: An Account of the Castro Communist Revolution* (1962).

Former U.S. ambassador to Cuba, Earl E. T. Smith, wrote the book *The Fourth Floor: An Account of the Castro Communist Revolution* in 1962. He wrote a letter to the *New York Times* several years after publishing his book stating the following: "Castro could not have seized power in Cuba without the aid of the United States. American government agencies and the United States press played a major role in bringing Castro to power... As the United States ambassador to Cuba during the Castro communist revolution of 1957-1959, I had first-hand knowledge of the facts which brought about the rise of Fidel Castro... The State Department constantly intervened-positively, negatively, and by innuendo- to bring about the downfall of President Fulgencio Batista, thereby was making it possible for Fidel Castro to take over the government of Cuba."

Ambassador Earl E. T. Smith blamed State Department officials, who worked on the fourth floor, for hiding the ideology of Fidel Castro and his followers. He said that Castro's victory was a disaster for both Cuba and the United States and could have been avoided.

Conclusion

The Council on Foreign Relations has controlled completely the State Department and the officials in the White House who have set the U.S. policy in Cuba. The American government agencies and the United States press played a major role in bringing Castro to power. James Perloff stated the following: "Perhaps the greatest shame of the Eisenhower administration was allowing Fidel Castro to transform Cuba into the Soviets' first outpost in the Western Hemisphere. Despite reasonable evidence, some of the president's apologist long contended that Castro had not been the communist when he originally to power."

The controversy was ultimately dispelled when Fidel Castro gave a speech on December 2, 1961, a few months after his victory at the Bay of Pigs. He said the following: "I have always been a Marxist Leninist since the days I was a student at University of Havana." Castro repeated the same during an interview with Barbara Walters in 1977.

Chapter 11

The Bay of Pigs Invasion, the October Missile Crisis, and Cuba's unknown role in the Vietnam War

On March 1960, President Eisenhower ordered the Central Intelligence Agency (CIA) to begin planning a regime change in Cuba. The CIA began recruiting anti-communist Cubans, who were trained in several places but mostly in the hills of Guatemala. This writer joined what would be later called the Assault Brigade 2506 on April 1, 1961. When this writer arrived in Guatemala, he met his older brother, Jorge de Varona, and many of his cousins and classmates from Cuba.

When President John F. Kennedy was elected in 1960, he filled his administration with members of the CFR, including several who gave him the advice to abandon the members of the Brigade 2506 at the Bay of Pigs. One of the worst ones was Dean Rusk, who was president of the Rockefeller Foundation and became Secretary of State.

Secretary of State Dean Rusk

Dean Rusk served as Secretary of State during the John F. Kennedy and Lyndon Baines Johnson administrations. Rusk was a Rockefeller Foundation trustee from 1950 to 1961. In 1952, he became president of the Rockefeller Foundation.

Secretary of State Dean Rusk and the high officials of the Department of State opposed from the very beginning the overthrow of the Castro bloody regime. Rusk asked President Kennedy to cancel the vital airstrikes against Castro Air Force, thus condemning the soldiers of the Brigade 2506 to a sure defeat. Rusk and Kennedy committed dereliction of duty and criminal negligence.

President John F. Kennedy changed completely the original plan prepared by the Joint Chiefs of Staff, the CIA, and the Eisenhower administration to overthrow the Castro regime in Cuba. In order for the invasion of Cuba to succeed, not a single change could be made to the plan due to the small number of soldiers in the Brigade 2506.

First, President Kennedy changed the landing at Trinidad. This city of 20,000 people in Cuba was next to the Escambray Mountains where many anti-communist rebels were already fighting. Trinidad had docks for the brigade´s obsolete Liberty type WW II cargo ships. It had hospitals to take care of the wounded. Trinidad only had two roads that led to Havana, which could have been easily defended.

Trinidad was the perfect place for the tiny brigade consisting of 1,500 soldiers. There were over 200,000 soldiers in the Castro regime equipped with Soviet Stalin heavy tanks, long-range artillery, and an air force that included jet aircraft and that was larger than the Brigade air force. The selection of the tiny villages of Playa Girón and Playa Larga in the Bay of Pigs area was a terrible site for the invasion since there were no docks for the ships, it has reefs, and there was no way to retreat.

Second, the original plan contemplated three air raids by the Brigade World War II B-26 bombers. A total of 48 sorties were to be conducted. Kennedy reduced the first surprise air attack of April 15, 1961 from 16 B-26s to only eight and from all airfields in Cuba to just three. Although the attack was successful, it left the Castro´s regime with two T-33 jets and several Sea Furies and B-26s. In order for the Bay of Pigs invasion to succeed, not one of Castro's planes could have been left operational since the enemy aircraft could completely destroy the obsolete cargo ships of the Brigade 2506.

CFR members Secretary of State Dean Rusk, White House Director of National Security Mac George Bundy, Ambassador to the United Nations Adlai Stevenson, and others urged President Kennedy to cancel all subsequent airstrikes after the first reduced surprise air raid. In spite of the strong objections by the CIA and the Joint Chiefs of Staff, President Kennedy followed the terrible advice given by the CFR members of his administration and cancelled all subsequent air strikes.

This writer, age 17 years old, was aboard the Liberty Ship type *Houston* with the Fifth Battalion at the Bay of Pigs. The *Houston* was attacked by enemy T-33 jets, B-26s, and Sea Fury aircrafts until it sank. He swam ashore but 26 others were killed by enemy planes, drown, and some were eaten sharks during the morning of April 17, 1961

This was a decision that doomed the small Brigade 2506. By sending the members of the Brigade to certain defeat, instead of cancelling the operation, President Kennedy committed criminal negligence. It was impossible for the Brigade to succeed. On April 17, 1961, two ships were sunk by enemy planes, including the *Houston* where this writer was on board. The soldiers who landed fought bravely during three days against 60,000 soldiers. When the brigadistas ran out of ammunition, they tried to escape to the swamps. However, practically all were captured, including this writer and his brother. One of this author's cousin, who was a pilot of a B-26, was shot down and killed at the age of 19.

The weakness shown by President Kennedy at the Bay of Pigs emboldened Soviet Premier Nikita Khrushchev, who built the Berlin Wall in August 1961 and introduced intercontinental ballistic missiles in Cuba in October 1962. During the October Missile Crisis, Kennedy made a pact with Khrushchev to never invade Cuba and dismantled the ICBMs U.S. missile bases in Turkey and Italy as the price for the Soviets to withdraw the missiles from Cuba. Unfortunately, subsequent presidents of the United States have abided by the diabolical Kennedy-Khrushchev Pact in which the United States promised never to invade Cuba or tolerate Cubans in the United States to attack the communist regime.

For many years, several U.S. presidents tried to restore diplomatic relations with the tyrannical regime of Fidel Castro. However, the bloody Cuban dictator was not interested and continued to support communist revolutions and help terrorists world-wide. CFR anti-communist Cuban American Néstor T. Carbonell (one of a few anti-communists among the 5,000 members) wrote an article entitled "The Cuba Deal: How Raúl Castro Duped Obama," which was published by *Forbes* as a guest post on February 27, 2015.

David Rockefeller shakes the bloody hand of Cuban dictator Fidel Castro.

Carbonell wrote the following: "Leading an impressive delegation of foreign policy heavy-weights, Rockefeller presented Fidel Castro in February 2001 a proposal developed by the CFR to normalize U.S. relations with Cuba. After five hours of marathon discussions which ended at 4:00 AM, Fidel rejected the "half-measures" proposed by the Council and demanded the unconditional lifting of the U.S. embargo without acquiescing to any significant economic and political reforms. A disillusioned Rockefeller wrote in his memoirs: Castro harangued us continuously throughout the night…I think there is little possibility for change while Castro remains in power…" During David Rockefeller's trip to Cuba, a delegation of 19 important members of the CFR who represented the financial, political, media and academic sectors came to talk with Cuban dictator bloody Fidel Castro.

What right did the late David Rockefeller and members of the CFR had to negotiate on behalf of the U.S. government with the totalitarian and oppressive communist regime of Fidel Castro? CFR, BG, and TC member David Rockefeller and other members of these globalist organizations violated the Logan Act by meeting numerous times with heads of nations. The Logan Act (1 Sta.613, 30 January 1799, currently codified at 18 U.S.C. & 953) is a federal law that forbids unauthorized citizens from negotiating with foreign governments. It was passed in 1799 and last amended in 1994. Violation of the Logan Act is a felony, punishable under federal law with imprisonment of up to three years. The Act was intended to prohibit United States citizens without authority from interfering in relations between the United States and foreign governments.

David Rockefeller invited Fidel Castro to his family home in Westchester County, New York. The billionaire introduced the Cuban bloody dictator to the social elite of Manhattan, individuals of the jet set, and others who represented the financial and political sector. The so-called "radical chic" enjoyed shaking the hand of and socializing with Fidel Castro, who was responsible with his brother Raúl Castro for the shooting and death of 17,000 freedom-loving Cubans and for the incarceration of more than 300,000 Cuban patriots.

Rockefeller also invited the bloody dictator Fidel Castro to the Pratt House in New York City, which is the headquarters of the Council on Foreign Relations, several times. One of Rockefeller's daughters, CFR member Peggy Rockefeller Dulany, invited several professors and organizational experts to travel to Cuba and meet there with officials in charge of heavy and light industry. David Rockefeller's eldest daughter, Abby Rockefeller, is a Marxist. She is a great admirer of Fidel Castro and has been involved in many radical organizations.

Carbonell failed to include in his article that Rockefeller and 14 other members of the CFR, BG, and TC wrote a letter to President Obama on May 19, 2014, which is discussed later on this book, requesting the president to lift the embargo and normalize relations with Cuba. Rockefeller and the CFR members were fully aware that Obama was secretly negotiating with Castro for several months. Thus, Rockefeller and the others who signed the letter to provide support to Obama are the ones responsible for Raúl Castro´s duping and making a fool of Obama. Carbonell is correct in saying that even though Cuba negotiated from a very weak position due to the fact that Venezuela is nearly broke, the bloody dictator Raúl Castro "got pretty much what he wanted."

Carbonell also failed to explain that Julia E. Sweig, who previously was Nelson and David Rockefeller Senior Fellow for Latin America, is now the Director for Latin American Studies at the CFR. She is a radical leftist who wrote two books on Cuba, in one of them praising many Cuban communists, including Josefina Vidal. Sweig has written many very friendly articles towards Cuba for the CFR, such as "A Reform Moment in Cuba?" She has advocated the same policy implemented by Obama.

Carbonell is a patriot and concluded his article by stating the following: "The only way out of the President's one-sided deal with Cuba is not to give the deceitful Cuban ruler a blank check, but to insist on a step-by-step quid pro quo that would safeguard the interests and security of the U.S. as well as the long-fought aspirations of freedom-loving Cubans."

Cuba's unknown role in the Vietnam War

On October 4, 1999, Michael D. Benge wrote an article titled "Cuban War Crimes against American POWs during the Vietnam War" for the National Alliance of Families for the Return of America's Missing Servicemen. Benge spent 11 years in Vietnam, over five years as a prisoner of war from 1968 to 1973, and follows the affairs of the region. While serving as a civilian Foreign Service Officer, he was captured in South Vietnam by the North Vietnamese, and held in numerous camps in South Vietnam, Cambodia, Laos and North Vietnam. He spent 27 months in solitary confinement and one year in a "black box." For efforts in rescuing several Americans before being captured, he received the Department of State's highest award for heroism and a second one for valor. He is an active Board Member of the National Alliance of Families for the Return of America's Servicemen.

Benge reported that Cuban officials during the Vietnam War brutally tortured and killed American POWs whom they beat senseless in a research program "sanctioned by the North Vietnamese." This was called the "Cuba Program" by the Department of Defense and the CIA, and it involved 19 American POWs (some reports state 20). Recent declassified secret CIA and DOD intelligence documents, obtained under the Freedom of Information Act, reveal the degree of communist Cuba's involvement with American POWs captured in Vietnam. A Defense Intelligence Agency (DIA) report stated that "The objective of the interrogators was to obtain the total submission of the prisoners..."

Benge said that according to former POW Air Force Colonel Donald "Digger" Odell, "two POWs left behind in the camp were 'broken' but alive when he and other prisoners were released [1973 Operation Homecoming]. ... They were too severely tortured by Cuban interrogators" to be released. The Vietnamese didn't want the world to see what they had done to them." Sadly, when the POWs were released during "Operation Homecoming" in 1973, they "were told not to talk about third-country interrogations. .... This thing is very sensitive with all kinds of diplomatic ramifications." Hence, the torture and murder of American POWs by the Cubans was swept under the rug by the U.S. Government! Very few Americans are aware of the crimes against humanity committed by Cuban regime communist assassins sent by Fidel and Raúl Castro to North Vietnam.

Brian Bobek, President of the Vietnam Veterans of America Chapter 154, left, and retired Lieutenant Colonel Donald "Digger" Odell visit Resurrection Cemetery POW memorial.

The Brutal Cuban Program in North Vietnam

Benge explained that the Cuban Program started around August 1967 at the Cu Loc POW camp known as "The Zoo", a former French movie studio on the southwestern edge of Hanoi. The American POWs gave their Cuban torturers the names "Fidel," "Chico," "Pancho" and "Garcia." U.S. reports indicated that testing "torture methods were of primary interest" of the Cuban Program. The Cuban leader of the Cuban Program, called "Fidel" was described in debriefing reports as "a professional interrogator," and a second team member was described as looking like a Czech "Chico". "The Cubans has the authority to order NVNS [North Vietnamese] to torture American POWs." The Vietnamese "catered" to the Cubans.

Benge wrote the following: "Several other documents corroborate that the CIA analysts identified two Cuban military attaches, Eduardo Morejón Esteves and Luis Pérez Jaen, who had backgrounds that seemed to correspond with information on "Fidel" and "Chico" supplied by returning POWs. Reportedly, in 1977-78, Esteves served under diplomatic cover as a brigadier general at the United Nations in New York and no attempt was made to either arrest or expel him…According to an expert on Cuba, "Fidel's" profile fits that of Cuban Dr. Miguel Angel Bustamante-O'Leary, President of the Cuban Medical Association. Dr. Miguel Bustamante is said to be an expert at extracting confessions through torture and he was compared to Nazi Dr. Joseph Mengale. Chico's profile fits that of Fernando Vecino Alegret. The torture and murder of American POWs in Vietnam by Cubans are unconscionable acts and are in direct violation of the Geneva Convention on Prisoners of War.

General Fernando Vecino Alegret later became Minister of Higher Education.

Fernando Vecino Alegret has been identified as one of the Cuban torturers of American POWS in North Vietnam. Sometimes identified as "Fidel" or as "Chico", Vecino Alegret became a general and minister of higher education. He has visited the United States and spoke at several universities. Why has this thug has not been arrested during his several visits to America?

Benge described the beatings and torture witnessed by other American POW as follows:

"The man could barely walk; he shuffled slowly, painfully. His clothes were torn to shreds. He was bleeding everywhere, terribly swollen, and a dirty, yellowish black and purple from head to toe. The man's head was down; he made no attempt to look at anyone. He had been through much more than the day's beatings. His body was ripped and torn everywhere; hell-cuffs appeared almost to have severed the wrists, strap marks still wound around the arms all the way to the shoulders, slivers of bamboo were embedded in the bloodied shins and there were what appeared to be tread marks from the hose across the chest, back and legs."

"Fidel smashed a fist into the man's face, driving him against the wall. Then he was brought to the center of the room and made to get down onto his knees. Screaming in rage, Fidel took a length of rubber hose from a guard and lashed it as hard as he could into the man's face. The prisoner did not react; he did not cry out or even blink an eye. Again and again, a dozen times, smashed the man's face with the hose. He was never released."

"Air Force ace Major James Kasler was also tortured by "Fidel" for days on end during June 1968. Fidel beat Kasler across the buttocks with a large truck fan belt until he tore my rear end to shreds. For one three-day period, Kasler was beaten with the fan belt every hour from 6 a.m. to 10 p.m. and kept awake at night. My mouth was so bruised that I could not open my teeth for five days." After one beating, Kasler's buttocks, lower back, and legs hung in shreds. The skin had been entirely whipped away and the area was a bluish, purplish, greenish mass of bloody raw meat."

American POWS taken to Havana

Benge pointed out that documents revealed that Cubans not only tortured and killed a number of American POWs in Vietnam, but may have also taken several POWs to communist Cuba in the mid-1960s. Benge said the following: "The POWs, mostly pilots, were reportedly imprisoned in Villa Marista, a secret Cuban prison run by Castro's G-2 intelligence service. According to a February 1971 State Department cable, a former aide to Fidel Castro offered to ransom POWs in North Viet Nam through the Castro Government. One intelligence source reportedly interviewed "Fidel", "Chico" and "Pancho" after they returned from Hanoi to Cuba and said they claimed that their real job was to act as gate-keepers to select American POWs who could aid international communism...Fidel, Chico and Pancho weren't the only Cubans who were involved with American POWs. As part of their propaganda program, Dr. Fernando Barral, a Spanish-born psychologist, interviewed Lt. Cmdr. John McCain Jr. (now a U.S. Senator) for an article published in Cuba's house-organ *Granma* on January 24, 1970. Barral was a card-carrying communist international residing in Cuba and traveling on a Cuban passport."

Cubans on the Ho Chi Minh Trail

Benge said that very few Americans are aware that Cuban soldiers were very involved in the Vietnam War. Communist Cuba had a very large contingent of combat engineers, the Girón Brigade, which was responsible for maintaining a large section of the Ho Chi Minh Trail; the supply line running from North Vietnam through Laos and Cambodia to South Vietnam. The contingent was so large that Cuba had to establish a consulate in the jungle.

Benge explained the following: "A large number of American personnel serving in both Vietnam and Laos were either captured or killed along the Ho Chi Minh Trail, and in all likelihood, many by the Cubans. One National Security Agency *SigNet* report states that 18 American POWs "are being detained at the Phom Thong Camp..." in Laos, and "...are being closely guarded by Soviet and Cuban personnel with Vietnamese soldiers outside the camp." Several reports indicate that Cubans were piloting MIGs in aerial combat with American pilots over North Vietnam... The involvement with American POWs was just a part of Cuba's long history of commitment to assist the Vietnamese communists, and just another chapter in their role as communist internationales on behalf of the Soviet Union."

Conclusion

The globalists who run the CFR have ignored the tremendous damage done by the communists in Cuba to the United States. The failure by the globalists in the Kennedy administration to support the Brigade 2506 during the Bay of Pigs invasion and the ignoring the torture and murder of Americans during the Vietnam War by the Department of State and Defense, are just two instances how Cuba has been given a free pass until today.

Chapter 12

President Donald J. Trump partially reversed Obama's Cuban policy

President Donald J. Trump is signing executive orders regarding his new Cuban policy after he spoke. From left to right in the picture: Secretary of Agriculture Sonny Perdue, Secretary of Commerce Wilbur Ross, Republican Congressman Mario Díaz Balart from South Florida, Governor of Florida Rick Scott, Republican Senator Marco Rubio from Florida, former political prisoner Cary Roque, Vice President Mike Pence, and Secretary of Labor Alex Acosta. In the back: Congressman Carlos Curbelo from South Florida, former political prisoner Ángel de Fana, and dissident Jorge Luis García Pérez "Antunez."

On June 16, 2017, President Donald J. Trump announced his new Cuban policy partially reversing Obama's shameful unilateral concessions to the Castro´s regime in return for nothing. President Trump said he would restrict travel to Cuba and prohibit U.S. business dealings with companies tied to the Cuban military and intelligence services. Diplomatic relations with Cuba, including renewed embassies in the respective country's capitals, will continue. President Trump pledged to reverse Obama's approach to Cuba as part of last year's presidential campaign, especially during appearances in Florida.

President Trump stated the following: "My administration's policy will be guided by key U.S. national security interests and solidarity with the Cuban people. I will seek to promote a stable, prosperous, and free country for the Cuban people. To that end, we must ensure that U.S. funds are not channeled to a regime that has failed to meet the most basic requirements of a free and just society."

President Donald J. Trump announced his new Cuban policy to about 1,000 enthusiastic mostly Cuban American supporters at the Manuel Artime Theater in Little Havana, Miami, Florida on June 16, 2017.

The White House Presidential Policy Directive has eight pages and five points. The directive stated the following: "The new policy centers on the belief that the oppressed Cuban people—rather than the oppressive Castro regime's military and its subsidiaries—should benefit from American engagement with the island.

From left to right in this picture appear some volunteers of the West Dade Trump Victory Office in Miami-Dade County ran by this writer: Xiomara Mastrapa, Chiqui Lamar, George Garces, Haydée Prado de Varona, and this writer at the Manuel Artime Theater in Little Havana, Miami, Florida.

When President Trump stepped off Air Force One at 12:25 p.m. on June 16, 2017, he was greeted by Florida Governor Rick Scott, Cuban dissident and former political prisoner Jorge Luis García Pérez "Antunez," and former political prisoners Ángel De Fana and Cary Roque. Waiting for him at the theater were dissidents Antonio Rodiles and Ailer González. President Trump announced that communist Cuba did not allow two others, José Daniel Ferrer and Berta Soler, to fly to the United States for the event.

Cuban opponent Jorge Luis García Pérez "Antunez", who was imprisoned for 17 years from 1990 to 2007, spoke with this writer at the Manuel Artime Theater.

Under a strict interpretation of the president executive orders, a United States citizen cannot stay in a hotel owned by the Cuban regime, eat at a government restaurant or nightclub, fly in a government aircraft, rent a government automobile, or use a tourist bus because they are run or controlled by the military Grupo de Administración Empresarial, S.A. (GAESA).

GAESA is administered by General Luis Alberto Rodríguez López Calleja, who is or was the son-in-law of Cuban bloody dictator Raúl Castro. GAESA is the business arm of the Cuban military that controls approximately 60% to 80% of all businesses in the island. The prohibition includes any subsidiaries or affiliated companies, along with other state-controlled entities.

GAESA operates in virtually every profitable area of the Cuban economy, controlling hotel chains, car rental agencies and sales companies, banks, credit card and remittance services, supermarkets, clothing shops, real estate development companies, gasoline stations, import and export companies, shipping and construction companies, warehouses, and even an airline. GAESA is the owner of the Gaviota hotel chain, which owns nearly 29,000 rooms in Cuba and serves an estimated 40% of the entire nation's foreign tourism. Gaviota has signed management contracts for 83% of its rooms with international hotel chains, including Spain's Meliá and the Swiss-based Kempinski.

General Luis Alberto Rodríguez López Calleja is or was the son-in-law of Cuban bloody dictator Raúl Castro. More than half of Cuba's business activities have to be run through General Rodríguez López Calleja.

The place chosen for the unveiling of President Trump's new Cuban policy was the Manuel Artime Theatre, named after a late leader of the Assault Brigade 2506. This writer participated at the age of 17, together with his brother and several cousins, in the Bay of Pigs invasion of April 17, 1961.

On late October 2016, at the Bay of Pigs Museum and Library in Little Havana, Republican candidate Donald Trump appeared before the Brigade 2506's Veterans Association, which had given him its endorsement. Presidential candidate Trump said the following: "The United States should not prop up the Castro regime economically and politically, as Obama has done and as Hillary Clinton plans to do. They don't know how to make a good deal, and they wouldn't know how to make a good deal if it was staring at them in the face."

Republican presidential candidate Donald Trump spoke at the Museum and Library of the Assault Brigade 2506 in Miami, Florida. Behind Donald Trump are the brigade flag and the pictures of the heroes who died trying to free Cuba. During Donald Trump's visit, he promised the Bay of Pigs veterans that he would make changes to the Cuban policy made by President Barack Obama and supported by Democratic candidate Hillary Clinton.

Cuban American Mercy Viana Schlapp, a *FoxNews* commentator, spoke before Donald Trump at the Museum and Library of the Assault Brigade 2506. In mid-September 2017, she was appointed White House Adviser for Strategic Communications. Mercy Viana Schlapp's father was a political prisoner in Cuba.

On June 17, 2017, Patricia Mazzei wrote an article titled "In Miami, Trump toughens Obama Cuba policy 'like I promised'" which was published in the *Miami Herald*. The reporter explained that President Trump gave a 38-minute speech in which he delighted in the crowd's energy. Trump said he would hold Cuban leaders accountable for human-rights violations and push them to open their economy to loud cheers from the crowd. The president stated the following:

"Effective immediately, I am canceling the last administration's completely one-sided deal with Cuba. Our policy will seek a much better deal for the Cuban people and for the United States of America."

"We will not lift sanctions on the Cuban regime until all political prisoners are free, freedoms of assembly and expression are respected, all political parties are legalized and free and internationally supervised elections are scheduled."

"We will not be silent in the face of communist oppression any longer. Last year I promised to be a voice against oppression ... and a voice for the freedom of the Cuban people. You heard that pledge. You exercised the right you have to vote. You went out and voted — and here I am, like I promised. To the Cuban government I say, put an end to the abuse of dissidents. Release the political prisoners. Stop jailing innocent people."

"Open yourselves to political and economic freedoms. Return the fugitives from American justice, including the return of the cop killer Joanne Chesimard. And finally, hand over the Cuban military criminals who shot down and killed four brave members of Brothers to the Rescue who were in unarmed, small, slow civilian planes."

Veterans of the Bay of Pigs invasion, veterans of the Armed Forces of the United States, Trump campaign workers, local politicians, and activists sat on risers behind the president and others were part of the audience. President Trump said during his speech that when rebels captured Santiago de Cuba in January 1959, they shot 73 individuals.

One of the men who were shot without due process was a police captain who had a five-year-old son named Luis Haza. Luis eventually became a virtuoso of the violin.

When he was 12 years old, the regime authorities asked him to play the violin during a communist meeting, but he refused. A communist took him out of his house and forced the boy to play the violin.

Famous orchestra conductor and violinist Luis Haza played "The Star-Spangled Banner"
to the delight of the audience.

Young Luis played the Star-Spangled Banner to the surprise of the communists, who remained silent. President Trump said that when this young boy grew up, he became a world famous violinist and orchestra conductor. At that point, President Trump asked dissident and violinist Luis Haza to join him in the stage. Haza then played "The Star-Spangled Banner" while many in the audience cried.

Joining President Donald Trump and Vice President Mike Pence on stage were the architects of the new Cuban policy, Republican Senator from Florida Marco Rubio and Congressman Mario Diaz-Balart from South Florida. In addition to Senator Rubio and Congressman Diaz-Balart, Florida Governor Rick Scott and Lieutenant Governor Carlos Lopez-Cantera also spoke at the event. Senator Marco Rubio, Representative Mario Diaz-Balart, Representative Carlos Curbelo, and Labor Secretary Alex Acosta flew from Washington, D.C. aboard Air Force One with President Trump.

Senator Marco Rubio and President Trump exchanged stories at the Manuel Artime Theater.

Speaking before President Trump announced the changes in the USA-Cuba policy, Senator Marco Rubio said President Trump's announcement may be the start of freedom for Cuba. Senator Rubio stated the following: "You mark my words: Whether it's in six months or six years, Cuba will be free. I believe that the people on the island —and history— will say that perhaps the key moment in that transition began on this day, here in this theater, with each of you and a president that was willing to do what needed to be done." Senator Marco Rubio wrote this writer and others a letter stating the following:

"Frank,

I am headed to Miami, Florida with President Trump to help him announce the strengthening of the United States' policy toward Cuba. It is very simple, this new policy directive reverses the Obama Administration's support for the communist Castro regime and its military apparatus, and aligns the United States with the Cuban people."

"The policy centers on the belief that the oppressed Cuban people-rather than the oppressive Castro regime's military and its subsidiaries-should benefit from American engagement with the island. This will be the first time in several decades that the Cuban people will have an economic advantage over the Cuban military."

"We will prohibit financial transactions with Group de Administración Empresarial, S.A. (GAESA) and its affiliates, subsidiaries, and successors. In turn, we will empower the Cuban people to develop greater economic independence and ultimate political liberty."

"With Raúl Castro and most of his closest advisors in their eighties, Cuba, one way or another, will soon have a new generation of leaders. By channeling funds away from the Castro regime and its military apparatus and towards the private citizens of Cuba, we will empower Cuba's rising generation economically in the near term and politically over the long term."

"This policy will better protect the United States' national security interests in the Western Hemisphere while advancing human rights and universal values that Americans hold dear. The Castro regime and its military apparatus continue to systematically suppress the Cuban people's legitimate aspirations for freedom, self-determination, and prosperity, and also continue to prop up the imploding Maduro dictatorship's violent efforts to crush the Venezuelan people's legitimate demands for elections and a return to democracy.

Finally, America's relationship with Cuba will depend entirely on the Cuban government's willingness to expand the Cuban people's political freedom, respect their universal rights, and allow freedom of press as well as free and fair democratic elections. Thank you for all of your support."

"

Congressman Mario Diaz-Balart remembering President Barack Obama trip to Havana, Cuba last year said, "You will no longer have to witness the embarrassing spectacle of an American president doing the wave at a baseball game with a ruthless dictator."

Berta Soler is the leader of the Ladies in White (Damas de Blanco), an effective dissent group.

Ladies in White write open letter to President Donald J. Trump

This letter reads as follows:

"Dear Mr. President,

In my capacity as leader of the Cuban non-violent human rights defenders, the Damas de Blanco, I am honored to convey to you the warmest thanks from all the members of our organization, including our four Damas recently sentenced to up to 3 years in prison, for your kind mention of our struggle.

These days, Mr. President, when most of the World responds with a deafening silence to the harassment, arbitrary detentions, beatings, house searches, and robberies against peaceful opponents, human rights activists and defenseless women, your words of encouragement are most welcomed.

Sadly, Mr. President, words of encouragement to the victims are not enough to placate the hateful ire of Raúl Castro. During his visit to Cuba, your predecessor, Barack Obama, showered us with beautiful words of good will, encouragement and great expectations for a better future through a new policy of improved relations and lifting of sanctions.

I, Berta Soler, was one of the few who told President Obama that his policy was condemned to failure; that the Castro regime would take as much as it could from the good will of the United States government without giving up a bit of control or reducing its repressive actions. Unfortunately, time proved that I was right.

Taking advantage of the lack of pressure from the United States, the Castro regime increased its repressive actions to levels not seen since the Black Spring of 2003 when 75 peaceful dissidents were sentenced to terms of imprisonment of up to 25 years. That was when our organization, the Damas de Blanco, was born to fight for the release of our husbands, fathers and sons imprisoned under miserable conditions far away from their families. Today, we continue to fight for all the political prisoners, more than a hundred, and for respect to the inalienable rights of the Cuban people.

But, we need your help Mr. President; we need your support. For more than half a century, our nation has suffered under a merciless totalitarian regime. We will continue to fight for our rights because we recognize it is our duty to free ourselves, but we can't do it alone. It is also the duty of the freedom loving peoples of the World.

The United States must continue to be the first defender of those who lack rights and freedoms in the world. The free world must isolate and punish unrepentant dictatorships and send a strong message to the tyrants that they will no longer be allowed to commit their crimes with impunity."

Sincerely yours,

Berta Soler,

Leader of the Ladies in White (Damas de Blanco)"

Ladies in White and other opponents of the Cuban tyranny are beaten up and arrested during President Barack Obama visit to Cuba in March 2016.

Letter to President Donald Trump from the Junta Patriótica Cubana (Cuban Patriotic Council)

This writer was asked at the National Convention of the Cuban Patriotic Council to write a letter to President Trump regarding his Cuban policy. Below is the letter that was sent to the White House.

June 26, 2017

President Donald J. Trump

The White House

1600 Pennsylvania Avenue N.W.

Washington, D.C. 20500

"Dear Mr. President,

Cuban Americans in the United States are very grateful to you for taking the first steps to partially reverse the shameful unilateral concessions given by President Barack Obama to the Cuban communist regime without a Quid Pro Quo. The three of us worked very hard in Miami-Dade County together with our organizations to elect you as president.

Frank de Varona worked full-time as Office Manager of the West Dade Trump Victory Office where he recruited over 200 volunteers. Brigade 2506 veteran Frank de Varona presented you, Mr. President, together with the president of the Brigade 2506 Bay of Pigs Veteran Association and another Bay of Pigs veteran with the insignia of the Brigade 2506 during your visit to the our Museum and Library. Frank de Varona spoke on your behalf at the Bayfront Park Rally in downtown Miami during your campaign. Frank de Varona, at the request of your Campaign Headquarters at Trump Tower, sent you an eight minute video with suggestions regarding your Cuban policy after your election as president. Frank de Varona has written 23 books, including six dealing with the Obama administration. His most recent book, *The Gathering Threat of Russia, China, and Their Allies Against America* (2016), has two chapters on Cuba.

Brigade 2506 veteran Raymond Molina attended the Republican Convention in July 2016 in Cleveland and met with members of your presidential campaign. Raymond Molina has worked for five Republican presidents and specifically advising CIA directors, including Bill Casey, on Latin Americans affairs.

Antonio D. Esquivel mobilized members of the Cuban Patriotic Council in 25 cities in the United States to assist in your presidential campaign. Antonio D. Esquivel was an adviser on communist infiltration to the Venezuelan government and its Armed Forces. Additionally, he served as an adviser on transportation to Dr. Leopoldo Sucre Figarala, President of the Venezuelan Corporation of Guayana.

Mr. President, we are grateful for the praise you gave to those of us who fought at the Bay of Pigs with the Brigade 2506 during your speech at the Manuel Artime Theater. We also remember your message to us in late October 2016 at the Bay of Pigs Museum and Library in Little Havana after the Brigade 2506 endorsed you for president. Mr. President, you said the following: "The United States should not prop up the Castro regime economically and politically, as Obama has done and as Hillary Clinton plans to do. They don't know how to make a good deal, and they wouldn't know how to make a good deal if it was staring at them in the face."

The three of us were present when you announced on June 16 at the Manuel Artime Theater that the United States would restrict travel to Cuba and prohibit U.S. business dealings with companies tied to the Cuban military and intelligence services. We applaud this policy. It was reassuring to hear you, Mr. President, saying that the United States commercial embargo would remain in place until the communist oppressive regime take steps to open up the island.

Mr. President, upholding the Helms-Burton Law and maintaining the commercial embargo are crucial to put pressure on the regime. You stated the following: "We will not lift sanctions on the Cuban regime until all political prisoners are free, freedoms of assembly and expression are respected, all political parties are legalized and free and internationally supervised elections are scheduled." We thank you for that strong message to the tyrannical communist regime. We also appreciated your denunciation of the tens of thousands of executions and incarcerations of freedom-loving Cubans by the Castro regime starting in 1959 and continuing until today.

Cuba is a merciless totalitarian state and its military and secret police continue to assassinate, beat up, and arrest peaceful opponents and systematically suppress the Cuban people's legitimate aspirations for freedom, self-determination, and prosperity. The Castro regime has an Occupation Army in Venezuela to prop up the imploding Maduro dictatorship and its violent efforts to crush the Venezuelan people's legitimate demands for freedom and democracy. Maduro follows orders from Cuban dictator Raúl Castro. Venezuela has become virtually a colony of Cuba.

Venezuela and Cuba are strong allies and both nations assist Islamic terror groups. There is a Hamas office in Havana. Cuba has always been a center of terrorism. Similar to Venezuela, the Cuban military participates in drug trafficking. On April 8, 1993, prosecutors at the U.S. Attorney's Office in Miami drafted a proposed indictment charging the Cuban government as a racketeering enterprise and Armed Forces Minister Raúl Castro as the chief of a 10-year conspiracy to send tons of Colombian cartel cocaine through Cuba to the United States. However, the case was later dropped.

Cuba sends intelligence agents to America to commit fraud with Medicare, Medicaid, other government services, and private businesses. Tens of millions of dollars have been stolen by Cuban agents with complete immunity.

The fates of the two communist regimes are interrelated. Venezuela and Cuba are a national security threat to the United States and both are close allies of North Korea, Iran, Syria, Russia, and China. Venezuela and Cuba have agents working with these countries.

Mr. President, the new Cuban policy has the goal of weakening the military dictatorship by denying it easy access to dollars through the military-owned tourist industry and by restricting travel. However, we would like to respectfully suggest for your consideration several other measures to strengthen the United States' policy toward Cuba. These suggestions are the following:

1) Add Cuba to the list of terrorist nations

Mr. President, in your speech you stated that the Cuba regime sent illegal weapons to North Korea and helps the regime in Venezuela to oppress its people. Cuba has a Hamas office in Havana and provides sanctuary to many American and foreign terrorists and murderers. The Cuban military and intelligence services assist Venezuela in providing financial support to Hezbollah, participating in drug trafficking, sending uranium to Iran, and engaging in subversion in Latin America.

2) Add Cuba to the list of nations involved in human trafficking

Mr. President, the Department of State in a previous Trafficking in Persons Report regarding Cuba stated the following: "Cuba is principally a source country for children subjected to trafficking in persons, specifically commercial sexual exploitation within the country... The Government of Cuba does not fully comply with the minimum standards for the elimination of trafficking and is not making significant efforts to do so."

Cuban medical doctors, dentists, nurses, engineers, sport trainers, musicians, and other professionals have stated that they are forced against their will to leave their families and are sent to nations in Latin America, Africa, Asia, and the Middle East. Cuba charges up to $5,000 per month for the "enslaved" medical professionals' involuntary postings abroad.

The Cuban doctors are paid $200 a month upon their return. The passports of the Cuban professionals are withheld while they perform their services. They live in miserable conditions while they are also watched by members of the intelligence services. The Cuban regime receives tens of millions each year as a result of "enslaving" Cubans from many professions. Communist Cuba is one of the worst nations in the world involved in human trafficking.

3) Stop U.S. cruise lines and private yachts from visiting Cuba

Mr. President, Carnival, Holland American, and other cruise lines have announced that they will increase their current sailings and services to Cuba. Nearly 200,000 Americans are expected to sail from the United States to Cuba this year. Mr. President, when these ships arrive at Cuban ports they will be forced to violate your stated policy of prohibiting U.S. business dealings with companies tied to the Cuban military and intelligence services. The cruise lines will pay fees to the regime for using its piers and disembarkation facilities. They will hire regime buses with intelligence agents as guides to take American tourists to military-owned restaurants, night clubs, bars, shops, and tourist sites such as Spanish fortresses.

Mr. President, there are no private companies in Cuba that have buses or large restaurants. The private restaurants known as "paladares" are too small to accommodate thousands of cruise liners tourists. American private yachts dock in military-own marinas, such as the Hemingway Marina in Havana harbor, and some of the yachts participate in fishing tournaments with Fidel Castro's sons. Private yachts pay fees and purchase food, supplies, and gasoline at these military-own marinas. The increased American tourism brought by cruise liners and private yachts to Cuba will enrich the oppressive communist regime that has been the worst and longest lasting unrepentant abuser of human and civil rights in the Western Hemisphere.

4) Work diplomatically with Western allied nations to condemn and impose economic sanctions on the rogue and illegitimate Cuban regime

Mr. President, the United States and its allies imposed severe economic sanctions and commercial restrictions to South Africa during Apartheid. Sadly, instead of implementing economic sanctions to Cuba, Western nations have continued to do business as usual with the military dictatorship for many years.

5) Impose economic sanctions and deny visas to high officials and high ranking military officers of the Cuban and Venezuelan regimes

Mr. President, high ranking government and high military officers from both nations come to the United States to travel and invest in property with the stolen funds from their nations. Freezing the assets of these oppressors is an effective way to punish those who abuse, incarcerate, and assassinate their fellow citizens.

6) Need to expedite the writing of the travel restrictions rules and strict enforcement of them to the full extent of the law by the Treasury Department

Mr. President, unless there are strong penalties, American tourists will continue to stay in military-owned hotels, using military-owned taxis, and eating and drinking in military-owned restaurants and nightclubs. There is a great need to expedite the writing of the travel regulations by the Treasury Department's Office of Foreign Assets Control since until that time Obama's travel policy remain in effect.

Tour companies that send American tourists to Cuba, such as Marazul, have bookings in military-owned hotels through 2019. The Cuban regime will change the designation of military-owned hotels to other government-control companies. It appears that tour operators are still permitted to book American tourists in Cuba hotels that are not affiliated with the military, such as Cubanacan and GranCaribe. Obviously, the Cuban regime will do whatever is necessary to get around the new travel rules. Therefore, the new travel rules should state that no American tourists are permitted to stay in any Cuban government hotel whether owned by the military or a non-military entity.

7) Limit the amount of remittances allowed to be sent to Cuba from the United States

Mr. President, previous presidents have suspended temporarily or limited the amount of remittances sent by Cuban Americans in the United States to Cuba. This is another way the Cuban oppressive regime earns tens of thousands of dollars each day. Current policy allows unlimited remittances to the island.

8) Implement regime change strategies in Cuba and Venezuela

Mr. President, please consider implementing regime change in Cuba and Venezuela. By declaring a total economic embargo to the narco military regime in Venezuela and ceasing the purchase of oil or the sale of gasoline and other goods, Maduro's dictatorial regime will collapse very soon and freedom and democracy will be restored. If democracy were to be restored in Venezuela, that nation would cease supplying free oil to communist Cuba. The Cuban regime would also collapse in a short time.

We know that implementing regime change in Cuba and Venezuela would be a very difficult step. We are aware that your administration will be severely criticized as inhumane by the increasingly radical Democratic Party, members of the Deep State in the federal government, and other nations. However, Mr. President, it is inhumane for the United States and its Western allies to remain silent to all the killings, beatings, and arrests and to conduct business as usual with these two unrepented bloody regimes. Each day, the Maduro's regime thugs, assisted by the Cuban Occupation Army and intelligence services, are killing women, men, and children in the bloody streets of cities across Venezuela. Mr. President, if such courageous regime change policy were implemented by your administration successfully, you will go down in history as the Liberator of two countries controlled by savage and bloody communist regimes that have brought much suffering to their peoples and other nations throughout the world.

Mr. President, we would be available to meet with any members of your administration to further discuss our concerns and these suggestions. Thank you for your consideration. Mr. President, please Make the Americas Great and Safe Again!"

Respectfully yours,

Antonio D. Esquivel,

President Cuban Patriotic Council

Raymond Molina,

Director of Inter-governmental Relations Cuban Patriotic Council

Chairman Miami-Dade Republican Conservative Coalition

Frank de Varona

Adviser and Member of the International Assembly Cuban Patriotic Council

Vice Chairman Miami-Dade Republican Conservative Coalition

South Florida Director of *Bear Witness Central*

Freedom-loving Cubans in the island and Cuban Americans in the United States are very grateful to President Donald J. Trump for the first steps taken to partially reverse the shameful unilateral concessions given by President Obama to the Cuban communist regime without a Quid Pro Quo or nothing in return. Today in Cuba there is more repression, beatings of peaceful opponents, and arbitrary arrests than before the restoration of diplomatic relations between the United States and the communist regime and the many concessions given by President Obama. The strengthening of the United States' policy toward Cuba is most welcome. As stated earlier, Cuba is a merciless totalitarian state.

As Senator Marco Rubio stated in a letter to this writer, "The Castro regime and its military apparatus continue to systematically suppress the Cuban people's legitimate aspirations for freedom, self-determination, and prosperity, and also continue to prop up the imploding Maduro dictatorship's violent efforts to crush the Venezuelan people's legitimate demands for elections and a return to democracy."

Cuban Americans were very pleased to hear President Trump blasting the enormous abuses of human and civil rights by the Castro regime. It was reassuring to hear the president saying that the United States commercial embargo would remain in place until the communist oppressive regime take steps to open up Cuba.

Upholding the Helms-Burton Law is crucial. Restating the important parts of the Helms-Burton Law was necessary and President Trump did it in his speech. The president stated the following: "We will not lift sanctions on the Cuban regime until all political prisoners are free, freedoms of assembly and expression are respected, all political parties are legalized and free and internationally supervised elections are scheduled."

President Trump spoke how Cuba sent illegal weapons to North Korea and helps the regime in Venezuela to oppress its people. Yet, the president did not state that he wants to place Cuba back in the list of terrorist-supporting nations, nor did he say that he plans to put Cuba back in the list of nations that participate in human trafficking. It is very important that President Trump takes these two actions very soon. The new Cuban policy of President Trump allows the United States airlines and cruise lines to continue providing service to the island. With the restrictions on travel, it is likely that the numbers of Americans visiting Cuba will diminish, thus reducing the cash flow to the Cuban military. However, the Treasury Department must strictly enforce the new travel restrictions to the full extent of the law. Otherwise, American tourists will continue to stay in military-owned hotels, use military-owned taxis, and eat in military-owned restaurants and nightclubs.

It is unfortunate that some Republican senators from farm states, such as Republican Senator John Boozman from Arkansas, criticized the president's new Cuban policy. These Republican and Democratic senators think that it is a great idea for farmers in their states to sell poultry, rice, and other products to Cuba on credit.

Cuba has never paid back any ill-advised nation or corporation which sold products on credit to the military in the island. Perhaps, the majority of Americans do not understand that the Export and Import Bank pays in cash when American corporations sell products on credit to nations that have no credit but they never pay back. American taxpayers are swindled in each of these transactions. This practice must be stopped. The Export and Import Bank needs to be abolished as it represents a welfare system for rich corporations. The Cuban corporations controlled by the military never pay back what they purchase. If American farmers want to sell their products in Cuba, they need to demand the military to pay them in cash for what they purchase.

The new Cuban policy has the goal of weakening the military dictatorship by denying it easy access to dollars through the military-owned tourist industry and by restricting travel. However, none of these announced measures will overthrow the Cuban communist regime, which is the longest and harshest military dictatorship in the Western Hemisphere. Cuba can still buy what it needs from other nations and receive their tourists in military-controlled businesses. It is important that all Western nations condemn the rogue and illegitimate Cuban regime as they did with South Africa during apartheid. Sadly, instead of implementing economic sanctions in Cuba, Western nations have continued to do business as usual with the military dictatorship for many years.

Venezuela and Cuba are strong allies and both nations assist Islamic terrorist groups. There is a Hamas office in Havana. Cuba has always been a center of terrorism. Similar to Venezuela, the Cuban military participate in drug trafficking. Cuba has an occupation Army in Venezuela assisted by its intelligence services. Venezuela sends financial help to Iran's militia Hezbollah. Venezuela sends uranium to Iran, its close ally. The fates of their communist regimes are interrelated. Venezuela and Cuba are a national security threat to the United States and both are close allies of Russia and China.

Obviously, the Cuban people need to take to the streets as the brave people in Venezuela are doing for over three months and demand freedom and democracy. Declaring a nation-wide strike and refusing to cooperate with the communist regime would be an important first step.

President Trump needs to sanction economically the high officials in the regime and high ranking military officers of both nations. Frequently, these oppressors come to the United States to invest in property with the stolen funds from their nations. Freezing the assets of the high-ranking oppressors in the United States is an effective way to punish those who abuse their fellow citizens. If President Trump wants to implement a regime change in communist Venezuela and Cuba, he needs to implement an economic embargo in Venezuela and stop purchasing petroleum from that terrorist narco nation. The communist regime in Venezuela could not survive a total economic embargo from the United States. If democracy were to be restored in Venezuela that nation would cease supplying free oil to communist Cuba. The Cuban regime would also collapse in a short time.

Conclusion

This writer realizes that those drastic steps are very difficult to implement by the Trump administration. International bankers, other nations, and the globalist elite of the New World Order would oppose such a policy labeling it as inhumane. It is inhumane for Western nations to remain silent in response to all the killings, beatings, and arrests and to conduct business as usual with these two unrepented bloody regimes. If such a courageous regime change policy were successfully implemented by President Donald Trump, he would go down in history as the Liberator of two savage and bloody communist regimes that have brought much suffering to their people and other nations throughout the world. Mr. President, Make the Americas Great and Safe Again!

Chapter 13

American and Canadian Diplomats were attacked in Cuba with sonic and ultrasonic or some other weapons and how America needs to respond

U.S. embassy in Havana, Cuba was reopened in 2015 as part of former President Obama's détente with the Cuban regime.

The Cuban bloody oppressive regime has a very long history of harassing and subjecting to surveillance American diplomats in Havana. Cuban intelligent agents have frequently entered American diplomats' homes and tampered with their computers, moved their books, and left feces. Often times, the electricity was cut off in their homes. Sometimes Cuban agents damaged their cars.

America tolerated these abuses for many years. The Castro brothers, who hated profoundly the United States, believed that they could continue to harass American diplomats forever with complete impunity.

Regime intelligence agents followed American diplomats as they drove in their cars. These agents would tailgate diplomats' vehicles and make it impossible to change lanes. However, attacking American diplomats with covert sonic weapons with the intent to seriously damage their health is a grave matter and substantial escalation that needs a very strong response from the United States.

Once again these events show clearly the total failure of former President Obama's Cuban policy of giving the bloody communist regime in Havana a series of unilateral concessions with no "Quid Pro Quo" or nothing in return. In fact, the brutal Cuban regime has increased the number of arbitrary arrests and beatings of peaceful opponents of the regime.

Ladies in White and other peaceful opponents of the Cuban tyranny are beaten up and arrested frequetly in Cuba.

The Cuban bloody dictator Fidel Castro and General Ramiro Valdes harassed American diplomats in
Cuba for many years..

Cuban Raúl Castro and Venezuelan Nicolás Maduro are two bloody dictators who are responsible for the deaths of tens of thousands of their people and others around the world.

American and Canadian diplomats were attacked with sonar and ultrasonic or other type of weapons in Havana

On August 9, 2017, the State Department revealed a new dispute between the America and Cuba when it said that American diplomats serving in Cuba were subjected to an "acoustic attack" in fall 2016 using a covert sonic weapon that left the Americans with severe hearing loss and mild traumatic brain injury. Canada also reported mysterious illnesses among its diplomats in Havana. The United States embassy in Havana reopened in 2015 as part of former President Obama's détente with the Cuban regime.

In the fall of 2016, a series of U.S. diplomats began suffering unexplained losses of hearing and memory problems. After months of investigation, U.S. officials concluded that the diplomats had been attacked with an advanced sonic weapon that operated outside the range of audible sound and had been deployed either inside or outside their residences and in at least one hotel.

CNN reported that "the employees affected were not at the same place at the same time, but suffered a variety of physical symptoms since late 2016, which resembled concussions." Along with investigating possible Cuban regime involvement, investigators are also exploring the possibility that the attack was carried out by a third country, such as Russia, operating without the Cuban regime's knowledge. The Foreign Ministry of the regime stated that "Cuba has never, nor would it ever, allow that the Cuban territory be used for any action against accredited diplomatic agents or their families."

On August 11, 2017, Frances Robles and Kirk Semple wrote an article titled "Health Attacks on U.S. Diplomats in Cuba Baffle Both Countries" which was published in the *New York Times*. The reporters explained that at least six American diplomats in Havana who were getting sick with headaches, dizziness and hearing loss were flown from Cuba to be treated at the University of Miami hospital in Miami. The illnesses may have been caused by some kind of sonic wave machine and the symptoms worsened with prolonged exposure. By mid-September, 2017, the number of American victims has now increased to at least 22 Americans.

Robles and Semple said that one of the diplomats had a more serious illness that involved a blood disorder. A University of Miami specialist went to Havana this month to examine others who work at the embassy because officials expect that more people were affected. The State Department stated that some American diplomats had symptoms of a mild traumatic brain injury. Canadian diplomats have reported experiencing similar incidents.

Russian Deputy Foreign Minister Sergei Ryabkov recently met with Cuban officials. Why?

State Department spokeswoman Heather Nauert said that U.S. authorities have not located any device nor they know the specific cause of these attacks and who is responsible. Cuba's top negotiator with the United States and other Cuban Officials met with Russian Deputy Foreign Minister Sergei Ryabkov. Was this meeting related to these attacks?

The reporters interviewed James Cason, who ran the United States Interests Section in Havana a decade ago. Carson stated the following regarding the Cuban intelligence agents: "They would come into your house and erase the pictures of your kids off your computer, or turn all the books around on your bookshelf, just to show you that you had no privacy. They never did anything physical to anybody. This sounds like a science experiment."

Secretary of State Rex W. Tillerson said in the fall of 2016 American diplomats were attacked with a covert sonar weapons. U.S. diplomats began suffering unexplained losses of hearing.

Two Cuban diplomats were expelled from Washington, D.C. in May 2017, yet the news of their expulsion and the sickness of U.S. diplomats in the fall of 2016 were not revealed until August 2017. Why were these events not reported earlier? On August 11, 2017, Secretary of State Rex W. Tillerson said the illnesses were a result of "health attacks," and added, "We've not been able to determine who's to blame." Was there a cover up?

This photo shows the Cuban embassy in Washington, D.C. The Trump administration expelled two Cuban diplomats from Washington, D.C. in May 2017 because Cuba had failed in its obligation to keep American diplomats safe.

Robles and Semple said that John Caulfield, who was chief of mission at the United States Interests Section in Havana from 2011 to 2014, stated it was "inconceivable" that a third government would have been able to act without the knowledge or cooperation of the Cubans. The Cuban government, he said, kept "such close tabs on us they would've immediately detected someone else." Caulfield added, "My speculation is that it was a surveillance effort that went bad."

The reporters pointed out that the State Department said many Americans cut their tours in Cuba short after falling ill in 2016. The Trump administration expelled two Cuban diplomats from Washington, D.C. because Cuba had failed in its obligation to keep American diplomats safe. The FBI is investigating these sonar attacks against American diplomats in Havana.

When asked about the sonar attack against American diplomats in Havana, Rhodes said the following: "It just doesn't strike me as something the Cuban government would do. They've been pragmatic about Trump." Once again, these remarks showed Rhodes' ignorance about the nature of the Castro totalitarian regime. The communist regime in the island has already caused immense damage to this nation and is very capable of inflicting even more damage driven by its enormous hatred of America.

Ben Rhodes negotiated secretly with Cuban officials to recognize the regime diplomatically. He may have been involved in the illegal unmasking of President Trump campaign officials. Rhodes continuous to be an appeaser of the brutal Cuban regime!

Sonic and ultrasonic weapons

Wikipedia has an article describing sonic and ultrasonic weapons of various types. *Wikipedia* explained the following:

"Sonic and ultrasonic weapons that use sound to injure, incapacitate, or kill an opponent. Some sonic weapons are currently in limited use or in research and development by military and police forces. Some of these weapons have been described as sonic bullets, sonic grenades, sonic mines, or sonic cannons. Some make a focused beam of sound or ultrasound; some make an area field of sound."

"Extremely high-power sound waves can disrupt or destroy the eardrums of a target and cause severe pain or disorientation. This is usually sufficient to incapacitate a person. Less powerful sound waves can cause humans to experience nausea or discomfort. The use of these frequencies to incapacitate persons has occurred both in counter-terrorist and crowd control settings."

"A long-range acoustic device has been used by the crew of the cruise ship *Seabourn Spirit* to deter pirates who chased and attacked the ship. More commonly this device and others of similar design have been used to disperse protesters and rioters in crowd control efforts."

"A similar system is called a "magnetic acoustic device. Mobile sonic devices have been used in in the United Kingdom to deter teenagers from lingering around shops in target areas.

High-amplitude sound of a specific pattern at a frequency close to the sensitivity peak of human hearing (2–3 kHz) is used as a burglar deterrent. Some police forces have used sound cannons against protesters, for example during the G20 summit in Pittsburgh and the Dakota Access Pipeline protest in South Dakota."

A long-range acoustic device (LRAD) is in use on the U.S. Navy *LCC-19 USS Blue Ridge*.

On September 2, 2017, Luis Mejer wrote an article titled "Sonic Technology" which he posted on his Facebook page. Mejer said that because of recent news regarding American diplomats in Cuba he did a bit of research on sonic technology. He explained that a variety of high powered sonic weapons (SW) exist spanning the infrasonic, ultrasonic, and audible ranges. These weapons which direct sound onto a target, and sound is energy, they can be considered directed-energy weapons. A variety of high powered sonic weapons (SW) exist spanning the infrasonic, ultrasonic, and audible ranges.

Mejer wrote that a long-range acoustic device (LRAD), such as the one use by the U.S. Navy, is a weapon emits a tightly-focused beam of audible sound to an individual or group at up to one kilometer. A focused beam, which can be transmitted directly into an individual's ear, would be inaudible to others in the area. It is to be used for behavior modification and psychological operations. Reportedly, at high power levels it can cause loss of equilibrium, migraines, nausea and vomiting.

Mejer pointed out that infrasonic and ultrasonic weapons can cause negative emotions such as fear, anxiety, or depression, as well as biological symptoms like nausea, vomiting, organ damage, burns, or death—depending on the frequency and power level. Most of these weapons function between the frequency ranges of about 1 Hz to 30 kHz. These frequencies occur within the following waves: Extremely Low Frequency (ELF) 1 Hz to 30 Hz, Super Low Frequency (SLF) 30 Hz to 300 Hz, Ultra Low Frequency (ULF) 300 Hz to 3 kHz, and Very Low Frequency (VLF) 3 kHz to 30 kHz1.

Ultrasonic weapons, Mejer argued, produce a variety of effects depending on the power level and frequency. Many are the same as those produced by infrasound, plus heating and burning. They include: tickling in the mouth/nose area, discomfort, heating of the skin, nausea, abdominal pains, and vomiting. At higher decibels it causes burns and heating of body up to lethal temperatures. Another very painful effect is bone resonation, which could cause a person's bones to literally explode.

Mejer explained that sonic projectiles are weapons basically of sonic rifles and canons which can transmit invisible energy over hundreds of meters, causing a blunt impact causing a variety of biological and psychological effects. It could also be adjusted to cause effects ranging from physical discomfort up to death. Effects short of death included abdominal pains, nausea, and vomiting. In addition, it could cause a person's bones to resonate, which is extremely painful.

Mejer said that the vortex gun is capable of transmitting an invisible whirlwind of force to affect a considerable blunt impact on a target. It will allegedly be used to disable or destroy personnel such as enemy combatants or disruptive crowds. Most of the current information pertaining to this technology is classified.

The electromagnetic personnel interdiction control (EPIC), Mejer wrote, is a portable acoustic weapon created by Invocon Incorporated. The U.S. Navy describes this as a developing technology which interferes with a person's equilibrium by sending acoustic pulses of energy which disrupt the chemical and mechanical processes of the vestibular system. This can result in disorientation, confusion, extreme motion sickness, and vomiting. The Navy declared that the weapon will operate through walls and other protective mediums that now provide cover for combatants in urban warfare situations.

The last weapon described in the article by Luis Mejer is the directed stick radiator (DSR). This weapon is a small portable acoustic weapon, which fires a focused, painful, audible sound up to 100 yards. Its kinetic effect is so intense that it can knock someone back and cause migraine headaches. In addition to being used to remotely incapacitate a specific individual it will be used for psychological operations.

More details on the attacks on American diplomats in Havana

On September 15, 2017, more details were revealed by the Trump administration on the unexplained attacks on the health on U.S. and Canadian diplomats and their families in Cuba. The Department of State said that at least 21 Americans were impacted and that it was possible that the number of victims would increase.

Heather Nauert is the State Department spokeswoman. She previously worked for *FoxNews*.

State Department spokeswoman Heather Nauert said America continuous to assess American personnel in Cuba. On September 14, 2017, Heather Nauert stated the following: "The investigation into all of this is still under way. It is an aggressive investigation. We will continue doing this until we find out who or what is responsible for this."

Associated Press reporters Josh Lederman, Michael Weissenstein, and Matthew Lee wrote an article titled "Details emerge on what befell U.S. diplomats in Cuba" which was published in the *Miami Herald* on September 15, 2017. The reporters said that one American diplomat heard a great blaring, grinding noise that jolted him from his bed in a Havana hotel. The diplomat moved just a few feet, and there was silence. He went back into bed and the agonizing sound hit him again. It was as if he had walked through some invisible wall cutting straight through his room.

Soon after that incident, the reporters said, the American diplomat was diagnosed hearing loss and speech problems, symptoms both similar and altogether different from others among at least 21 American victims of "health attacks." New details learned by the *Associated Press* show that at least some of the "health attacks" were confined "to specific rooms or even parts of rooms with laser-like specificity, baffling U.S. officials who say the facts and the physics don't add up."

Fulton Armstrong, a former CIA official who served in Cuba long before the United States re-opened an embassy there, stated, "None of this has a reasonable explanation." He added, "It's just mystery after mystery after mystery."

At first the Trump administration suspected that a sonic weapon might have been used. However, the diagnosis of mild brain injury, considered unlikely to result from sound, has confounded the FBI, the State Department and intelligence agencies involved in the investigation.

Some American diplomats "now have problems concentrating or recalling specific words, several officials explained, the latest signs of more serious damage than the U.S. government initially realized", said the reporters.

This writer wonders why the U.S. government reported the "health attacks" nine months after symptoms were first reported and why the Trump administration still has not identified who was responsible or the weapon or weapons to explain the attacks.

Reporters Lederman, Weissenstein, and Lee explained the following: "In fact, almost nothing about what went down in Havana is clear. Investigators have tested several theories about an intentional attack — by Cuba's government, a rogue faction of its security forces, a third country like Russia, or some combination thereof. Yet they've left open the possibility an advanced espionage operation went horribly awry, or that some other, less nefarious explanation is to blame."

U.S. officials said that in addition to Americans being attacked from their homes. U.S. diplomats were attacked at the recently renovated Hotel Capri, a 60-year-old concrete tower steps from the famous Havana's Malecon, the waterside promenade.

The incidents vary deeply with different symptoms, different recollections of what happened. In several episodes explained by U.S. officials, victims knew it was happening in real time, and there were strong indications of a sonic attack, said the reporters.

Lederman, Weissenstein, and Lee wrote the following: "Some felt vibrations, and heard sounds — loud ringing or a high-pitch chirping similar to crickets or cicadas. Others heard the grinding noise. Some victims awoke with ringing in their ears and fumbled for their alarm clocks, only to discover the ringing stopped when they moved away from their beds. The attacks seemed to come at night. Several victims reported they came in minute-long bursts. Yet others heard nothing, felt nothing. Later, their symptoms came… Some have mild traumatic brain injury, known as a concussion, and others permanent hearing loss."

Investigators could not explained why fewer than 10 Canadian were harmed, too, including some who reported nosebleeds since Canada has had warm relations with the bloody communist regime for many years. Following the American complain to the Cuban mass murdering regime earlier this year, Canada detected its own cases. Then the FBI and the Royal Canadian

Mounted Police traveled to Havana to investigate. FBI investigators swept the rooms, looking for weapons but found nothing.

After the brutal Cuban tyrant Fidel Castro died, Canadian Prime Minister Justin Trudeau praised him as a great leader. Some have speculated that Justin Trudeau may be Fidel Castro's son since the look very much alike and his leftist mother visited Cuba frequently and met with the brutal tyrant.

The Embassy of the United States of America in Havana, Cuba

The reporters pointed out that sound and health experts are equally perplexed since "targeted, localized beams of sound are possible, but the laws of acoustics suggest such a device would probably be large and not easily concealed." "And no single, sonic gadget seems to explain such an odd, inconsistent array of physical responses", they explained. Other symptoms have included brain swelling, dizziness, nausea, severe headaches, balance problems and tinnitus, or prolonged ringing in the ears. Many American victims have shown improvement since coming back to America and some suffered only minor or temporary symptoms.

Cuba's regime declined to answer specific questions about the incidents, pointing to a previous Foreign Affairs Ministry statement denying any involvement, promising full cooperation and saying it was treating the situation "with utmost importance." The tyrannical regime's statement said that "Cuba has never, nor would it ever, allow that the Cuban territory be used for any action against accredited diplomatic agents or their families, without exception."

United States Senate

SELECT COMMITTEE ON INTELLIGENCE

WASHINGTON, DC 20510-6475

September 14, 2017

The Honorable Rex Tillerson
Secretary of State
United States Department of State
2201 C Street, NW
Washington, DC 20520

Secretary Tillerson:

We write today concerning the injuries sustained by multiple U.S. diplomatic personnel posted to the U.S. Embassy in Havana, Cuba. Our officials and their families have been the targets of unacceptable levels of harassment and "acoustic" attacks that, in some cases, have caused permanent hearing damage and other significant injuries.

The safety of U.S. diplomatic personnel and their families posted overseas remains one of our high priorities and a shared responsibility of those nations that host U.S. diplomatic facilities. We urge you to remind the Cuban government of its obligation and to demand that it take verifiable action to remove these threats to our personnel and their families. Furthermore, we ask that you immediately declare all accredited Cuban diplomats in the United States persona non grata and, if Cuba does not take tangible action, close the U.S. Embassy in Havana.

Cuba's neglect of its duty to protect our diplomats and their families cannot go unchallenged. We appreciate your attention to this important national security matter and look forward to your timely response.

Sincerely,

On September 15, 2017, Susan Crabtree wrote an article titled "GOP Senators Urge Trump to Expel Cuban Diplomats from U.S., Threaten to Shutter Embassy" which was published in the *Washington Free Beacon* website. The reporter said that five important Republican senators asked the Trump administration to expel Cuban diplomats from Washington, D.C. immediately and even close the American embassy in Havana if the Cuban regime is not more forthcoming about mysterious "acoustic" attacks that have seriously harmed the health of many U.S. diplomats.

Senator John Cornyn from Texas is a member of the Senate Select Committee on Intelligence. He also serves as the Senate majority whip and is the Number Two Republican leader in the upper chamber.

Crabtree wrote that on September 15, 2017, GOP Senators John Cornyn of Texas, Marco Rubio of Florida, Tom Cotton of Arkansas, Richard Burr of North Carolina, and James Lankford of Oklahoma sent a letter to Secretary of State Rex Tillerson asking him to take action regarding the harassment and acoustic attacks on American diplomats in Cuba. The senators want Secretary Tillerson to immediately declare all accredited Cuban diplomats in the United States as "persona non grata", and expelled them from America.

The Republican senators wrote "that if Cuba does not take tangible action to remove these threats to the diplomats and their families, to take the decisive step of closing the U.S. embassy in Havana." They also said that Secretary Tillerson needs to remind the Cuban regime of its obligation to protect U.S. diplomats and their families under international treaties.

The letter written by the five GOP senators stated the following: "Our officials and their families have been the targets of unacceptable levels of harassment and 'acoustic' attacks that, in some cases, have caused permanent hearing damage and other significant injuries. The safety of U.S. diplomatic personnel and their families posted overseas remains one of our high priorities and a shared responsibility of those nations that host U.S. diplomatic facilities."

"Cuba's neglect of its duty to protect our diplomats and their families cannot go unchallenged. We appreciate your attention to this important national security matter and look forward to your timely response."

Crabtree pointed out that the five senators "have waited more than a month to request that President Donald Trump threaten to close the embassies, a step that would reverse much of the efforts to normalize diplomatic relations taken by President Barack Obama." She also said that in mid-August 2017, the *Washington Free Beacon* was the first to report that the "U.S. government was hiding key details of the mystery attacks on U.S. diplomats in Cuba and may have misled the public and Congress on the full scope and nature of the attacks."

Crabtree explained that U.S. officials in early August 2017 said approximately six Americans were the victims of the attacks when the actual number of U.S. diplomats was far higher—in the double digits. Crabtree stated the following: "In addition to the greater number of U.S. persons harmed by the sonic device, sources told the *Washington Free Beacon* that some Americans stationed in Havana began experiencing symptoms months earlier than the State Department has publicly admitted, and that the symptoms they suffered included permanent hearing loss, sleeplessness as well as damage to some diplomats› brain function and cognitive abilities."

Republican senators who wrote the letter to Secretary of State Tillerson serve on the Senate Intelligence Committee and on Senate Foreign Relations Committee. Senator Richard Burr from North Carolina is the chairman of the Senate Select Committee on Intelligence. Senator Marco Rubio from Florida is also a member of the Senate Foreign Relations Committee, which has jurisdiction over the State Department and diplomatic personnel.

Senator John Cornyn from Texas also serves as the Senate majority whip, the Number Two GOP leader in the upper chamber. James Lankford from Oklahoma serves on the Senate Select Committee on Intelligence. Senator Tom Cotton from Arkansas serves on the Senate Foreign Relations Committee.

Senator Richard Burr from North Carolina is the chairman
of the Senate Select Committee on Intelligence.

On September 17, 2017, Secretary of State Rex Tillerson said that the Trump administration is considering shutting down the American embassy in Havana. Tillerson said the following regarding the closing of the U.S. embassy in Cuba: "We have it under evaluation. It is a very serious issue with respect to the harm that certain individuals have suffered. We've brought some of those people home. It's under review."

This is great news to this writer and other Cuban Americans freedom fighters. Enough is enough! America should not tolerate any more attacks from the bloody tyranny in Cuba.

President Donald J. Trump has already ordered the expulsion of two Cuban diplomats from Washington, D.C. However, if the FBI investigation discovers that the Castro regime ordered such uncivilized, unprecedented, and brutal attacks against American diplomats, attacks that Cuban thugs are very capable of having done, then America must consider a range of responses.

Possible actions by the United States recommended by this writer to three officials in the White House if the Cuban regime ordered the attacks against American diplomats or allowed a third country to do it

Below are some of the suggested action(s) by this writer that could be taken by America:

1) Add Cuba to the list of terrorist nations.

President Donald J. Trump in his speech in Miami stated that the Cuba regime sent illegal weapons to North Korea and helps the regime in Venezuela to oppress its people. Cuba has a Hamas office in Havana and provides sanctuary to many American and foreign terrorists and murderers. The Cuban military and intelligence services assist Venezuela in providing financial support to Hezbollah, participate in drug trafficking, send uranium to Iran, and engage in subversion in Latin America.

2) Add Cuba to the list of nations involved in human trafficking.

The Department of State in a previous Trafficking in Persons Report regarding Cuba stated the following: "Cuba is principally a source country for children subjected to trafficking in persons, specifically commercial sexual exploitation within the country... The Government of Cuba does not fully comply with the minimum standards for the elimination of trafficking and is not making significant efforts to do so."

Cuban medical doctors, dentists, nurses, engineers, sport trainers, musicians, and other professionals have stated that they are forced against their will to leave their families and sent to nations in Latin America, Africa, Asia, and the Middle East. Cuba charges up to $5,000 per month for the "enslaved" medical professionals' involuntary postings abroad. The Cuban doctors are paid $200 a month upon their return.

The passports of the Cuban professionals are withheld while they perform their services. These doctors live in miserable conditions while they are also watched by members of the intelligence services. The Cuban regime receives tens of millions each year as a result of "enslaving" Cubans from many professions. Communist Cuba is one of the worst nations in the world involved in human trafficking.

3) Stop U.S. cruise lines and private yachts from visiting Cuba

Carnival, Holland American, and other cruise lines have announced that they will increase their current sailings and services to Cuba. Nearly 200,000 Americans are expected to sail from the United States to Cuba this year.

When these ships arrive at Cuban ports they will be forced to violate President Trump stated policy of prohibiting U.S. business dealings with companies tied to the Cuban military and intelligence services. The cruise lines will pay fees to the regime for using its piers and disembarkation facilities. Cruise lines are hiring and will continue to hire regime buses with intelligence agents as guides to take American tourists to military-owned restaurants, night clubs, bars, shops, and tourist sites such as Spanish fortresses.

There are no private companies in Cuba that have buses or large restaurants. The private restaurants known as "paladares" are too small to accommodate thousands of cruise liners tourists. American private yachts dock in military-own marinas, such as the Hemingway Marina in Havana harbor, and some participate in fishing tournaments with Fidel Castro's sons.

American owners of private yachts pay fees and purchase food, supplies, and gasoline at these military-owned marinas. The increased American tourism brought by cruise liners and private yachts to Cuba will enrich the oppressive communist regime that has been the worst and longest-lasting unrepentant abuser of human and civil rights in the Western Hemisphere.

4) Work diplomatically with Western allied nations to condemn and impose economic sanctions on the rogue and illegitimate Cuban regime.

The United States and its allies imposed severe economic sanctions and commercial restrictions to South Africa during Apartheid. Sadly, instead of implementing economic sanctions to Cuba, Western nations have continued to conduct business as usual with the military dictatorship for many years. America and its allies must isolate and punish the unrepentant and oppressive Cuban dictatorship.

5) Impose economic sanctions and deny visas to high officials and high ranking military officers of the Cuban and Venezuelan regimes.

High ranking government and high military officers from both nations travel to the United States and invest in property with the stolen funds from their nations. Freezing the assets of these oppressors is an effective way to punish those who abuse, incarcerate, and assassinate their fellow citizens.

6) Limit the amount of remittances allowed to be sent to Cuba from the United States

Previous presidents have suspended temporarily or limited the amount of remittances sent by Cuban Americans in the United States to Cuba. This is another way the Cuban oppressive regime earns tens of thousands of dollars each day. Current policy allows unlimited remittances to the island. In 2016, over $3.5 billion were sent to Cuba by Cuban Americans who had relatives and friends in the island.

7) Break diplomatic relations with Cuba

President Dwight D. Eisenhower broke diplomatic relations with Cuba when Fidel Castro ordered the America embassy in Havana to drastically reduce the numbers of its employees. Attacking American diplomats with sonic wave weapons to harm their health is far more serious.

8) Implement regime change strategies in Cuba and Venezuela

By declaring a total economic embargo to the narco military regime in Venezuela and ceasing the purchase of oil or the sale of gasoline and other goods, Maduro's dictatorial regime will collapse and freedom and democracy will be restored. If democracy were to be restored in Venezuela that nation would cease supplying free oil to communist Cuba. The Cuban regime could also collapse in a short time.

Conclusion

It is disconcerting to this writer why America has tolerated so much abuse from the mass murdering Cuban totalitarian regime for almost 60 years. Even now the United States has taken pains not to accuse Havana of perpetrating the attacks. Nothing in Cuba occurs without the late tyrant Fidel Castro's and later his equally brutal brother dictator Raúl Castro's permission. This writer agrees with the five prominent Republican senators who told Secretary Tillerson that "Cuba's neglect of its duty to protect our diplomats and their families cannot go unchallenged."

The FBI investigation must be conducted quickly to determine if the Castro regime was responsible for the attacks on American diplomats. If it is determined that the Cuban regime was involved, then the Trump administration will need to consider some or all of the recommendations outlined by this writer. America should not tolerate such an abuse to at least 22 of its diplomats.

Cuba has an Occupation Army in Venezuela led by generals and assisted by its intelligence services. Venezuela sends financial help to Iran's militia Hezbollah. Venezuela sends uranium to Iran, a close ally. The fates of their communist regimes are interrelated. Venezuela and Cuba are national security threats to the United States and both are close allies of Russia and China.

If such a courageous regime change policy were implemented successfully by President Donald Trump, he would go down in history as the Liberator of two savage and bloody communist regimes that have brought much suffering to their people and other nations throughout the world. This writer hopes and prays that President Donald J. Trump will Make the Americas Great and Save Again!

Chapter 14

The roles of the Council on Foreign Relations, the Bilderberg Group, and the Trilateral Commission in Obama's Cuba Policy

Under former President Barack Obama, the powerful members of the CFR, the Bilderberg Group, and the Trilateral Commission interfered with Cuban affairs. On May 19, 2014, 46 powerful business people, former politicians, and government officials, among them 17 Hispanics (mostly Cuban Americans) wrote an open letter to the President Obama requesting him to end the embargo as a way of improving relations with Cuba and open this country to U.S. multinationals to build factories on the oppressed island.

This letter was rejected by anti-communist Cuban Americans in the United States and by almost all of the opponents of the tyranny in Cuba. Among this group were 15 individuals who belong to the three very powerful organizations that are so influential in the United States and the world, the Council on Foreign Relations (CFR), the Trilateral Commission (TC), and the Bilderberg Group (BG).

This is the reason why a secret and well-coordinated campaign went on for several months, which involved multiple editorials written by Colombian journalist Ernesto Londoño in the *New York Times*. It is well known that this important newspaper in New York City is the voice of the CFR. Other newspapers controlled by these powerful elitist globalists also demanded ending the embargo, releasing the three remaining spies, and restoring diplomatic relations with Cuba.

It was all about money, without regards to the immense suffering of the Cuban people. These individuals knew that what Obama was doing was helping the Cuban tyranny to remain in power for years to come. This tyranny may continue with Raúl Castro's son, Coronel Alejandro Castro, waiting to succeed his father.

All of these individuals want to make Cuba the China of the Caribbean by building factories in the island where workers receive a salary of $20 a month and where there are no unions or any other human rights organizations. The fact that the workers in Cuba are oppressed and exploited by the bloody dictatorship is of no concern to the multinational corporations that want to move into the island to maximize profits.

These multinationals that built factories in China did not care about the oppressed Chinese workers and their miserable wages or about the environmental violations of Beijing. However, now that China is stronger economically and militarily, the dictator Xi Jinping is demanding higher salaries for the Chinese workers and more concessions from the multinationals.

Cuba offered a unique opportunity. With the Cuban economy seriously at risk due to the imminent bankruptcy of Venezuela, Cuban dictator Raúl Castro wanted to mend fences with the United States to save his brutal regime. Brazil invested $980 million to build the port of Mariel, one of the best in the world, with modern gigantic cranes, rail, etc. to accommodate large containers ships. Everything was prepared for the change of U.S. policy towards Cuba.

The following are the most powerful individuals in our nation who are part the elitist groups (some belong to the three or two groups) and who were responsible for the measures taken by Obama:

• David Rockefeller [BG, TC, and CFR] – The late David Rockefeller was founder of the BG and TC and long-time president of the CFR, honorary member of the Council of the Americas, and one of the most powerful individuals in the United States and the world.

• Richard Feinberg [BG and CFR] – Former White House Official on Latin America and professor at the University of California in San Diego.

• Dan Glickman [BG and CFE] – Former Secretary of Agriculture and former congressman from Kansas.

• Lee Hamilton [BG, TC, and CFR] – Former chairman of the House of Representatives Foreign Relations Committee and Intelligence Committee.

• Jane Harman [TC and CFR] – Former United States representative.

• John Negroponte [TC and CFR] – Former Deputy Secretary of State and former Director of the National Intelligence Agency.

- Ambassador Thomas Pickering [BG, TC, and CFR] – Former Under Secretary of State for Political Affairs. He participated in the Benghazi cover-up when he was appointed by Secretary Clinton to a panel and eventually the panel's conclusions favored Clinton.

- Susan Segal [CFR] – President and CEO of Americas Society/Council of the Americas.

- Anne-Marie Slaughter [TC and CFR] – President and CEO of New America Foundation and former Director for Policy Planning of the Department of State.

- Admiral James Stavridis [CFR] – Former Head of the Southern Command of the United States from 2006 to 2009, former Supreme Allied Commander de NATO from 2009 to 2013, and Dean of Fletcher School at Tufts University.

- Alan Stoga [CFR] – President and founder of Zemi Communications and Vice President of Americas Society.

- Strobe Talbott [TC and CFR] – President of the Brookings Institution and former Deputy Secretary of State.

- Arturo Valenzuela [CFR] – Former Assistant Secretary of State for Western Hemisphere Affairs and professor of government and international relations at Georgetown University.

- Alexander Watson [CFR] – Assistant Secretary of State for Western Hemisphere Affairs.

- George Weiksner [CFR] – Vice President of Credit Suisse.

The Council on Foreign Relations, which is the establishment of this nation, has controlled completely the State Department and the officials in the White House, who set the U.S. policy in Cuba under former President Obama. As Perloff indicated, most of the members of the CFR have sympathized with socialism and Marxism in carrying out the goal of bringing about a one-world government.

Conclusion

Americans need to fight this diabolical idea of allowing the United States to lose its sovereignty, Constitution, laws, and wealth. Freedom-loving Cubans on both sides of the Straits of Florida need to continue fighting for a free Cuba as members of the CFR and the other two groups, the BG and TC, want to invest in Cuba and do not care about restoring a democracy in this country. Additionally, anti-communist Cubans need to understand that the United States government has not been and is not currently an ally in overthrowing the bloody, tyrannical and oppressive regime of the Castro brothers. It is up to the Cubans to establish a free and democratic nation in the island.

Ambassador Thomas Pickering [BG, TC, and CFR] is a former Under Secretary of State for Political Affairs. He participated in the Benghazi cover-up when he was appointed by Secretary Clinton to a panel and eventually the panel's conclusions favored Clinton.

Chapter 15

The Bilderberg Group

The Bilderberg Group (BG) was founded in 1954 by Polish-born Joseph Retinger to promote a greater understanding between Europe and the United States. The organizers met at the Hotel Bilderberg for a three-day meeting in Oosterbeek, Netherlands and that is why it received that name. A founding member was German-born ex-Nazi Prince Bernhard, husband of Queen Juliana of Holland. During their first meeting, very powerful individuals from the United States and Europe decided that the group would determine all issues regarding the politics and economic policies that their nations would follow and their strategy for ruling the world and eventually create a planetary one government.

The late Prince Bernhard, a former Nazi and husband of Queen Juliana of Holland, was a founding member of the Bilderberg Group.

Since 1954 the Bilderbergers meet once a year in different cities in Europe, Canada and the United States. The members of the BG have represented the wealthy elite of the Western World, bankers, industrialists, financiers, prime ministers, presidents, monarchs, key politicians, owners of the media, presidents of the European Union, World Bank and the International Monetary Fund, heads of the Federal Reserve Bank and other presidents of European central bankers, secretary generals of NATO, and important cabinet and military leaders. Similar to the CFR, the BG meetings are secret. All U.S. presidents since Eisenhower have belonged to BG global ruling class or sent representatives to the meetings

The late David Rockefeller, the billionaire banker, former president of the Council on Foreign Relations, was one of the founders of the Bilderberg Group. He later founded the Trilateral Commission.

David Rockefeller always advocated for a global government. In his book, *Memoirs* (2003), he stated the following: "Some even believe we are a part of the secret cabal working against the best interests of the United States, characterizing my family and me as internationalists and of conspiring with others around the world to build a more integrated global political and economic structure-one-world, is you will. If that's the charge, I stand guilty, I am proud of it."

There are about 130 participants in these meetings, of which about 80 are regulars such as Henry Kissinger. Many Obama´s advisors, cabinet members, and important White House officials are Bilderbergers, such as Obama's Godfather George Soros, the late Zbigniew Brzezinski, Hillary Clinton, Robert Gates, Timothy Geithner, Janet Napolitano, Susan Rice, Paul Volcker, and James Jones. Approximately 2/3 of the participants come from Europe and the rest from the United States and Canada.

Promising politicians are invited and interviewed by the BG, such as the governors of small states Jimmy Carter of Georgia and Bill Clinton of Arkansas. If these politicians support the one-world government objective of the BG, then the BG will give them enormous financial support and, with the established media owned by them, massive positive coverage to make them presidents. Of course, after Carter and Clinton were elected president, they staffed their administration with CFR, TC and BG members and consulted with BG members constantly on matters of domestic and international affairs.

The most powerful individuals in the planet, such as the late David Rockefeller, were members of these three organizations. The Americans that participate in the BG, CFR and TC meetings with head of nations and high government officials are in violation of the U.S.'s Logan Act that prohibits elected officials to meet in private with influential business and banking executives to debate and design public policy.

Baron Edmond de Rothschild

From the very beginning of the BG various members of the Rockefeller families and their allies, the Rothschild dynasty in Europe, have been the most powerful force of the organization. Baron Edmond de Rothschild, the French-born financier who was said to be the wealthiest of the surviving descendants of the legendary banking family, has been a most active member of the BG. Baron Edmond de Rothschild died in Geneva in 1997 at the age of 71.

Many years ago, in an interview, Baron Edmond de Rothschild said that of all the countries in the world where he did business, the United States appealed to him most. "For me it symbolizes free enterprise, where a man is responsible only to himself, a place of endless opportunity and limitless space," he said. Then he added, "I am fundamentally a citizen of the world, devoted to France, where I was born, to Switzerland, where I was made welcome, and to Israel because I am a Jew." These two families, the Rockefellers and Rothschilds, as well as European monarchs and a small group of very wealthy individuals determine who will be invited to participate in the BG meetings.

John Coleman described in his book *Conspirators' Hierarchy: The Story of the Committee of 300* (1992) how the BG´s Committee of 300 resurrected the comeback of Francois Mitterrand to power in France. This socialist French president had stated many times his hatred for capitalism. He specifically stated the following: "Industrial capitalism development is the opposite of freedom. We must put an end to it."

George Soros

George Soros was born on August 12, 1930, as Schwartz György, in Hungary. He is a billionaire business magnate who is chairman of Soros Fund Management. Currently, Soros and his very rich allies are funding over 170 communist and radical organizations to undermine and, if possible, destroy the presidency of Donald Trump.

George Soros is known as "The Man Who Broke the Bank of England" because of his short sale of U.S. $10 billion worth of pounds, resulting in a profit for him of $1 billion during the 1992 Black Wednesday United Kingdom currency crisis. Soros is one of the 30 richest people in the world. Soros is a well-known supporter of progressive and extreme radical political causes. He is also known as Obama's godfather.

The Bilderberg Group (BG) official website explains the following:

"Founded in 1954, the Bilderberg conference is an annual meeting designed to foster dialogue between Europe and North America. Every year, between 120-150 political leaders and experts from industry, finance, academia and the media are invited to take part in the conference. About two thirds of the participants come from Europe and the rest from North America; approximately one third from politics and government and the rest from other fields."

"The conference is a forum for informal discussions about major issues facing the world. The meetings are held under the Chatham House Rule, which states that participants are free to use the information received, but neither the identity nor the affiliation of the speaker(s) nor any other participant may be revealed. Thanks to the private nature of the conference, the partici-pants are not bound by the conventions of their office or by pre-agreed positions. As such, they can take time to listen, reflect and gather insights. There is no desired outcome, no minutes are taken and no report is written. Furthermore, no resolutions are proposed, no votes are taken, and no policy statements are issued."

But is this an accurate description of the BG and its objectives? Not at all. There is a desired outcome that all individuals will implement!

According to Daniel Estulin, author of The Bilderberg Group (2009), the major objectives of the Bilderbergers to achieve a one-world government under them are the following:

- One international identity. All national identities will be eliminated to establish one set of universal values.

- Centralized control of the people. Using mind control methods, they plan to direct humanity to obey their wishes.

- A zero-growth society. In a post-industrial period, zero growth will be necessary to destroy progress. American and Canadian industries will be moved to poor Latin American coun-tries to use slave labor, such as in Cuba.

- A state of perpetual imbalance. They will manufacture constant crises to keep the people un-der duress and bring about apathy. Again, look at Cuba where people are constantly looking for food and are being told that the United States is about to invade them or that rich Cubans are coming back to take away their homes and enslave them. Most Cubans hate the regime but very few try to overthrow the most horrible and oppressive tyranny of the Americas that has lasted more than 58 years. Some writers think the Cuban regime was installed by these powerful organizations as a model for Latin America. No one has explained why the late Da-vid Rockefeller traveled to Cuba so many times to meet with the bloody dictator Fidel Castro.

- Centralized control of all education. Indoctrination will be implemented in schools and uni-versities to erase the past and the lessons of history regarding constitutional rights, liberties, and freedom. Many think that Obama´s common core curriculum for all public school stu-dents was being pushed by globalists, including its biometric invasion of privacy, an aspect that reminds this writer of George Orwell's book, *1984*.

- Centralized control of all foreign and domestic policies. This objective was adopted by previous U.S. presidents. President Obama pushed for the approval in the Senate of a series of U.N. treaties that are harmful to the United States since they take away its sovereignty, liberties and wealth.

- Empowering the United Nations. This has been done slowly for many years.

- Expansion of NATO and western trading bloc. This has been going on as the European Union incorporated Eastern European and Mediterranean nations.

- One legal system. The U.N. International Court of Justice will become the sole legal system of the world.

- One socialist welfare state. The BG envisions the creation of a socialist one-world government where obedient slaves will be rewarded and non-conformists will be exterminated.

The Europeans have long supported the concept of giving up the sovereignty of their individual nations as they formed the European Union. Barack Obama, as he stated in Berlin during the 2008 presidential campaign, believes that "he is a citizen of the world." Obama agreed that the United States needs to move toward a world socialist government.

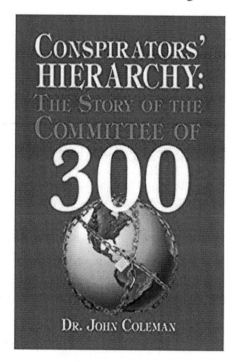

John Coleman wrote the book *Conspirators' Hierarchy: The Story of the Committee of 300* (1992).

Chapter 16

The 2017 Bilderberg Conference at the Westfields Marriott in Chantilly, Virginia

The **65th Bilderberg** Conference took place at the Westfields Marriott in Chantilly, Virginia.

The 65th Bilderberg Conference took place at the Westfields Marriott in Chantilly, Virginia with 131 participants from 21 countries. The wealthy members of the globalist elite met from June 1 to June 4, 2017.

On June 1, 2017, the British newspaper the *Guardian* wrote an article about this conference. It reported that the meeting was going to evaluate the presidency of Donald Trump among other issues. The secretive three-day summit of the globalist political and economic elite started on June 1, 2017 at the Westfields Marriott, a luxury hotel a short distance from the White House Oval Office. The hotel was already on lockdown while an army of landscapers have been busy planting fir trees around the perimeter to protect globalist billionaires from any prying lenses.

As usual, a multitude of guards protected the globalists from the press and protesters who always follow the elite of the New World Order. The members of the globalist elite at the Bilderberg meeting did not want the decisions that they made to be known by the citizens of their nations.

Anti-globalist demonstrations, such as the one shown in this picture, are now common each time the Bilderberg Group meets.

The *Guardian* reported that at the top of the conference agenda this year were the following words: "The Trump administration: a progress report." The newspaper asked the following questions: "Is the president going to be put in detention for tweeting in class? Held back a year? Or told to empty his locker and leave? If ever there's a place where a president could hear the words "you're fired!," it's Bilderberg." It explained that the White House took no chances. The president sent three high White House officials to the **Bilderberg** Conference. They were Director of National Security Council General H.R. McMaster, Commerce Secretary Wilbur Ross, and **Assistant to the President and Director of Strategic Initiatives** Chris Liddell. Henry Kissinger, the very powerful Bilderberger, visited President Trump at the White House a few weeks ago to discuss "Russia and other things."

The Bilderbergers have summoned the head of NATO, Jens Stoltenberg, to give feedback. Stoltenberg led the session on "The transatlantic defense alliance: bullets, bytes and bucks". He was joined by the Dutch minister of defense and other senior European politicians and party leaders.

Perhaps the most significant name on the list was Cui Tiankai, China's ambassador to the United States. According to the *Guardian*, China was discussed at a summit attended by the Chinese ambassador, White House Director of National Security General H.R. McMaster, Commerce Secretary Wilbur Ross, Republican Senator Tom Cotton, Republican Senator Lindsey Graham, former CIA Director John Brennan (who is now is a Senior Advisor of the Kissinger Associates, Inc)., Governor of Virginia Terry McAuliffe, and many important American investors in the country, including the heads of the financial services firms of the Carlyle Group and KKR and the boss of Google.

The *Guardian* reported the following: "Eric Schmidt, the executive chairman of Alphabet, Google's holding company, has just come back from a trip to Beijing, where he was overseeing Google. He declared it "a pleasure to be back in China, a country that I admire a great deal". Three days spent chatting to the Chinese ambassador certainly won't harm his ambitions there. All this is the kind of thing that should be headline news, but with the president of Turner International attending, we can be fairly sure Bilderberg won't make many ripples at *CNN*. … You could of course complain about a lack of press coverage of Bilderberg…So will Trump be given his marching orders at Bilderberg, or will he be kept on as a useful doofus?"

The agenda of the 2017 Bilderberg annual meeting

The key topics for discussion this year included:

1. The Trump Administration: A progress report
2. Trans-Atlantic relations: options and scenarios
3. The Trans-Atlantic defense alliance: bullets, bytes and bucks
4. The direction of the EU
5. Can globalization be slowed down?
6. Jobs, income and unrealized expectations
7. The war on information
8. Why is populism growing?
9. Russia in the international order
10. The Near East

11. Nuclear proliferation

12. China

13. Current events

Participants to the 2017 Bilderberg annual meeting

Castries, Henri de (FRA), Chairman of the Steering Commitee and President of Institut Montaigne; Former Chairman and CEO, AXA

Achleitner, Paul M. (DEU), Chairman of the Supervisory Board, Deutsche Bank AG; Treasurer, Bilderberg Meeting

Adonis, Andrew (GBR), Chair, National Infrastructure Commission

Agius, Marcus (GBR), Chairman, PA Consulting Group

Akyol, Mustafa (TUR), Senior Visiting Fellow, Freedom Project at Wellesley College

Alstadheim, Kjetil B. (NOR), Political Editor, Dagens Næringsliv

Altman, Roger C. (USA), Founder and Senior Chairman, Evercore

Arnaut, José Luis (PRT), Managing Partner, CMS Rui Pena & Arnaut

Barroso, José M. Durão (PRT), Chairman, Goldman Sachs International

Bäte, Oliver (DEU), CEO, Allianz SE

Baumann, Werner (DEU), Chairman, Bayer AG

Baverez, Nicolas (FRA), Partner, Gibson, Dunn & Crutcher

Benko, René (AUT), Founder and Chairman of the Advisory Board, SIGNA Holding GmbH

Berner, Anne-Catherine (FIN), Minister of Transport and Communications

Botín, Ana P. (ESP), Executive Chairman, Banco Santander

Brandtzæg, Svein Richard (NOR), President and CEO, Norsk Hydro ASA

Brennan, John O. (USA), Senior Advisor, Kissinger Associates Inc.

Bsirske, Frank (DEU), Chairman, United Services Union

Buberl, Thomas (FRA), CEO, AXA

Bunn, M. Elaine (USA), Former Deputy Assistant Secretary of Defense

Burns, William J. (USA), President, Carnegie Endowment for International Peace

Çakiroglu, Levent (TUR), CEO, Koç Holding A.S.

Çamlibel, Cansu (TUR), Washington DC Bureau Chief, Hürriyet Newspaper

Cebrián, Juan Luis (ESP), Executive Chairman, PRISA and El País

Clemet, Kristin (NOR), CEO, Civita

Cohen, David S. (USA), Former Deputy Director, CIA

Collison, Patrick (USA), CEO, Stripe

Cotton, Tom (USA), Senator

Cui, Tiankai (CHN), Ambassador to the United States

Döpfner, Mathias (DEU), CEO, Axel Springer SE

Elkann, John (ITA), Chairman, Fiat Chrysler Automobiles

Enders, Thomas (DEU), CEO, Airbus SE

Federspiel, Ulrik (DNK), Group Executive, Haldor Topsøe Holding A/S

Ferguson, Jr., Roger W. (USA), President and CEO, TIAA

Ferguson, Niall (USA), Senior Fellow, Hoover Institution, Stanford University

Gianotti, Fabiola (ITA), Director General, CERN

Gozi, Sandro (ITA), State Secretary for European Affairs

Graham, Lindsey (USA), Senator

Greenberg, Evan G. (USA), Chairman and CEO, Chubb Group

Griffin, Kenneth (USA), Founder and CEO, Citadel Investment Group, LLC

Gruber, Lilli (ITA), Editor-in-Chief and Anchor "Otto e mezzo", La7 TV
Guindos, Luis de (ESP), Minister of Economy, Industry and Competitiveness

Haines, Avril D. (USA), Former Deputy National Security Advisor

Halberstadt, Victor (NLD), Professor of Economics, Leiden University;

Hamers, Ralph (NLD), Chairman, ING Group

Hedegaard, Connie (DNK), Chair, KR Foundation

Hennis-Plasschaert, Jeanine (NLD), Minister of Defence, The Netherlands

Hobson, Mellody (USA), President, Ariel Investments LLC

Hoffman, Reid (USA), Co-Founder, LinkedIn and Partner, Greylock

Houghton, Nicholas (GBR), Former Chief of Defence

Ischinger, Wolfgang (INT), Chairman, Munich Security Conference

Jacobs, Kenneth M. (USA), Chairman and CEO, Lazard

Johnson, James A. (USA), Chairman, Johnson Capital Partners

Jordan, Jr., Vernon E. (USA), Senior Managing Director, Lazard Frères & Co. LLC

Karp, Alex (USA), CEO, Palantir Technologies

Kengeter, Carsten (DEU), CEO, Deutsche Börse AG

Kissinger, Henry A. (USA), Chairman, Kissinger Associates Inc.

Klatten, Susanne (DEU), Managing Director, SKion GmbH

Kleinfeld, Klaus (USA), Former Chairman and CEO, Arconic

Knot, Klaas H.W. (NLD), President, De Nederlandsche Bank

Koç, Ömer M. (TUR), Chairman, Koç Holding A.S.

Kotkin, Stephen (USA), Professor in History and International Affairs, Princeton University

Kravis, Henry R. (USA), Co-Chairman and Co-CEO, KKR

Kravis, Marie-Josée (USA), Senior Fellow, Hudson Institute; President, American Friends of Bilderberg

Kudelski, André (CHE), Chairman and CEO, Kudelski Group

Lagarde, Christine (INT), Managing Director, International Monetary Fund

Lenglet, François (FRA), Chief Economics Commentator, France 2

Leysen, Thomas (BEL), Chairman, KBC Group

Liddell, Christopher (USA), Assistant to the President and Director of Strategic Initiatives

Lööf, Annie (SWE), Party Leader, Centre Party

Mathews, Jessica T. (USA), Distinguished Fellow, Carnegie Endowment for International Peace

McAuliffe, Terence (USA), Governor of Virginia

McKay, David I. (CAN), President and CEO, Royal Bank of Canada

McMaster, H.R. (USA), National Security Advisor

Micklethwait, John (INT), Editor-in-Chief, *Bloomberg* LP

Minton Beddoes, Zanny (INT), Editor-in-Chief, The Economist

Molinari, Maurizio (ITA), Editor-in-Chief, La Stampa

Monaco, Lisa (USA), Former Homeland Security Officer

Morneau, Bill (CAN), Minister of Finance

Mundie, Craig J. (USA), President, Mundie & Associates

Murtagh, Gene M. (IRL), CEO, Kingspan Group plc

Netherlands, H.M. the King of the (NLD)

Noonan, Peggy (USA), Author and Columnist, The *Wall Street Journal*

O'Leary, Michael (IRL), CEO, Ryanair D.A.C.

Osborne, George (GBR), Editor, London Evening Standard

Papahelas, Alexis (GRC), Executive Editor, Kathimerini Newspaper

Papalexopoulos, Dimitri (GRC), CEO, Titan Cement Co.

Petraeus, David H. (USA), Chairman, KKR Global Institute

Pind, Søren (DNK), Minister for Higher Education and Science

Puga, Benoît (FRA), Grand Chancellor of the Legion of Honor and Chancellor of the National Order of Merit

Rachman, Gideon (GBR), Chief *Foreign Affairs* Commentator, *The Financial Times*

Reisman, Heather M. (CAN), Chair and CEO, Indigo Books & Music Inc.

Rivera Díaz, Albert (ESP), President, Ciudadanos Party

Rosén, Johanna (SWE), Professor in Materials Physics, Linköping University

Ross, Wilbur L. (USA), Secretary of Commerce

Rubenstein, David M. (USA), Co-Founder and Co-CEO, The Carlyle Group

Rubin, Robert E. (USA), Co-Chair, Council on Foreign Relations and Former Treasury Secretary

Ruoff, Susanne (CHE), CEO, Swiss Post

Rutten, Gwendolyn (BEL), Chair, Open VLD

Sabia, Michael (CAN), CEO, Caisse de dépôt et placement du Québec

Sawers, John (GBR), Chairman and Partner, Macro Advisory Partners

Schadlow, Nadia (USA), Deputy Assistant to the President, National Security Council

Schmidt, Eric E. (USA), Executive Chairman, Alphabet Inc.

Schneider-Ammann, Johann N. (CHE), Federal Councillor, Swiss Confederation

Scholten, Rudolf (AUT), President, Bruno Kreisky Forum for International Dialogue

Severgnini, Beppe (ITA), Editor-in-Chief, 7-Corriere della Sera

Sikorski, Radoslaw (POL), Senior Fellow, Harvard University

Slat, Boyan (NLD), CEO and Founder, The Ocean Cleanup

Spahn, Jens (DEU), Parliamentary State Secretary and Federal Ministry of Finance

Stephenson, Randall L. (USA), Chairman and CEO, AT&T

Stern, Andrew (USA), President Emeritus, SEIU and Senior Fellow, Economic Security Project

Stoltenberg, Jens (INT), Secretary General, NATO

Summers, Lawrence H. (USA), Charles W. Eliot University Professor, Harvard University

Tertrais, Bruno (FRA), Deputy Director, Fondation pour la recherche stratégique

Thiel, Peter (USA), President, Thiel Capital

Topsøe, Jakob Haldor (DNK), Chairman, Haldor Topsøe Holding A/S

Ülgen, Sinan (TUR), Founding and Partner, Istanbul Economics

Wahlroos, Björn (FIN), Chairman, Sampo Group, Nordea Bank, UPM-Kymmene Corporation

Wallenberg, Marcus (SWE), Chairman, Skandinaviska Enskilda Banken AB

Walter, Amy (USA), Editor, The Cook Political Report

Weston, Galen G. (CAN), CEO and Executive Chairman, Loblaw Companies Ltd and George Weston Companies

White, Sharon (GBR), Chief Executive, Ofcom

Wieseltier, Leon (USA), Isaiah Berlin Senior Fellow in Culture and Policy, The Brookings Institution

Wolf, Martin H. (INT), Chief Economics Commentator, *Financial Times*

Wolfensohn, James D. (USA), Chairman and CEO, Wolfensohn & Company

Wunsch, Pierre (BEL), Vice-Governor, National Bank of Belgium

Zeiler, Gerhard (AUT), President, Turner International

Zients, Jeffrey D. (USA), Former Director, National Economic Council

Zoellick, Robert B. (USA), Non-Executive Chairman, AllianceBernstein L.P.

Chapter 17

The 2016 Bilderberg Group meeting and the United States presidential elections

The 2016 Bilderberg conference took place from June 9 to June 12, 2016 in Dresden, Germany. The conference venue was the five-star Taschenbergpalais Hotel, which is located in Dresden's historic city center, the "Innere Altstadt."

The 64th Bilderberg meeting included around 130 participants from 20 countries. According to the official website, the participants were a diverse group of political leaders and experts from industry, finance, academia, and the media.

The key topics for discussion this year included:

1. Current events (Even though not announced, the U.S. presidential election was be in the agenda).
2. China
3. Europe: migration, growth, reform, vision, unity
4. Middle East
5. Russia
6. US political landscape, economy: growth, debt, reform
7. Cyber security
8. Geo-politics of energy and commodity prices
9. Precariat and middle class
10 Technological innovation

Final list of participants in the 2016 Bilderberg conference, as announced in the Bilderberg Group official website

The invited individuals were as follows:

CHAIRMAN

Castries, Henri de (FRA), Chairman and CEO, AXA Group

Aboutaleb, Ahmed (NLD), Mayor, City of Rotterdam

Achleitner, Paul M. (DEU), Chairman of the Supervisory Board, Deutsche Bank AG

Agius, Marcus (GBR), Chairman, PA Consulting Group

Ahrenkiel, Thomas (DNK), Permanent Secretary, Ministry of Defence

Albuquerque, Maria Luís (PRT), Former Minister of Finance; MP, Social Democratic Party

Alierta, César (ESP), Executive Chairman and CEO, Telefónica

Altman, Roger C. (USA), Executive Chairman, Evercore

Altman, Sam (USA), President, Y Combinator

Andersson, Magdalena (SWE), Minister of Finance

Applebaum, Anne (USA), Columnist *Washington Post*; Director of the Transitions Forum, Legatum Institute

Apunen, Matti (FIN), Director, Finnish Business and Policy Forum EVA

Aydin-Düzgit, Senem (TUR), Associate Professor and Jean Monnet Chair, Istanbul Bilgi University

Barbizet, Patricia (FRA), CEO, Artemis

Barroso, José M. Durão (PRT), Former President of the European Commission

Baverez, Nicolas (FRA), Partner, Gibson, Dunn & Crutcher

Bengio, Yoshua (CAN), Professor in Computer Science and Operations Research, University of Montreal

Benko, René (AUT), Founder and Chairman of the Advisory Board, SIGNA Holding GmbH

Bernabè, Franco (ITA), Chairman, CartaSi S.p.A.

Beurden, Ben van (NLD), CEO, Royal Dutch Shell plc

Blanchard, Olivier (FRA), Fred Bergsten Senior Fellow, Peterson Institute

Botín, Ana P. (ESP), Executive Chairman, Banco Santander

Brandtzæg, Svein Richard (NOR), President and CEO, Norsk Hydro ASA

Breedlove, Philip M. (INT), Former Supreme Allied Commander Europe

Brende, Børge (NOR), Minister of *Foreign Affairs*

Burns, William J. (USA), President, Carnegie Endowment for International Peace

Cebrián, Juan Luis (ESP), Executive Chairman, PRISA and El País

Charpentier, Emmanuelle (FRA), Director, Max Planck Institute for Infection Biology

Coeuré, Benoît (INT), Member of the Executive Board, European Central Bank

Costamagna, Claudio (ITA), Chairman, Cassa Depositi e Prestiti S.p.A.

Cote, David M. (USA), Chairman and CEO, Honeywell

Cryan, John (DEU), CEO, Deutsche Bank AG

Dassù, Marta (ITA), Senior Director, European Affairs, Aspen Institute

Dijksma, Sharon A.M. (NLD), Minister for the Environment

Döpfner, Mathias (DEU), CEO, Axel Springer SE

Dyvig, Christian (DNK), Chairman, Kompan

Ebeling, Thomas (DEU), CEO, ProSiebenSat.1

Elkann, John (ITA), Chairman and CEO, EXOR; Chairman, Fiat Chrysler Automobiles

Enders, Thomas (DEU), CEO, Airbus Group

Engel, Richard (USA), Chief Foreign Correspondent, *NBC* News

Fabius, Laurent (FRA), President, Constitutional Council

Federspiel, Ulrik (DNK), Group Executive, Haldor Topsøe A/S

Ferguson, Jr., Roger W. (USA), President and CEO, TIAA

Ferguson, Niall (USA), Professor of History, Harvard University

Flint, Douglas J. (GBR), Group Chairman, HSBC Holdings plc

Garicano, Luis (ESP), Professor of Economics, LSE; Senior Advisor to Ciudadanos

Georgieva, Kristalina (INT), Vice President, European Commission

Gernelle, Etienne (FRA), Editorial Director, Le Point

Gomes da Silva, Carlos (PRT), Vice Chairman and CEO, Galp Energia

Goodman, Helen (GBR), MP, Labour Party

Goulard, Sylvie (INT), Member of the European Parliament

Graham, Lindsey (USA), Senator

Grillo, Ulrich (DEU), Chairman, Grillo-Werke AG; President, Bundesverband der Deutschen Industrie

Gruber, Lilli (ITA), Editor-in-Chief and Anchor "Otto e mezzo", La7 TV

Hadfield, Chris (CAN), Colonel, Astronaut

Halberstadt, Victor (NLD), Professor of Economics, Leiden University

Harding, Dido (GBR), CEO, TalkTalk Telecom Group plc

Hassabis, Demis (GBR), Co-Founder and CEO, DeepMind

Hobson, Mellody (USA), President, Ariel Investment, LLC

Hoffman, Reid (USA), Co-Founder and Executive Chairman, LinkedIn

Höttges, Timotheus (DEU), CEO, Deutsche Telekom AG

Jacobs, Kenneth M. (USA), Chairman and CEO, Lazard

Jäkel, Julia (DEU), CEO, Gruner + Jahr

Johnson, James A. (USA), Chairman, Johnson Capital Partners

Jonsson, Conni (SWE), Founder and Chairman, EQT

Jordan, Jr., Vernon E. (USA), Senior Managing Director, Lazard Frères & Co. LLC

Kaeser, Joe (DEU), President and CEO, Siemens AG

Karp, Alex (USA), CEO, Palantir Technologies

Kengeter, Carsten (DEU), CEO, Deutsche Börse AG

Kerr, John (GBR), Deputy Chairman, Scottish Power

Kherbache, Yasmine (BEL), MP, Flemish Parliament

Kissinger, Henry A. (USA), Chairman, Kissinger Associates, Inc.

Kleinfeld, Klaus (USA), Chairman and CEO, Alcoa

Kravis, Henry R. (USA), Co-Chairman and Co-CEO, Kohlberg Kravis Roberts & Co.

Kravis, Marie-Josée (USA), Senior Fellow, Hudson Institute

Kudelski, André (CHE), Chairman and CEO, Kudelski Group

Lagarde, Christine (INT), Managing Director, International Monetary Fund

Levin, Richard (USA), CEO, Coursera

Leyen, Ursula von der (DEU), Minister of Defence

Leysen, Thomas (BEL), Chairman, KBC Group

Logothetis, George (GRC), Chairman and CEO, Libra Group

Maizière, Thomas de (DEU), Minister of the Interior, Federal Ministry of the Interior

Makan, Divesh (USA), CEO, ICONIQ Capital

Malcomson, Scott (USA), Author; President, Monere Ltd.

Markwalder, Christa (CHE), President of the National Council and the Federal Assembly

McArdle, Megan (USA), Columnist, *Bloomberg* View

Michel, Charles (BEL), Prime Minister

Micklethwait, John (USA), Editor-in-Chief, *Bloomberg* LP

Minton Beddoes, Zanny (GBR), Editor-in-Chief, The Economist

Mitsotakis, Kyriakos (GRC), President, New Democracy Party

Morneau, Bill (CAN), Minister of Finance

Mundie, Craig J. (USA), Principal, Mundie & Associates

Murray, Charles A. (USA), W.H. Brady Scholar, American Enterprise Institute

Netherlands, H.M. the King of the (NLD)

Noonan, Michael (IRL), Minister for Finance

Noonan, Peggy (USA), Author, Columnist, The *Wall Street Journal*

O'Leary, Michael (IRL), CEO, Ryanair Plc

Ollongren, Kajsa (NLD), Deputy Mayor of Amsterdam

Özel, Soli (TUR), Professor, Kadir Has University

Papalexopoulos, Dimitri (GRC), CEO, Titan Cement Co.

Petraeus, David H. (USA), Chairman, KKR Global Institute

Philippe, Edouard (FRA), Mayor of Le Havre

Pind, Søren (DNK), Minister of Justice

Ratti, Carlo (ITA), Director, MIT Senseable City Lab

Reisman, Heather M. (CAN), Chair and CEO, Indigo Books & Music Inc.

Rutte, Mark (NLD), Prime Minister

Sawers, John (GBR), Chairman and Partner, Macro Advisory Partners

Schäuble, Wolfgang (DEU), Minister of Finance

Schieder, Andreas (AUT), Chairman, Social Democratic Group

Schmidt, Eric E. (USA), Executive Chairman, Alphabet Inc.

Scholten, Rudolf (AUT), CEO, Oesterreichische Kontrollbank AG

Schwab, Klaus (INT), Executive Chairman, World Economic Forum

Sikorski, Radoslaw (POL), Senior Fellow, Harvard University; Former Minister of *Foreign Affairs*

Simsek, Mehmet (TUR), Deputy Prime Minister

Sinn, Hans-Werner (DEU), Professor for Economics and Public Finance, Ludwig Maximilian University of Munich

Skogen Lund, Kristin (NOR), Director General, The Confederation of Norwegian Enterprise

Standing, Guy (GBR), Co-President, BIEN; Research Professor, University of London

Svanberg, Carl-Henric (SWE), Chairman, BP plc and AB Volvo

Thiel, Peter A. (USA), President, Thiel Capital

Tillich, Stanislaw (DEU), Minister-President of Saxony

Vetterli, Martin (CHE), President, NSF

Wahlroos, Björn (FIN), Chairman, Sampo Group, Nordea Bank, UPM-Kymmene Corporation

Wallenberg, Jacob (SWE), Chairman, Investor AB

Weder di Mauro, Beatrice (CHE), Professor of Economics, University of Mainz

Wolf, Martin H. (GBR), Chief Economics Commentator, *Financial Times*

The Bilderberg Group chose Hillary Clinton to be the next president

Republican Senator Lindsey Graham from South Carolina

Republican Senator Lindsey Graham from South Carolina initially endorsed Donald Trump but later withdrew his endorsement. The attendance of anti-Trump Senator Lindsey Graham to the 2016 Bilderberg Group meeting was an obvious sign that the Bilderberg Group tried to prevent Donald Trump from defeating Bilderberg's chosen candidate, Hillary Clinton. Senator Graham also attended the 2017 Bilderberg Group meeting.

The secretive Bilderberg Group discussed in 2016 how to prevent Donald Trump from becoming president, the possibility of mass riots as a result of wealth inequality, and the migrant crisis as well as the United Kingdom's vote on leaving the European Union. Donald Trump's self-funded campaign and his public opposition to globalism and internationalist trade deals like NAFTA shocked the Bilderberg globalist elitists. Three other interesting participants on the list were Richard Engel, *NBC* News' chief foreign correspondent; Vernon E. Jordan, Jr., Senior Managing Director, Lazard Frères & Co.; and Roger Charles Altman.

Richard Engel, *NBC* News' chief foreign correspondent, also worked for *ABC* News. Both television organizations are part of the mainstream pro-Democratic Party news media.

Roger Charles Altman is an American investment banker, the founder and executive chairman of Evercore, and a former Democratic politician. He served as Assistant Secretary of the Treasury in the Carter administration and as Deputy Secretary of the Treasury in the Clinton administration from January 1993 until he resigned in August 1994, amid the Whitewater controversy. He supported Hillary Clinton for president.

Vernon E. Jordan, Jr., is a Senior Managing Director, Lazard Frères & Co. LLC

Vernon E. Jordan, Jr., is a civil rights activist who was chosen by President Bill Clinton as a close adviser. Jordan, a member of the Democratic Party, has become an influential figure in American politics.

Thomas E. "Tom" Donilon is an attorney and former high government official who served as White House National Security Advisor in the Obama administration.

Thomas E. "Tom" Donilon served as Agency Review Team Lead for the State Department in the Obama transition team. Obama appointed Donilon as Deputy to National Security Advisor James Jones. Donilon replaced Jones as National Security Advisor on October 8, 2010. Donilon tendered his resignation as National Security Adviser on June 5, 2013. He was followed by Susan Rice. Donilon is a former member of the Steering Committee of the Bilderberg Group.

This writer pointed out that Hillary Clinton was the chosen presidential candidate of the BG. Two very powerful Democrats were invited to attend the 2015 Bilderberg Group meeting held in Austria. One of the two Democrats was Tom Donilon, a Democrat operative, who served in the Obama White House as National Security Director. The other was Jim Messina, a Democratic Party operative and chief advisor to Hillary Clinton. Many suspect that the BG may have decided to place the very corrupt former Secretary of State in the White House to continue to advance the agenda of the BG for a planetary government.

Who is Jim Messina and why was he invited to the 2015 BG meeting in Austria?

Jim Messina

Jim Messina was the White House Deputy Chief of Staff for Operations under President Barack Obama from 2009 to 2011. He was hired as National Chief of Staff for the Obama campaign in the 2008 general election. He later became campaign manager of Obama's 2012 re-election campaign. After Obama was elected, Messina was named Director of Personnel for the Obama-Biden Transition team, helping Obama pick his cabinet.

Messina became President Obama's White House Deputy Chief of Staff and earned the nickname "the fixer." Dan Pfeiffer called Messina "the most powerful person in Washington that you have heard of." He also said that Messina and Chief of Staff Rahm Emanuel (present mayor of Chicago) had a "crazy relationship" and explained that "You'd be in a meeting, and Rahm would bark out that something needed to be done; Jim would disappear from Rahm's office, pop through the door a few minutes later and say, 'Got it!' or 'Got him!'" Messina had a crucial role in the passage of the disastrous Affordable Care Act or ObamaCare and was widely credited with the effort to repeal Don't Ask Don't Tell regarding gays in the Armed Forces.

Jim Messina celebrated Obama's reelection in November 2012

Messina was Obama's campaign manager during the 2012 presidential election. In January 2013, Messina became head of Organizing for Action (OFA), using the Obama for America database and other resources to support Obama's dangerous legislative agenda in his second term. While OFA was formed in 2009 by Obama, it was reformed as a political-action non-profit group in January 2013. Obama is the only president in history to have created such an organization.

Obama has continued pushing his destructive anti-American, pro-Muslim, Marxist, and New World Order agenda after leaving the White House. His former White House and campaign official founded The Messina Group, a full-service consulting firm with offices in Washington, D.C., New York, San Francisco, and London.

Steve Watson wrote an article entitled "Bilderberg Backs Hillary for 2016 Presidency" which was published in *InfoWars* on June 8, 2015. He explained that Jim Messina of The Messina Group was the chief advisor to Hillary Clinton. Messina also headed the super PAC Priorities USA, which supported Barack Obama and was firmly involved in the Hillary Clinton camp.

Messina led the unpopular United Kingdom Prime Minister David Cameron to a surprise majority victory in British elections. Messina said on MS*NBC*'s "Morning Joe" program the following: "I'm coming home tomorrow and it's whatever it will take to get Hillary [elected]." Watson wrote that "Messina's presence at Bilderberg will be focused around ensuring none of Hillary's potential challengers get the big bucks from the innumerable transnational banks and corporations that will also be represented at Bilderberg."

As it has been reported by many, including this writer, in June 2008, the Bilderberg Group met in secret with both Hillary Clinton and Barack Obama while the globalists were meeting in Chantilly in Northern Virginia. As always, the nation's press was shunted. Watson pointed out that it is believed that the group endorsed Barack Obama over Hillary Clinton, as a more immediate candidate, with the plan of having Hillary Clinton essentially pick up as president for a third Obama term. A powerful Bilderberg member and top corporate elitist, James A. Johnson, also had a direct hand in selecting Obama's running mate for the 2008 election, acting as kingmaker for America's then future president.

Hillary Clinton has a deep rooted connection to the Bilderberg New World Order globalist elitist. Bill Clinton attended the 1991 meeting in Germany. Shortly before becoming president, he attended again in 1999 the BG annual meeting held in Sintra, Portugal (despite Clinton's lie that he had not attended in 15 years). It is rumored that Hillary Clinton attended the 2006 meeting in Ottawa, Canada. It is important to note that some individuals attend the meetings and their names are not published in the official list of attendees.

Some of the individuals who attended the 2015 and those who attended the 2016 Bilderberg Group meetings were strong supporters of the very corrupt Hillary Clinton. It is obvious that she is the one this globalist elite wanted in the White House. This writer believes that the Bilderberg Group, the Council of Foreign Relations, and the Trilateral Commission are part of the New World Order's objective of a one-world government to enslave humanity. If Hillary Clinton would have been elected president the road to a world government would have to continue full speed ahead. Unfortunately, the United States is similar to the nation described in George Orwell's book *1984*, a Big Brother surveillance society and police state!

The world may be on the verge of an economic collapse in the near future as a result of the United States and European central bankers' decisions, such as the printing of over $11 trillion out of thin air. These banks are controlled by the private banking cartels, which are the owners of these financial institutions. The economic crisis in Greece, Spain, Portugal, Italy, and other European countries could also contribute to this impending economic catastrophe.

Americans need to fight the global government being planned under the United Nations, but controlled by the members of the Bilderberg Group, Council of Foreign Affairs, and Trilateral Commission. If this diabolical plan is ever successful, the United States will lose its sovereignty, wealth, Constitution, and laws.

The Bilderberg Group selected the very corrupt Hillary Clinton as the next president. Both Hillary and former president Bill Clinton have always believed that they are above the law and that rules and regulations that apply to others do not apply to them. It is clear why Hillary Clinton's destruction of 30,000 e-mails was a risk she was willing to take. Bill and Hillary are devious, unprincipled, and dishonest liars who have committed many crimes. The Clinton Foundation is a criminal enterprise as Hillary Clinton traded favors in exchange for millions for the corrupt foundation when she served as Secretary of State. Both of them should be indicted.

Similar to Barack Obama, Hillary Clinton lies frequently. Similar to Barack Obama, Hillary Clinton has been involved in numerous scandals and has committed crimes. Similar to Barack Obama, Hillary Clinton believes that she is above the law. Similar to Obama, she has ties to the Muslim Brotherhood. Hillary Clinton, unlike her husband, is not a charming and charismatic politician. No matter how hard she tried to connect with ordinary people, many felt that she lacked authenticity. Together with her campaign staffers, Hillary Clinton tried very hard to distance herself from the many scandals involving Bill Clinton and her. However, Hillary Clinton has a very serious problem and that is that her many scandals will simply never go away.

The fact that the Clinton Foundation has accepted millions from foreign countries and shady individuals over a number of years, which constitute a major scandal, hurt Hillary Clinton's presidential campaign. How did Hillary Clinton pretend to be a defender of the rights of women in the United States when she accepted millions of dollars from Middle Eastern countries where women are severely oppressed and stoned to death for infidelity?

Never before in U.S. history had a presidential candidate been campaigning while 147 FBI agents were investigating that candidate for misusing classified top secret information in an illegal private server at her home and for corruption while serving as secretary of state. More than likely, China, Russia, Iran, North and other enemy nations that have cyber capabilities have all the Clinton's e-mails. Some of the top secret emails had the names of many of the CIA spies in foreign enemy countries. Most likely, the CIA spies have already been killed or imprisoned due to Hillary's criminal negligence as in Benghazi and Libya.

Conclusion

In spite of the immense support by the globalists Hillary Clinton lost the presidential election.

Chapter 18

The Council on Foreign Relations, the Bilderberg Group, and the Trilateral Commission have as their main objectives to achieve a one-world socialist government

The Trilateral Commission (TC) was founded in 1973 by David Rockefeller, former secretary of State Henry Kissinger, and former National Security Advisor Zbigniew Brzezinski. The TC has about 350 members from Europe, Asia, and the Americas, who want to foster a closer cooperation among these three continents. The inner circle of the TC, as with the CFR and BG, has as its main objective to achieve a one-world socialist government. As stated earlier, former presidential candidate Barry Goldwater, who previously had criticized the CFR, said the following about the TC: "David Rockefeller's newest international cabal is intended to be the vehicle for multinational consolidation of the commercial and banking interests by seizing control of the political government of the United States."

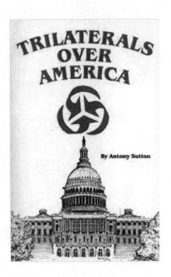

Antony Sutton is the author of *Trilaterals over America* (1995).

Antony Sutton's book titled *Trilaterals over America* (1995) concluded that the TC's real objective is to collaborate with the CFR and BG to establish policies for the implementation of a one-world government. In the first few years, the TC issued six positions papers which were later incorporated in a book titled Triangle Papers. Estulin cited Gary Allen´s book, *The Rockefeller File* (1976), which stated the following: "If the Triangle Papers are any indication we can look for four major thrusts toward world economic controls." Allen described that, first, the

TC would pursue a new world monetary system; second, it would raid or steal U.S. resources and wealth to share with Third World countries; third, it would increase trade with communist countries; and last, it would use the energy crisis to gain international control.

Estulin wrote that since the publication of Allen's book, the United States has sent billions of dollars of its technology to China and Russia and has heavily subsidized and forgiven debts to Third World countries. Obama forgave Muslim Brotherhood-dominated Egypt one billion that the nation owed the U.S., besides giving Egypt $2.5 billion in aid along with 200 Abraham tanks and modern jet aircraft.

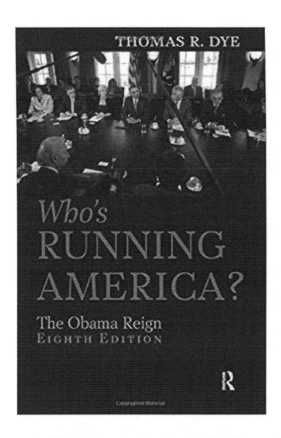

Thomas R. Dye wrote *Who's Running America*? : The Obama Reign in 2014.

Amazon describes this book as follows:

"A classic book of American government, *Who's Running America?* continues to demonstrate how power is concentrated in large institutions no matter who inhabits the White House. The eighth edition of this best-selling text focuses on the Obama administration and the ways in which it is different from but also similar to administrations that have come before."

"Based on years of exhaustive data compilation and analysis, *Who's Running America?* explores the influence and impact of governmental leaders, corporate officials, and other elites both inside and outside the United States. Employing an oligarchic model of national policymaking, Tom Dye doesn't just lay out theory and data. He very consciously "names names" in describing the people who inhabit the White House, the Cabinet, the leaders of Congress, members of the Supreme Court, as well as the board rooms of the nation's largest corporations and banks including leading media lights as well as "fat cat" political contributors. Dye argues that big institutions run America, but also that these institutions are made up of real people. *Who's Running America?* puts the flesh and bones on the statistics and delivers the inside scoop on the Obama reign."

Thomas Dye had written a previous book titled Who is Running America? Institutional Leadership in the United States in 1976. He described the process how public opinion is created in America as follows:

"This opinion is formulated by the dominant Council on Foreign Relations members who belong to an inner circle called Special Group that plan and coordinate the psycho-political operations used to manipulate the American public, and through a vast intergovernmental undercover infrastructure called the Secret Team that include the legislative, executive, and judicial branches of government, such as the Secretary of State, the Secretary of Defense, the Secretary of the Treasury, and the Director of the CIA; those who control television, radio, and the newspapers corporations; who head the largest law firms; who run the largest and most prestigious universities and think tanks; who direct the largest private foundations and who direct the largest public corporations."

Estulin explained that the CFR "Secret Team" follows the same pattern of all secret societies. The CFR is organize as circles within circles, with the "exterior layer (Secret Team) always protecting the more dominant inner membership (Special Group) that coordinates the psycho-political operations".

Estulin wrote the following:

"By keeping the objectives, the identities and the roles by members of Secret Team hidden from other team members, the CFR Special Group protects itself from hypothetical prosecution by denying its participation in the operations. To further protect itself from possible prosecution, the CFR does not reveal to every Council member what psycho-political operations are being planned or what their exact role in the operation is. The more exclusive Bilderberg Group operates under identical criteria."

The Rio+ 20 Conference

In June 2012, Secretary of State Hillary Clinton travelled to Rio de Janeiro, Brazil to attend the 20th anniversary of the original Rio Conference on global sustainability. This conference was known as Rio+20. Without the approval of Congress, Secretary Clinton, on behalf of President Barack Obama, committed the United States to give the United Nations Environment Programme (UNEP) $2 billion towards an eventual fund of $100 billion.

The U.S. contribution would go to a Green Climate Fund, which is located in Switzerland. This institution was created by the United Nations Climate Conference in Durban, South Africa in December 2011.

The Green Climate Fund would be run by a 24-nation interim board. The money towards this United Nations agency would come from developed nations, such as the United States. It will then distributed to Third World countries, many of which are led by dictators, to be used to fight climate change. The United States would have no control as to where its money is spent. Much of U.S. foreign aid in the past was wasted. Instead of going to the poor people, this aid went to the pockets of Third World dictators.

Achim Steiner, United Nations Under-Secretary General and United Nations Environmental Programme (UNEP) executive director, stated the following at the Rio+20 Conference: "World leaders and governments have today agreed that a transition to a green economy, backed by strong social provisions, offers a key pathway towards a sustainable 21st century." Dick Morris and Eileen McGann in their book, *Here Come the Black Helicopters!: UN Global Governance and the Loss of Freedom* (2012), described the statement by Steiner as a new form of global extortion and the first major step in "a global scheme to redistribute resources from the First World nations, whose industry and hard work has created them, to Third World dictators who can stash the money in Swiss bank accounts." The plan is for developed nations, which do not include China or India, to have a major transfer of wealth using the environment as an excuse.

Agenda 21

The first Rio Conference in 1992 created Agenda 21, a most ambitious global initiative in an effort to fight climate change. Agenda 21 is the United Nations' plan to take over the world and create a world government using phony science with respect to global warming.

All of the United Nations' studies on global warming have been discredited since the scientists who prepared them falsified the data. If this plan is fully implemented, Americans would lose their sovereignty and independence, wealth, and land to the United Nations and to a group of powerful elites who would enslave all.

Even though Agenda 21 was never ratified by the United States Senate, many states and local zoning and planning boards are implementing some of the recommendations as they prepare policies for land use. In order to bypass the United States Senate, President Bill Clinton signed Executive Order Number 12852 to implement Agenda 21.

Morris and McGann explained that Agenda 21 spells out how each of us must live in the New World Order as follows: "We need to leave rural areas, low density suburbs, and leafy small towns and aggregate in big cities and crowded urban areas." The United Nations by means of Agenda 21 threatens the sovereignty of the United States and wishes to control our food supply, financial institutions, land, oceans, and rivers, all using the threat to the environment.

The 2030 Agenda of the United Nations and its implications

On July 8, 2015, Bolivia's Marxist Evo Morales gave Pope Francis a cross with a hammer and a sickle at the bottom. Pope Francis took it back to the Vatican saying it was just "protest art."

The United Nations launched "The 2030 Agenda" at a major conference from September 25 to September 27, 2015 in New York City with the participation Marxist Pope Francis. Pope Francis traveled to New York to deliver an address which kicked off this conference since he is a supporter of the socialist multi-polar planetary one-world government that is being pushed by the New World Order.

On July 8, 2015, Bolivia's Marxist Evo Morales gave Pope Francis a cross with a hammer and a sickle at the bottom. Pope Francis did not reject this cross and gladly accepted this monstrosity. The sacrilegious cross was designed by Father Luis Espinal, a communist Jesuit, who was assassinated in 1980 in Bolivia for conspiring with communists to overthrow the government of that nation. When he returned to Rome, Pope Francis called the repugnant sacrilegious cross "an art of protest" and not a communist symbol of the Marxist Liberation Theology of the Catholic Church. The Pope also accepted and thanked Bolivia's Marxist Evo Morales for giving him the Order of the Condor and the Order of Luis Espinal, both of them decorated with a hammer and sickle.

On August 14, 2015, Michael Snyder wrote an article titled "In September 2015, Agenda 21 will be transformed into the 2030 Agenda" which was published in the website *Bear Witness Central*. Snyder pointed out the following: "Unlike Agenda 21, which primarily focused on the environment, the 2030 Agenda is truly a template for governing the entire planet. In addition, to addressing climate change, it also sets ambitious goals for areas such as economics, health, energy, education, agriculture, gender equality and a whole host of other issues. As you will see below, this global initiative is being billed as a new universal Agenda for humanity. If you are anything like me, alarm bells are going off in your head right about now. This new agenda is solidly rooted in a document known as Agenda 21 that was originally adopted by the United Nations back in 1992."

United Nations Treaties

The United Nations and the dictators of the Third World cannot wait to steal the U.S. money. To add injury to insult, Third World dictators have insisted that when they receive money from the United States, they want to be immune from legal challenges and lawsuits or outside inspections. What they mean is to have a free hand to use this money for personal gains. Unfortunately, Barack Obama did not only want to redistribute wealth inside the United States but also redistribute the wealth of this country among Third World countries.

Obama also wanted to sign many United Nations treaties, such as the Law of the Sea (LOST), that would have place the United States on the road to a world government. The LOST treaty, which was negotiated in the 1970s, would abruptly place two thirds of the oceans under the control of the United Nations. When this treaty was presented to President Ronald Reagan in 1982, he rejected it as did Prime Minister Margaret Thatcher of Great Britain.

The treaty created another United Nations agency called the International Seabed Authority (ISA) with the purpose of transferring the wealth from developed nations to Third World countries. The ISA will have the right to impose taxes or collect royalties on offshore oil and gas wells that are more than 200 nautical miles from the coasts of the United States. If this treaty were to be approved by the United States Senate, over time billions of dollars would be taken from U.S. multinational corporations that drill for oil and gas far away from our coasts and given to the United Nations instead of going to the U.S. Treasury. Additionally, the United States would be forced to share its technology for free with the entire world.

The treaty would become a massive global welfare program to Third World nations and be handled by the often corrupt bureaucrats from the United Nations. Additionally, this treaty would endanger U.S. national security since its wealth could go to enemy nations that would use it to attack the United States. Sadly, the Obama administration supported the Law of the Sea as did previous administrations.

The Second Amendment of the U.S. Constitution, the right to bear arms, was also under assault by the Obama administration. Obama had a new ally in the disarmament of the United States in the form of the Arms Trade Treaty (ATT), which was approved by the United Nations. One of the largest impediments to the establishment of a U.N.'s socialist world government is the fact that Americans possess weapons. Obama pushed the Senate to ratify the ATT, which includes registering, banning, and eventually confiscating all guns by the United Nations. Should the Senate ever pass this diabolical treaty, it is over for freedom-loving patriots in the United States. Americans need to keep their weapons just as the Founders intended in order to defend their liberty against domestic and foreign enemies.

The United Nations, as well as Iran, China, Russia, and most Arab nations, wants the U.N. agency, the International Telecommunication Union, to take over the internet and restrict its usage and regulate its content. Dictators and tyrants, such as the late Fidel and Raúl Castro, want to control the flow of information to its people. The internet in the United States, while is not perfect, serves as a vehicle to provide information to its citizens that the established liberal press does not cover. As explained earlier, the media in the United States is controlled by the CFR, TC, and BG. Americans read and watch in television what these groups want they to know. Thank God for the internet! The Obama administration would have liked to have restricted the information that Americans receive but so far laws have not been passed to do just that.

The United Nations would also like to have supremacy over U.S. courts and place this nation under the jurisdiction of the International Criminal Court and the International Court of Justice. President George W. Bush renounced the treaty but former President Obama and the globalists wanted the Senate to approve it. If the U.S. Senate were to approve such a treaty Americans would lose their sovereignty.

The United Nations would like to have the ability to tax individuals without their approval to transfer their wealth to Third World dictators. Perhaps U.N. officials should read the U.S. history to discover how Americans fought for their independence over the issue of taxation without representation.

Globalists in the European Union and elsewhere would like Americans to adopt a Code of Conduct for Outer Space Activities. This Code would restrict their ability to place satellites and other objects in space. Unbelievably, Obama said he was not going to ask the Senate for approval and was going to simply follow the Code voluntarily. This is, of course, another violation of the U.S. Constitution since this Code is a treaty.

The United Nations Environment Programme (UNEP) wants to accelerate international cooperation and implement regulations worldwide. In essence, UNEP would like to become a global Environmental Protection Agency. This action would also end the sovereignty of Americans and allow the United Nations to dictate them what to do in regards to their industries and impose strict regulations on U.S. businesses and industries. Obama's EPA was filled with socialists and radicals that were constantly harassing American energy companies and blocking the development of their energy resources in the United States.

The socialist and communist globalists and radical environmentalists at the United Nations have been working over the years to take away the sovereignty of the United States. As explained by Morris and McGann, the United Nations' Commission on Global Governance published its final report, named *Our Global Neighborhood*, in 1995. This diabolical document recommends, among other actions, the following:

• Establishing an Economic Security Council to oversee worldwide economies.

• Authorizing the United Nations and its agencies to impose global taxes.

• Instituting a U.N. Army.

• Terminating the power of the permanent members of the United Nations.

• Creating an International Criminal Court.

• Creating a new body of the United Nations for civil society by which advocates for the environment, population control, etc. can play a role in policy making.

• Placing the authority for regulating the production and distribution of arms on the United Nations as well as of gun control.

• Granting mandatory jurisdiction in the International Court of Justice to all members.

• Ceding jurisdiction over the global commons, such as oceans, space, and the environment, to the Trusteeship Council.

Unfortunately, extremely powerful organizations, such as the Trilateral Commission and the Bilderberg Group which are made up of billionaires and millionaires bankers, industrialists, members of the media, CEOs of multinationals, and high government officials from all over the world, also want a world government that, as they believe, they will control.

Maurice Strong

Maurice Strong

The late Maurice Strong served as Undersecretary General of the United Nations. He died in 2015 at the age of 86. The late socialist is the so-called godfather of the environmental movement. He was involved in the Stockholm conference in 1971 that led to the establishment of the United Nations Environment Programme the following year. Strong organized the United Nations Conference on Environment and Development, known as the Earth Summit, which was held in Rio de Janeiro, Brazil in June 1992.

The late Maurice Strong, the late David Rockefeller, and other powerful individuals became members of the Club of Rome. In 2005, Strong became involved in the investigation of the Oil-for-Food scandal of the United Nations. It was discovered that Strong, while working for the Secretary-General of the United Nations Kofi Annan, had endorsed a check to himself for $988,885. Although he was not indicted, he resigned to his U.N. post. He then moved to Beijing, China where he teaches at Chinese universities and advices the Chinese government. Should Americans trust Maurice Strong and his socialist and communist friends at the United Nations and throughout the world?

President Donald J. Trump has appointed some globalists in the White House and to his cabinet

Even though, President Donald J. Trump ran on an anti-globalist, nationalistic, and America first platform, he has also named several members of the Council of Foreign Relations, the Trilateral Commission, and others who have attended Bilderberg Group meetings to the White House and his cabinet. This writer is convinced that President Trump is a patriot. However, no president in the United States has been able to disregard the very powerful globalist elite that runs the world. The Trump administration includes anti-globalist and globalist officials.

Gary Allen wrote the book *The Rockefeller File* (1976)

Chapter 19

Goldman Sachs Bank and other international banks that assisted the Maduro regime in Venezuela and are part of the New World Order

Goldman Sachs headquarters is located at 200 West Street in Manhattan, New York City.

On May 30, 2017, Venezuelans protested in front of the New York City headquarters of the banking firm Goldman Sachs over its purchase of Petróleos de Venezuela (PDVSA) bonds. Opponents of the bloody regime of dictator Nicolás Maduro in Venezuela have requested Wall Street banks not to purchase Venezuelan bonds that would assist the regime to continue to oppress and kill freedom-seeking protesters in cities across Venezuela. The National Assembly of Venezuela, which is controlled by opponents of the cruel and oppressive Maduro regime, has requested international financial institutions to avoid any transactions that might help the regime financially. This regime is responsible for a multitude of assassinations and other human-rights abuses.

On May 28, 2017, Goldman Sachs purchased $2.8 billion bonds from Petróleos de Venezuela (PDVSA) at a discount. Goldman Sachs's asset-management division paid the Venezuelan communist regime about $865 million for $2.8 billion worth of bonds—or 31 cents on the dollar. The bonds that were issued by state oil company Petróleos de Venezuela, S.A. in 2014 will mature in 2022.

Goldman Sachs is a very powerful international investment bank whose former employees are working in the Trump administration. They have also worked in all previous Democratic and Republican administrations. A former Goldman Sachs employee is **Mario Draghi,** who is the President of the European Central Bank which is located in Frankfurt, Germany.

Draghi previously worked at Goldman Sachs from 2002 until 2005 before becoming the governor of the Bank of Italy in December 2005, where he served until October 2011. In 2014 Draghi was listed as the 8th most powerful person in the world by *Forbes*. In 2015 *Fortune* magazine ranked him as the world's second greatest leader.

Mark Carney, a former employee of Goldman Sachs, is the Governor of the Bank of England. Carney had a 13 year career with Goldman Sachs in its London, Tokyo, New York and Toronto offices. Goldman Sachs is part of the New World Order.

Julio Borges, who appears sitting, is president of the National Assembly of Venezuela, which is controlled by opponents of the dictatorial Maduro regime. The National Assembly was illegally abolished by the Maduro regime.

On May 30, 2017, Kejal Vyas and Anatoly Kurmanaev in Caracas, Venezuela and Julie Wernau in New York wrote an article titled "Goldman Sachs under Fire for Venezuela Bond Deal." This article was published in the *Wall Street Journal*.

The reporters explained that the President of National Assembly of Venezuela, Julio Borges, wrote a letter to Goldman Sachs CEO, Lloyd Blankfein, and stated the following: "It is apparent Goldman Sachs decided to make a quick buck off the suffering of the Venezuelan people. I also intend to recommend to any future democratic government of Venezuela not to recognize or pay on these bonds." Mr. Borges said National Assembly would launch an investigation into the Goldman Sachs transaction. He also warned that any future opposition government "would not forget where Goldman Sachs stood when it had to choose between supporting the Maduro dictatorship and democracy for our country."

Lloyd Blankfein is the Chief Executive Officer of Goldman Sachs.

Venezuela is near bankruptcy and there is a tremendous need for hard currency. Julio Borges stated that the financial assistance given by Goldman Sachs to the tyranny in Venezuela will make them stronger. Borges said that up to now 57 people have been assassinated, 13,000 have been wounded, and about 2,000 have been arrested and prosecuted by military tribunals since the massive protests began two months ago.

Goldman Sachs responded in a statement saying said it had bought the securities, which are held in funds and accounts that the bank manages on behalf of clients, from a broker and did not interact with the Venezuelan government. "We recognize that the situation is complex and evolving and that Venezuela is in crisis," the bank indicated. "We agree that life there has to get better, and we made the investment in part because we believe it will," Goldman Sachs added.

The reporters pointed out that Goldman Sachs has been increasing its Venezuelan holdings in recent months. Moreover, a government official said that the regime is looking at all options to raise money it owes to key allies such as Russia and China.

Other financial institutions have purchased Venezuelan bonds, including J.P. Morgan Chase and Company, Fidelity Investments, **BlackRock**, Inc., T. Rowe Price Group, HSBC Holdings PLC, and Pacific Investment Management Co. Representatives for BlackRock, Fidelity, HSBC, and Pimco declined to comment.

The reporters explained that Ricardo Hausmann, who is a former Venezuelan planning minister and a critic of the Maduro government, recently urged J.P. Morgan Chase and Company to remove Venezuelan bonds from its benchmark emerging-market debt index. That would allow investors who trade entire asset classes to avoid holding debts issued by a government accused of major human rights abuses.

The globalist international bank Goldman Sachs created the BRICS

The powerful international globalist bank created the BRICS. The term "BRIC" is the acronym that stands for Brazil, Russia, India, and China—the four rapidly developing countries that have come to symbolize the shift in global economic power away from the developed G-7 economies. Not well known is the fact that the creation of this association of nations is part of the New World Order.

The acronym "BRIC" was invented in 2001 by then-chairman of Goldman Sachs Asset Management, Baron Terence Jim O'Neill, in his publication Building Better Global Economic BRICs. The foreign ministers of the initial four BRIC states, which were Brazil, Russia, India, and China, met in New York City in September 2006. A full-scale diplomatic meeting was held in Yekaterinburg, Russia, on June 16, 2009.

As *Wikipedia* explained, originally the first four BRIC nations were Brazil, Russia, India, and China, before adding South Africa in 2010. The BRICS members are all leading developing or newly industrialized countries, but they are distinguished by their large, sometimes fast-growing economies and significant influence on regional affairs. The five BRICS nations are G-20 members. Since 2009, the BRICS nations have met annually at formal summits. China hosted the 9th BRICS summit in Xiamen from September 3 to September, 2017.

Wikipedia said that as of 2015, the five BRICS countries represent over 3.6 billion people, or about 40% of the world population. The five nations have a combined nominal GDP of $16.6 trillion, equivalent to approximately 22% of the gross world product. The BRICS are expected to expand 4.6% in 2016, from an estimated growth of 3.9% in 2015. The World Bank expects BRICS growth to pick up to 5.3% in 2017.

Terence James O'Neill, Baron O'Neill of Gatley who was born March 17, 1957, is former chairman of Goldman Sachs Asset Management and former British Conservative government minister. In 2014, O'Neill was named an Honorary Professor of Economics at the University of Manchester. He was appointed Commercial Secretary to the Treasury, a position he held until his resignation on September 23, 2016.

Jim O' Neill wrote the book *The Growth Map Economic Opportunity in the BRICs and Beyond* in 2011 (see picture of book cover above). Ten years before Jim O'Neill predicted the fastest growing economies of the past decade.

Amazon describes *The Growth Map* as follows:

"It's been ten years since Jim O'Neill conceived of the BRIC acronym. He and his team made a startling prediction: Four developing nations- Brazil, Russia, India, and China (with the later addition of South Africa) would overtake the six largest Western economies within forty years. The BRIC analysis permanently changed the world of global investing, and its accuracy has stood the test of time."

"*The Growth Map* features O'Neill's personal account of the BRIC phenomenon, how it has evolved, and where those four key nations currently stand after a turbulent decade. And the book also offers an equally bold prediction about the "Next Eleven" countries: Bangladesh, Egypt, Indonesia, Iran, Mexico, Nigeria, Pakistan, Philippines, South Korea, Turkey, and Vietnam. These developing nations may not seem exceptional today, but they offer exciting opportunities for investors over the next decade, just as BRIC did before them."

"O'Neill also shares several compelling insights about the world economy. He reveals the value for growing countries in being willing to play by meaningfully committing to policies that encourage further growth and engagement with globalization. He explains how the G-20 can adjust to better incorporate the BRICs and to better reflect the balance of the global economy."

"Finally, O'Neill makes the counterintuitive claim that good things can quite often come from crises. While established economic powers may see the rise of the BRICs as a threat, international trade benefits us all over the long term. Likewise, the recent financial crisis revealed deep problems in our economic systems, problems we now have the opportunity to fix."

"A work of astute and absorbing analysis, *The Growth Map* is an indispensable guide for every investor and every participant in the global economy. Anyone who wants to understand the developing world would do well to heed the man called "one of the most sought-after economic commentators on the planet."

Former Goldman Sachs executives are working in the Trump administration

Gary David Cohn, former president of Goldman Sachs, is the Director of the National Economic Council at the White House. When he left the bank he was given $124 million in compensation.

There are several former employees of Goldman Sachs working in the Trump administration. One of them is Gary Cohn who was born on August 27, 1960. He was formerly the president and chief operating officer of Goldman Sachs from 2006 to 2017. He is the chief economic advisor to President Donald Trump and Director of the National Economic Council. Cohn is a registered Democrat, but has donated extensively to Republican politicians as well.

The current Secretary of the Treasury is Steven Mnuchin.

Another former Goldman Sachs executive is Secretary of the Treasury Steven Mnuchin. He was born on December 21, 1962. After he graduated from Yale University in 1985, Mnuchin worked for the globalist international investment bank Goldman Sachs for 17 years, eventually becoming its Chief Information Officer. After he left Goldman Sachs in 2002, he worked for and founded several hedge funds. During the financial crisis of 2007–2008, Mnuchin bough the failed residential lender IndyMac. He changed the name to OneWest Bank and rebuilt the bank, then sold it to CIT Group in 2015. Mnuchin joined Trump's presidential campaign in 2016, and was named national finance chairman for the campaign. On February 13, 2017, Mnuchin was confirmed as Secretary of the Treasury by a 53–47 vote in the Senate.

Another former Goldman Sachs executive working in the White House is Dina Habib Powell.

Dina Habib Powell is the current White House Deputy National Security Advisor for Strategy. In 2007, she joined Goldman Sachs as a managing director and became a partner in 2010, recently serving as the president for the Goldman Sachs Foundation and Goldman Sachs Impact Investing team working primarily on philanthropic efforts. Powell worked with the Clinton Foundation in various projects.

Dina Habib Powell was born on June 12, 1973 in Cairo, Egypt. In January 2017, she was appointed Deputy National Security Advisor for Strategy to President Donald Trump. She is also an Assistant to the President and Senior Counselor for Economic Initiatives.

Prior to accepting these White House positions, Powell was a managing director and partner at Goldman Sachs and president of their non-profit subsidiary, the Goldman Sachs Foundation. In that capacity she ran the Foundation's 10,000 Women program. Previously, she served in the George W. Bush administration as Assistant Secretary of State for Educational and Cultural Affairs, Deputy Undersecretary of State for Public Affairs and Public Diplomacy, and an Assistant to the President for Presidential Personnel. Powell was born in Egypt and immigrated with her family to Texas at a young age.

Globalist insider Dina Powell was linked to Hillary Clinton, **Valery Jarrett**, and Huma Abedin.

Roger Stone wrote an article titled "Who is Dina Habib Powell and why should you care" which was published in his website on June 13, 2017. Stone asked the following questions: "How did this ex-Bush White House aide who is best friends with Hillary's gal pal, confidant, advisor, and vice chair of her 2016 campaign for the presidency Huma Abedin, Obama White House Chief of Staff Valery Jarrett and discredited Bush National Security Advisor Condi Rice who walked us into the Iraq war over weapons of mass destruction that did not exist get this job? How did this globalist insider and ardent neo-con land a key spot in the Trump circle?"

Stone said that the answer lies in President Trump son-in-law Jared Kushner and his wife Ivanka. Dina Powell was born in Cairo, Egypt on June 23, 1973. Her family moved to the United States when she was four, settling in Texas. In 1988 she married Richard Powell, a senior public affairs executive. She interned with Texas Republican Senator Kay Bailey Hutchison. During George W. Bush's presidency, Powell served as Assistant Secretary of State for Education and Cultural Affairs and at 29, became the youngest person to direct the White House personnel office.

Stone pointed out that Goldman Sachs was a major funding source for Hillary Clinton's campaign as well as paying her $675,000 for a speech whose content she refused to release. President Trump said in a statement the following about Powell: "Dina Powell is a tremendous talent and has a stellar record of public service as well as a great career in the private sector.

She has been recognized for her strategic oversight of key programs and initiatives and is a leader in both economic growth and the crucial empowerment of women in various aspects of business development and entrepreneurial endeavors."

Stone wrote that "clearly, the President knows little of Powell's pedigree or background." Stone ended his article by stating the following: "Trump's White House has been leaking since the start and it's no surprise that Dina Powell has long been considered a leaker. In 1990 she got in trouble for leaking negative stories on Ginny Thomas, the wife of Justice Clarence Thomas. Now she and National Security Advisor H. R. McMaster have been pegged by sources at the National Security Council as two of Trump's major leakers! President Trump has surrounded himself with double crossing double agents who will do him harm. Let's hope he wakes up before it is too late."

Dina Powell worked closely with the Clinton Foundation

Dina Habib Powell and Valerie Jarrett have a close relationship.

On September 7, 2017, Aaron Klein wrote an article titled *"Clinton Cash*: Dina Powell Partnered with the Clinton Foundation for Goldman Sachs Globalist Initiative" that was published by *Breitbart*. Klein explained that when Dina Powell served as president of the Goldman Sachs Foundation, she "repeatedly partnered with the Clinton Global Initiative for a globalist women's project that served as the centerpiece of Goldman's charitable foundation."

Dina Powell's Goldman Sachs Foundation also gave donations directly to the Clinton Foundation and partnered with Hillary Clinton's State Department. Powell herself was associated with numerous groups and projects linked to the Clintons.

Klein said that Powell received a salary of $2 million per year from Goldman Sachs. Her financial disclosure form showed salary, benefits, cash bonuses and equity from Goldman Sachs totaling $6,128,950. The Goldman Sachs Foundation was set up to make up for its terrible conduct during the financial crisis of 2008. The international bank agreed to pay a $5 billion settlement to the Justice Department for "its serious misconduct in falsely assuring investors that securities it sold were backed by sound mortgages, when it knew that they were full of mortgages that were likely to fail, acting associate attorney general Stuart Delery announced in a statement when the settlement was finalized." Klein pointed out that Dina Powell has been described in the media as having a good relationship with Valerie Jarrett, Barack Obama's most important advisers during his presidency.

Goldman Sachs and the Clintons

Klein wrote that Powell joined Goldman Sachs as a managing director in 2007 and was named partner in 2010. In coming to Goldman Sachs, Powell joined an international banking firm that has long been deeply tied to the Clintons.

Klein stated the following: "Bill and Hillary Clinton raked in massive speaking fees from Goldman Sachs, with *CNN* documenting a total of at least $7.7 million in paid speeches to big financial firms, including Goldman Sachs and UBS. Hillary Clinton made $675,000 from speeches to Goldman Sachs specifically, and her husband secured more than $1,550,000 from Goldman speeches. In 2005 alone, Bill Clinton collected over $500,000 from three Goldman Sachs events. Goldman's chief executive, Blankfein, provided a major boost to Clinton's failed 2008 presidential bid when he endorsed her over Barack Obama and held a fundraiser in his apartment for her 2008 campaign."

Conclusion

It is shameful that while Venezuelan patriots are demonstrating and dying in the streets throughout many cities of that nation, international bankers are giving financial assistance and oxygen to the tyrannical Maduro regime. Obviously, these international bankers do not care about the freedom and liberty of Venezuela. All that these international bankers want is to maximize profits by buying bonds at a tremendous discount and enormous interest rates for their international financial institutions. This writer hopes that when Venezuela becomes a democratic country, the bonds that were purchased by these international bankers will not be paid.

The fact that international bankers are propping up the communist regime in Venezuela at a time when it is almost bankrupt and could fall has happened many times in history. Oftentimes, many, but not all, international bankers have assisted communist regimes come to power and have kept helping them financially to stay in power. International bankers financed the Bolshevik Revolution in the Soviet Union. They continued supporting the Soviet Union as its economy deteriorated in spite of the many crimes and millions of Soviet citizens who were killed. International bankers have also supported the bloody Castro regime in Cuba.

It is also very concerning the appointment of several former employees of Goldman Sachs to the Trump administration. One former Goldman Sachs executive, Dina Habib Powell, worked with the corrupt and criminal Clinton Foundation as well as having a close relationship with Valerie Jarrett. This writer hopes that these individuals do not harm the president or changes his nationalist anti-globalist America First agenda!

Chapter 20

The Visit of Vice President Mike Pence to Doral, Florida

Vice President Mike Pence delivered an address denouncing the bloody Maduro regime in Venezuela to hundreds of Hispanics at Our Lady of Guadalupe Catholic Church in Doral, Florida. The photo was taken by this writer.

On August 23, 2017, Vice President Mike Pence came to the City of Doral in South Florida to discuss the ongoing crisis in Venezuela and the atrocities committed by the bloody regime of the dictator Nicolás Maduro. He spoke to a crowd of over 1,800 Venezuelans, Cuban Americans, and other Hispanics. There were also Americans of non-Hispanic origin. The visit took place in the beautiful Our Lady of Guadalupe Catholic Church located at 11691 NW 25th St. in Doral, Florida.

Previously, Vice President Pence had met with members of the Venezuelan exile community, recent Venezuelan migrants, other local leaders, and officials. The visit came following Pence's wide-ranging trip to Latin American where he addressed leaders of Panama, Colombia, Argentina, and Chile.

Our Lady of Guadalupe has a Venezuelan-born pastor, the Reverend Israel Mago. Father Mago spoke in English and Spanish as did Archbishop Thomas Wenski. The Archbishop pointed out that Our Lady of Guadalupe, which painting can be seen in the altar, is the Patron of all Latin America. Archbishop Thomas Wenski prayed with the audience for the liberation of Venezuela. The city of Doral in Miami-Dade County has so many immigrants and refugees from Venezuela that the city is known as Doralzuela.

On August 21, 2017, Patricia Mazzei wrote an article titled "Pence hints of economic sanctions against Venezuela" which was published in the *Miami Herald*. The reporter explained that before delivering his remarks, Vice President Mike Pence — joined by Senator Marco Rubio, Congressman Mario Diaz-Balart, and Governor Rick Scott — spent more than an hour listening to 15 local Venezuelans telling him about the violence, assassinations, repression, tortures and rapes in prisons, and political persecution carried out by the bloody dictator Maduro's security forces.

María Eugenia Tovar fought back tears as she told Vice President Pence how her 22-year-old daughter, Génesis Cardona, was killed during a 2014 protest by a gunshot to the head.

Mazzei said that María Eugenia Tovar told Vice President Pence how her beautiful 22-year-old daughter, Génesis Cardona, was assassinated during a 2014 protest by a gunshot to the head. During his speech Vice President Pence recognized Ms. Tovar and asked her to stand. Francisco

Márquez talked about his four months imprisonment during which he was tortured. Márquez stated the following about the inhumane imprisonment: "What I can only describe as a putrid, mosquito-infested jungle. I got dengue fever. I was made to run amid gunfire, just to mess with my head. I shared prison cells with people that talked about how they were beaten for hours. How they put a Ziploc bag over their head with insecticide. How women had been raped."

Political prisoners in Cuba have also been tortured, starved, assassinated, denied medicines, and women brutally raped. This writer spent two years in different prisons in Cuba, along with almost 1,200 soldiers from the Brigade 2506, and he too was tortured.

The reporter wrote that two exiled judges, Antonio Marval Jiménez and Alejandro Jesús Rebolledo, and three opposition mayors — Warner Jiménez of Maturín, Gustavo Marcano of Lechería, and Ramón Muchacho of Chacao — met with the Vice President. All these Venezuelans had fled to Miami after the lives of the judges were at risk and the three mayors were sentenced by the regime courts to prison for failing to curtail street protests.

Mayor Warner Jiménez, who escaped Venezuela by boat in a storm, said the following: "We're fighting against gangsters. We'd like to ask for your help. Please don't let Venezuela turn into another Cuba."

Alejandro Jesus Rebolledo, a Venezuelan judge who fled the country recently, accused the Maduro regime of crimes such as money laundering and drug trafficking. Carlos Vecchio, a well-known leader of an opposition party, said that Venezuela is a failed state where criminals have taken control of the country. Vecchio said the following: "It is a criminal state. It is led by a mafia involved in drug trafficking and close to terrorist groups." Ramon Muchacho was the mayor of the municipality of Chacao since 2013 but fled in July 2017, saying he was being persecuted by the government. "There is no way to get the regime out by democratic means," Muchacho said, asking for more help from Latin America, the United States, and Europe for Venezuela.

During the meeting, Ernesto Ackerman, a local leader of Venezuelan-Americans, approached Pence and gave him a black hat with the colors of the Venezuelan flag. It read, "Make Venezuela Great Again."

All of them urged Vice President Pence for additional economic and financial sanctions to punish Venezuela for installing a new, all-powerful constitutional assembly on August 4, 2017.

The members of the so-called constitutional assembly were elected in a fraudulent election that usurped the power of the opposition-controlled parliament. The democratically elected assembly was abolished by the regime.

Dictator Nicolás Maduro appointed Islamic terrorist and drug trafficker
Tarek El Aissami as Vice President of Venezuela.

On February 13, 2017, Vice President El Aissami was sanctioned by the Treasury Department under the Foreign Narcotics Kingpin Designation. U.S. officials after accusing him of facilitating drug shipments from Venezuela to Mexico and America, froze tens of millions of dollars of assets under El Aissami's control. A day later, Venezuela's opposition-controlled National Assembly (that was later illegally abolished by the regime) voted in favour of opening an investigation into El Aissami's alleged involvement in drug trafficking. Tarek El Aissami was being accused of running a drug trafficking network of corrupt officials in Venezuela.

Vice President listened to the Venezuelans' horror stories and to each individual, he offered words of comfort, and reiterated the Trump administration's commitment to doing more. "The United States is helping," Pence said. "And more help is on the way," he added.

The White House, according to the *Wall Street Journal*, is considering banning any trades in U.S. dollars of Venezuelan debt. Mazzei stated the following: "That's the sort of financial sanction — short of prohibiting Venezuelan oil imports and exports — that Rubio and other

South Florida politicians have pushed to starve Maduro of cash. The Treasury Department has already slapped individual financial and travel restrictions on 30 Venezuelans tied to the government…Vice President Mike Pence hinted at soon-to-come economic sanctions against the Venezuelan government, but he offered little in the way of specifics of what a more robust U.S. response might look like or when it might come, choosing instead to deliver a broader message of hope to increasingly despondent Venezuelans."

Vice President Pence pointed out that the Trump administration intends to further punish Venezuelan dictator Nicolás Maduro and members of his regime for destroying the South American country's democracy. More sanctions could come as early as this week. But Pence did not detail any potential penalties.

"Our resolve is unwavering," Vice President Pence told the over 1,800 people at Our Lady of Guadalupe Catholic Church. Vice President Pence stated the following:

"You may be assured: Under the leadership of President Donald Trump, the United States of America will continue to bring the full measure of American economic and diplomatic power to bear until democracy is restored in Venezuela. We hear you, we stand with you. We will not stand by as Venezuela crumbles. As other countries in Latin America have improved their economies, Venezuela has gone downhill." The Vice President called Maduro's presidency, a dictatorship.

Venezuelan woman showed a sign asking for U.S. military assistance against the Maduro regime.

A woman held a sign at the event that read, "Venezuelan resistance asks for military assistance. We can't do it alone," an apparent reference to Trump's remarks earlier this month that there was a possibility for the United States to invade Venezuela.

The week before Vice President Pence visited Colombia, Argentina, Chile, and Panama in an attempt to rally the region against Venezuela. President Trump's comments that a military option has not been discarded alarmed some Latin American leaders. However, it is not well known that Iran has military bases in Venezuela with ballistic missiles pointed at U.S. cities. Retired four-star Admiral James Lyons has denounced these bases and asked for a surprise American strike to destroy them.

Many individuals responded with an enthusiastic applause to the Vice President. Women brought the tricolor Venezuelan flag and others draped the flag over their shoulders. The crowd frequently chanted "Libertad. Libertad!"

In this picture appear three Venezuelan women and my friends and campaign volunteers Ana María "Chiqui" Lamar and Raquel Barreto Melero. We are holding the flag of Venezuela.

Mazzei pointed out that Vice President Pence noted with satisfaction that Panamanian President Juan Carlos Varela announced on August 22, 2017, that Venezuelans will be soon required to obtain travel visas into his country — a move denounced by Maduro's regime. "While President Trump has said that 'We have many options for Venezuela,'" Vice President Pence said, "we remain confident that working with all of our allies across Latin America, we can achieve a peaceable solution to the crisis facing the Venezuelan people."

In Doral, Vice President Pence spent about an hour at the U.S. Southern Command privately debriefing generals about his trip to South America and thanking local service members. The U.S. Southern Command is responsible for all of Latin America.

Major General U.S. Air Force Chief of Staff Jon A. Norman, left; Lieutenant General Joseph P. DiSalvo, Deputy Commander of U.S. Southern Command; Vice President Mike Pence, and Brigade General Juan Pablo Forero, right, Director of Exercises and Coalition Affairs, at the U.S. Southern Command in Doral. These generals met with Vice President Pence prior to his speech at the church.

Mazzei said that Vice President Pence did not give any specifics about upcoming action. However Congressman Mario Diaz-Balart and Senator Marco Rubio praised the White House for imposing four rounds of individual sanctions in seven months in office.

Senator Marco Rubio spoke in support of the Trump administration sanctions against the communist regime in Venezuela. The picture was taken by this writer.

Senator Rubio spoke in English and Spanish and received a warm welcome from the audience as he spoke in front of the altar of the church. Senator Rubio said that he has spoken with the president seven or eight times on how to deal with Venezuela at his request. Senator Rubio said that the Maduro regime is totally isolated. There is not a democratic nation in Latin America that has not raised its voice to condemn the regime. America will do whatever it is necessary to assure that democracy will be restored in Venezuela, he added.

Senator Marco Rubio stated the following: "I have 100 percent confidence that the president and vice president of the United States will take the appropriate measures. They will do it at the right time, and they will do it in the right way, but they will do it. It is going to happen. I am confident that one day, in a Venezuela that is free, many of us will be able to gather in a setting such as this."

Republican Congressman Mario Diaz-Balart from South Florida, Florida Republican Senator Marco Rubio and Florida Republican Governor Rick Scott gave Vice President Mike Pence a standing ovation following Vice President Pence's remarks on Venezuelan crisis, at Our Lady of Guadalupe Catholic Church in the city of Doral in South Florida.

The four individuals of the Trump campaign in Miami-Dade were invited by the White House to hear the Vice President, from right to left Manager Coral Gables Office Ron Gawronski, Manager Hialeah Office George Morffiz, former Mayor of Hialeah and Miami-Dade Campaign Chairman Julio Martinez, Manager West Dade Office Frank de Varona, and a campaign volunteer.

Who is Vice President Mike Pence?

Michael R. Pence is the 48th and current Vice President of the United States.

According to his official biography, Michael R. Pence was born in Columbus, Indiana, on June 7, 1959, one of six children born to Edward and Nancy Pence. As a young boy he had a front row seat to the American Dream. After his grandfather immigrated to the United States when he was 17, his family settled in the Midwest. The future Vice President watched his Mom and Dad build everything that matters – a family, a business, and a good name. Sitting at the feet of his mother and his father, who started a successful convenience store business in their small Indiana town, he was raised to believe in the importance of hard work, faith, and family.

Vice President Pence set off for Hanover College, earning his bachelor's degree in history in 1981. While there, he renewed his Christian faith which remains the driving force in his life. He later attended Indiana University School of Law and met the love of his life, Second Lady Karen Pence.

After graduating, Vice President Pence practiced law, led the Indiana Policy Review Foundation, and began hosting The Mike Pence Show, a syndicated talk radio show and a weekly television public affairs program in Indiana. Along the way he became the proud father to three children, Michael, Charlotte, and Audrey.

Vice President Mike Pence is coming down from Air Force Two airplane.

Growing up in Indiana, surrounded by good, hardworking Hoosiers, Vice President Pence always knew that he needed to give back to the state and the country that had given him so much. In 2000, he launched a successful bid for his local congressional seat, entering the United States House of Representatives at the age of 40.

The people of East-Central Indiana elected Vice President Pence six times to represent them in Congress. On Capitol Hill he established himself as a champion of limited government, fiscal responsibility, economic development, educational opportunity, and the U.S. Constitution. His colleagues quickly recognized his leadership ability and unanimously elected him to serve as Chairman of the House Republican Study Committee and House Republican Conference Chairman. In this role, the Vice President helped make government smaller and more effective, reduce spending, and return power to state and local governments.

In 2013, Vice President Pence left the nation's capital when Hoosiers elected him the 50th Governor of Indiana. He brought the same limited government and low tax philosophy to the

Indiana Statehouse. As Governor, he enacted the largest income tax cut in Indiana history, lowering individual income tax rates, the business personal property tax, and the corporate income tax in order to strengthen the State's competitive edge and attract new investment and good-paying jobs. Due to his relentless focus on jobs, the state's unemployment rate fell by half during his four years in office, and at the end of his term, more Hoosiers were working than at any point in the state's 200-year history.

As Governor of Indiana, Vice President Pence increased school funding, expanded school choice, and created the first state-funded Pre-K plan in Indiana history. He made career and technical education a priority in every high school. Under Vice President Pence's leadership, Indiana, known as "The Crossroads of America," invested more than $800 million in new money for roads and bridges across the state. Despite the record tax cuts and new investments in roads and schools, the state remained fiscally responsible, as the Vice President worked with members of the Indiana General Assembly to pass two honestly balanced budgets that left the state with strong reserves and AAA credit ratings that were the envy of the nation.

It was Indiana's success story, Vice President Pence's record of legislative and executive experience, and his strong family values that prompted President Donald Trump to select Mike Pence as his running mate in July 2016. The American people elected President Donald Trump and Vice President Pence on November 8, 2016. President Donald Trump and Vice President Pence entered office on January 20, 2017.

Vice President Mike Pence remains grateful for the grace of God, the love and support of his family, and the blessings of liberty that are every American's birthright. He looks forward to working with the American people as together they seek to Make America Great Again.

Conclusion

The speeches made by Vice President Mike Pence, Senator Marco Rubio, Congressman Mario Diaz-Balart and Governor Rick Scott lifted the spirits of Venezuelans and other Hispanics in the audience. They look forward to the Trump administration increasing economic and financial sanctions against the oppressive and brutal Maduro regime that is committing genocide against the people of Venezuela. This writer hopes and has recommended to some White House officials to implement a complete economic embargo against the communist regime in Venezuela as a means of overthrowing the bloody chavistas from power.

Chapter 21

United States imposed severe economic sanctions against Venezuela

President Donald J. Trump signed an Executive Order imposing strong,
new financial sanctions on the dictatorship in Venezuela.

The Statement by the Press Secretary on New Financial Sanctions on Venezuela

The statement by the White House press secretary stated the following:

"The Maduro dictatorship continues to deprive the Venezuelan people of food and medicine, imprison the democratically-elected opposition, and violently suppress freedom of speech. The regime's decision to create an illegitimate Constituent Assembly—and most recently to have that body usurp the powers of the democratically-elected National Assembly—represents a fundamental break in Venezuela's legitimate constitutional order."

"In an effort to preserve itself, the Maduro dictatorship rewards and enriches corrupt officials in the government's security apparatus by burdening future generations of Venezuelans with massively expensive debts. Maduro's economic mismanagement and rampant plundering of his nation's assets have taken Venezuela ever closer to default. His officials are now resorting to opaque financing schemes and liquidating the country's assets at fire sale prices."

Vice President Mike Pence spoke at Our Lady of Guadalupe Church in the City of Doral in South Florida on the future economic sanctions against the communist regime of Venezuela.

The Statement by the Press Secretary also said the following:

"As Vice President Mike Pence has said, in Venezuela, we're seeing the tragedy of tyranny play out before our eyes. No free people have ever chosen to walk the path from prosperity to poverty. No free people have ever chosen to turn what was once, and should still be, one of South America's richest nations into its poorest and most corrupt."

"We will not stand by as Venezuela crumbles. The President's new action prohibits dealings in new debt and equity issued by the government of Venezuela and its state oil company. It also prohibits dealings in certain existing bonds owned by the Venezuelan public sector, as well as dividend payments to the government of Venezuela."

"To mitigate harm to the American and Venezuelan people, the Treasury Department is issuing general licenses that allow for transactions that would otherwise be prohibited by the Executive Order. These include provisions allowing for a 30-day wind-down period; financing for most commercial trade, including the export and import of petroleum; transactions only involving Citgo; dealings in select existing Venezuelan debts; and the financing for humanitarian goods to Venezuela."

"These measures are carefully calibrated to deny the Maduro dictatorship a critical source of financing to maintain its illegitimate rule, protect the United States financial system from complicity in Venezuela's corruption and in the impoverishment of the Venezuelan people, and allow for humanitarian assistance."

"The United States is not alone in condemning the Maduro regime. Through the Lima Declaration of August 8, 2017 our friends and partners in the region refused to recognize the illegitimate Constituent Assembly or the laws it adopts. The new United States financial sanctions support this regional posture of economically isolating the Maduro dictatorship."

"The United States reiterates our call that Venezuela restores democracy, hold free and fair elections, release all political prisoners immediately and unconditionally, and end the repression of the Venezuelan people. We continue to stand with the people of Venezuela during these trying times."

On August 25, 2017, President Donald J. Trump issued an Executive Order which was implemented by the Treasury Department. It imposed economic sanctions against the bloody communist regime in Venezuela. The Treasury Department prohibited the purchase of bonds issued by the Venezuelan regime and its state-owned oil company, Petróleos de Venezuela, S.A. (PEDEVESA).

Treasury Secretary Steven Mnuchin stated the following: "Maduro may no longer take advantage of the American financial system to facilitate the wholesale looting of the Venezuelan economy at the expense of the Venezuelan people. These measures will undermine Maduro's ability to pay off political cronies, and regime supporters, and increase pressure on the regime to abandon its disastrous path."

On August 26, 2017, Patricia Mazzei and Franco Ordoñes wrote an article titled "U.S. imposes first economic sanctions against Venezuela" which was published by the *Miami Herald*. The reporters explained that the Trump administration stated on August 25, 2017 that it will not help to underwrite "tyranny" and restricted Venezuela's ability to borrow money from American banks, a prohibition intended to deny the regime of dictator Nicolás Maduro of much-needed funds. Treasury Secretary Steven Mnuchin stated that "Maduro may no longer take advantage of the American financial system to facilitate the wholesale looting of the Venezuelan economy at the expense of the Venezuelan people."

Venezuela is almost bankrupt and the prohibition by United States of purchasing Venezuelan debt could push Venezuela closer to complete economic collapse. This writer has recommended the imposition of a total economic embargo against the Venezuelan regime. However, such a measure, which has been threatened by America, has not been implemented yet. The communist regime in Venezuela, which has been denounced by the United States and its Latin American allies as a dictatorship, will now have to turn to China and Russia to finance their billions of debt.

In this picture appears Venezuelan dictator Nicolás Maduro (left), next to his vice president, who is a drug-trafficking Islamic terrorist, Tarek El Aissami. Maduro appears presenting Russian dictator Vladimir Putin with the Key of the City of Caracas in April 2010.

Mazzei and Ordoñes pointed out that Venezuela is suffering an unprecedented economic collapse "caused by plunging oil prices and rampant mismanagement that has led to hyperinflation, violent crime and widespread food and medicine shortages." Dictator Nicolás Maduro stated the following: "The illegal measures President Donald Trump took today against the Venezuelan people simply violate international law. They ratify an imperial path of aggression against Venezuela."

Venezuelan dictator Maduro said on August 25 that he will prosecute for treason his opponents, who he accused of being behind the sweeping U.S. financial sanctions. Maduro accused President Donald J. Trump of trampling with international law and relations with Latin America by taking actions that he said would cause "great damage" to the Venezuelan oil economy as well as to American investors who own the country's bonds.

Maduro singled out the president of Venezuela's freely-elected National Assembly, Julio Borges, as being the "mastermind" of the financial and economic "blockade." He further called on the communist regime-stacked Supreme Court and a new, all-powerful and illegal Constitutional Assembly to initiate proceedings against opponents who have lobbied in favor of the sanctions. "You've got to be a big traitor to your country to ask for sanctions against Venezuela," Maduro said."

President Trump's Executive Order also restricts the Venezuelan oil giant's American subsidiary, Citgo, from sending dividends back to Venezuela — a move that Maduro said would lead to the "virtual closure" of a company responsible for thousands of American jobs. "They're committing robbery, fraud," dictator Maduro stated, adding that Venezuela would reach out to its American partners to make sure decades of business relationships are not broken. If necessary the government would find new markets for the roughly 700,000 barrels of oil it sends daily to the U.S.," he added.

The Venezuelan regime and its state-owned oil company, Petróleos de Venezuela S.A. (PEDEVESA), have about $4 billion in debt payments due before the end of the 2017 with only $9.7 billion in international reserves on hand, the vast majority consisting of gold ingots that are hard to trade immediately for cash.

The Department of State was ignored by the White House on the issue of Venezuelan economics sanctions

The Under Secretary for Political Affairs Thomas Shannon serves as the day-to-day manager of overall regional and bilateral policy issues, and oversees the bureaus for Africa, East Asia and the Pacific, Europe, and Eurasia, the Near East, South and Central Asia, the Western Hemisphere, and International Organizations.

Tom Shannon was go-between for Caracas and Washington of the then-Secretary of State John Kerry. On June 14, 2015, it was reported that Shannon met with Venezuela's second-most powerful official the then-National Assembly President Diosdado Cabello and the then-*Foreign Affairs* Minister Delcy Rodríguez in Haiti. Shannon also met a few times with dictator Nicolás Maduro in Caracas.

Prior to the meeting in Haiti, Venezuela accused the United States of plotting a coup d'etat and ordered Washington to reduce its embassy staff and imposed a visa requirement on U.S. visitors. America in turn declared Venezuela a national security threat and ordered economic sanctions against seven chavistas officials accusing them of corruption and human rights abuses.

Shannon's meetings with Maduro and other regime officials were failures as the communist regime continues to assassinate and incarcerate members of the peaceful opposition and elected officials. Venezuela continues to send part of the millions obtained by exporting drugs to America and many other countries to Iran's Hezbollah militia in Lebanon and Syria and continuous to export uranium to Iran.

In spite of the increased repression and genocide against the people of Venezuela, Shannon wanted more dialogue with the mass-murdering communist regime. He also opposed strong economic sanctions against Venezuela. Secretary of State Rex Tillerson supported Shannon and previously called him his best advisor at the department. Secretary Tillerson allowed Shannon to deal with Cuba and Venezuela while he concentrated in North Korea and other nations.

Diosdado Cabello had been accused of plotting the assassination of Senator Marco Rubio. He is the head of the Cartel de los Soles, the drug-trafficking enterprise, which is run by high-ranking generals and regime officials.

On August 26, 2017, Franco Ordoñez and Nora Gámez Torres wrote an article titled "U.S. diplomat's effort to save dialogue fell flat" which was published in the *Miami Herald*. The reporters explained that on July 23, 2017, as the White House and Senator Marco Rubio and his allies in Congress were drawing up plans for a broad and strong set of economic sanctions against the Maduro regime, Under Secretary of State for Political Affairs Tom Shannon was meeting in private with the Venezuela's foreign minister Samuel Moncada.

As explained earlier, Shannon implemented the failed policy of Obama with Venezuela and Cuba and met frequently with officials from the communist regime from Venezuela. Shannon is an appeaser to both regimes and always insists on more dialogue with the unrepented brutal tyrants of those two countries.

Ordoñez and Gámez Torres said that even though President Donald Trump had promised "strong and swift" economic sanctions, including potentially oil sanctions, against Venezuela, Shannon opposed it. The inter-agency group was nearly agreed on what that package of punishments would be. Tom Shannon, however, kept advocating a more limited punishment that could allow more dialogue to continue.

Shannon wanted the lines of communication with the Venezuelan brutal regime to remain open. He kept fighting for more dialogue with Caracas and pushing back against pressure from the White House National Security Council (NSC) and Senator Rubio.

Shannon warned that aggressive economics sanctions could close diplomatic channels with Caracas. However, Shannon was fighting a losing battle since Senator Rubio was aligned with a group at the White House that included National Security Adviser H.R. McMaster in arguing for strong economic sanctions.

What is there to dialogue with the bloody dictator Maduro and with his boss the assassin-in-series Raúl Castro? The time to talk to these tyrants is over. The time to act forcefully has arrived!

During the discussions between Shannon and the National Security Council officials in the White House were intense. At one point, Fernando Cutz, the NSC's Director for South America Western Hemisphere Affairs, criticized strongly the State Department officials, in front of approximately 30 senior officials.

Fernando Cutz is the NSC's Director for South America Western Hemisphere Affairs.

Ordoñez and Gámez Torres concluded their article by stating the following:" Ultimately, Trump's Chief of Staff John Kelly joined Pence and McMaster to overrule Shannon and encourage Trump to sign off on the sanctions package announced on August 25, 2017. According to several sources, Tillerson joined in their decision. And the White House delivered the tougher, broader set of sanctions that NSC wanted. And in the end, rather than be there to witness his own defeat, Shannon went on vacation."

Dictator Nicolás Maduro's nephews, Franqui Flores and Efraín Campos Flores are found guilty of trying to send 800 kilograms of cocaine to America

The *Miami Herald* reported on August 29, 2017, that Franqui Francisco Flores de Freitas and Efraín Antonio Campos Flores were found guilty to trying to send 800 kilograms of cocaine to America by a New York jury. The two criminals are nephews of Maduro's wife, Cilia Flores, and both of them are also implicated in assassinations.

Franqui Flores and Efraín Campos Flores are expected to be sentenced to life in prison in September 2017. The prosecution of the two criminals was a hard blow to the Maduro regime.

Conclusion

The globalists who supported the brutal Maduro regime in Venezuela were defeated by the Trump administration. This writer is in agreement with the economic sanctions implemented by the Trump administration against the Maduro dictatorship. Trump administration stated that it will not help to underwrite "tyranny" and restricted Venezuela's ability to borrow money from American banks. Thus international banks, such as Goldman Sachs, will not be able to buy Venezuelan bonds that help the Maduro dictatorship to remaim in power. The Department of State is filled with globalists who served under the Obama administration. Secretary Tillerson has not replaced them. One of the worst senior officials is Undersecretary for Political Affairs Thomas Shannon.

There are still no nominees for assistant secretary of state for Western Hemisphere Affairs and for director of the Office of Cuban Broadcasting who is responsible for Radio and Television Martí. Tillerson should recommend individuals for these two positions.

Defense Secretary James Mattis needs to fill the position of deputy assistant secretary of defense for Western Hemisphere Affairs. Both the communist regimes of Venezuela and Cuba represent national security dangers to America. After more than 200 days in office, the president needs to recommend qualified individuals for these positions.

This writer would like to see a complete economic embargo against the genocidal Maduro regime. The United States has called for the restoration of democracy in Venezuela. The Maduro regime needs to hold free and fair elections, release all political prisoners immediately and unconditionally, and end the repression of the Venezuelan people. Since obviously the communist regime, with the assistance of a Cuban Occupation Army, will not restore freedom and liberty, the United States needs to implement regime change strategies.

Chapter 22

The Bank for International Settlements That Rules the World

Adam Lebor wrote *Tower of Basel: The Shadowy History of the Secret Bank that Runs the World* in 2013.

Adam Lebor's book is the first critical investigative history of the most secretive and powerful global financial institution in the world. Lebor conducted many interviews of international central bankers and their employees, including Paul Volcker, the former chairman of the Federal Reserve Bank (the Fed), and Sir Mervyn King, former governor of the Bank of England. He also conducted extensive archival research of the Bank for International Settlements (BIS) in Basel, Switzerland and other libraries in the United States and Great Britain. His book includes biographies on the major central bankers who founded the bank and the important officials who worked at the BIS.

The sordid history of the Bank for International Settlements (BIS)

The Bank for International Settlements was created on May 17, 1930 to administer or "settle" the World War I reparations imposed on Germany under the Treaty of Versailles. There were four very powerful individuals who played a very important role in the founding of BIS. They were Charles Gates Dawes, Owen Daniel Young, Hjalmar Schacht, and Montagu Norman.

President Calvin Coolidge is shown on the left in the picture and on the right is Vice President Charles Gates Dawes. Dawes was one of the two Americans who founded the BIS.

The first of these individuals was Charles Dawes. He was born on August 27, 1865 and died on April 23, 1951. Dawes was a powerful banker, politician, and military general. Charles G. Dawes was the director of the United States Bureau of the Budget in 1921 and later served on the Allied Reparation Commission in 1923. He subsequently worked on stabilizing the German economy. For his work on the Dawes Plan for Germany's World War I reparations, he won the Nobel Peace Prize in 1925.

Charles Dawes was elected vice president under President Calvin Coolidge from 1925 to 1929. Two years later, he was appointed ambassador to England. In 1932, Dawes resumed his banking career as chairman of the board of the City National Bank and Trust in Chicago, where he remained until his death in 1951.

Owen D. Young was the other American who founded the BIS.

The other American who founded the BIS was Owen D. Young. He was born on October 27, 1874 and died on July 11, 1962. Young served as a member of the German Reparations International Commission during the Second Reparations Conference in 1929.

In addition to his work on the German Reparations Commission, Young founded the Radio Corporation of America (RCA) as a subsidiary of General Electric in 1919. Young was appointed as first chairman of RCA and continued in this position until 1933. Owen D. Young was chairman of the board of General Electric from 1922 to 1939. He tried to obtain the nomination as president of the Democratic Party but lost to Franklin Delano Roosevelt in 1932.

German Hjalmar Schacht was one of the founders of the BIS.

The third individual who founded the BIS was Hjalmar Schacht. He was born on January 22, 1877 and died on June 3, 1970. He was a German economist, banker, politician, and co-founder of the German Democratic Party in 1918. He served as the Currency Commissioner and President of the Reichsbank under the Weimar Republic. He was a fierce critic of his country's post-World War I reparation obligations. Schacht became a supporter of the bloody dictator Adolf Hitler.

Schacht served in Hitler's regime as President of the Reichsbank from 1933 to 1939 and Minister of Economics from 1934 to 1937. He was responsible for the economic recovery of Germany that allowed Adolf Hitler to rearm the German Armed Forces and lounge World War II.

Schacht opposed Hitler's policy for the re-armament of Germany due to its violation of the Treaty of Versailles and because he believed that it disrupted the German economy. He was dismissed as President of the Reichsbank in January 1939. Hjalmar Schacht remained as a minister without portfolio and received the same salary until he was fully dismissed from the government in January 1943. After the war, he was tried at Nuremberg but acquitted.

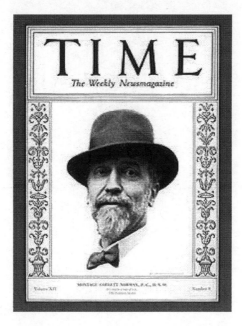

British Montagu Norman was one of the founders of the BIS.

The fourth individual who founded the BIS was Montagu Norman. He was born on September 6, 1871 and died on February 4, 1950. He served as Governor of the Bank of England from 1920 to 1944. During those years, he was one of the most influential central bankers of the world. His power was so enormous that a single speech made by Norman could affect the New

York Stock Exchange in the United States and other stock exchanges in the world. Before and during World War II, Montagu Norman's allegiance was to the Bank of International Settlements and not to Great Britain.

In addition to Adam Lebor outstanding book, *Tower of Basel: The Shadowy History of the Secret Bank that Runs the World* (2013), other books have been written on the operations of the Bank of International Settlements. James C. Baker is the author of a pro-BIS book entitled The Bank for International Settlements: Evolution and Evaluation (2002). Baker wrote a comprehensive history of BIS.

James C. Baker wrote the book The Bank for International Settlements:
Evolution and Evaluation, in 2002.

Amazon described this book as follows: "In a world of increasing cross-border financial transactions, the Bank for International Settlements stands out as the oldest existing international financial institution and among the most controversial. For many it is a mystery: What does it actually do? For others it poses an ethical dilemma: What did it do to aid the Nazis during World War II? Baker examines the history, administration, evolution, and operations of this reclusive institution. He discusses the work of its permanent committees, such as the Basel Concordats of 1975 and 1983 and the Basel Capital Accords of 1988 and 2001."

"Among other products and services he notes the BIS's studies of the use of derivatives by banks, its analysis of payment and settlement systems worldwide, and its supervision of the insurance and investment banking businesses. Then, in a cool and balanced appraisal, he looks at the Bank's operations during World War II, its relationship with the Nazis in their gold and foreign exchange transactions. Throughout, he underlines the importance of the BIS and its value in maintaining stability of the international monetary system. The result is a major academic study, a work of special interest to scholars, teachers, and students, and an important, readable, engrossing account for finance and investment professionals as well."

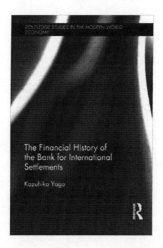

Kazuhiko Yago wrote the book *The Financial History of the Bank for International Settlements* in 2012.

Another book on the BIS was written by a Japanese scholar. A review of Kazuhiko Yago book, *The Financial History of the Bank for International Settlements* (2012), by Financial History Review said the following: "One of the most 'Europeanised' Japanese scholars, benefited from a grant which helped him delve into the archives of the Bank for International Settlements (organized by Piet Clement) and of a few central banks. His book does not compete with Gianni Toniolo's overall history commissioned by the BIS ... or with the papers delivered by either Toniolo or Clement. Nevertheless, it makes a contribution to the construction of the history of the BIS and to that of the cooperation between central banks, in Europe and across the Atlantic, and its bibliography, collected in the endnotes, serves as a toolkit."

Amazon described Yago's book as follows: "The Bank for International Settlements (BIS), founded in 1930, works as the Bank for Central Banks. The BIS is an international forum where central bankers and officials gather to cope with international financial issues, and a bank which invests the funds of the member countries. This book is a historical study on the BIS, from its foundation to the 1970s. Using archival sources of the Bank and financial institutions of the member countries, this book aims to clarify how the BIS faced the challenges of contemporary international financial system."

"The book deals with following subjects: Why and how the BIS has been founded? How did the BIS cope with the Great Depression in the 1930s? Was the BIS responsible for the looted gold incident during WWII? After the dissolution sentence at the Bretton Woods Conference in 1944, how did the BIS survive? How did the BIS act during the dollar crisis in the 1960s and the 1970s? A thorough analysis of the balance sheets supports the archival investigation on the above issues."

"The BIS has been, and is still an institution which proposes an alternative views: crisis manager under the Great Depression of the 1930s, peace feeler during the WWII, market friendly bank in the golden age of the Keynesian interventionism, and crisis fighter during the recent world financial turmoil. Harmonizing the methodology of economic history, international finances and history of economic thoughts, the book traces the past events to the current world economy under financial crisis."

Gianni Toniolo wrote with Piet Clement the book *Central Bank Corporation at the Bank for International Settlements 1932-1973* in 2005.

Another book on the BIS was written by Gianni Toniolo with Piet Clement. This book was *Central Bank Corporation at the Bank for International Settlements 1932-1973* (2005). These two professors wrote the history of the BIS from 1932 to 1973.

Geoffrey Wood reviewed *Central Bank Corporation at the Bank for International Settlements 1932 to 1973* (2005) for the *EH:NET* website and expressed the following:

"This book covers the history of the Bank of International Settlements (BIS) from its birth in 1930 to 1973, a date determined by the thirty year rule. There is, before the historical study proper starts, a fascinating opening chapter which very briefly describes international monetary systems between 1870 and 1973, discusses what central bank cooperation can mean, and reviews that cooperation under the classical gold standard and for the years 1914 to 1922, as well as setting out A BIS View of Cooperation. Let it be said immediately that this is a useful and interesting book. It is also very detailed, and, except for the specialist, for dipping into rather than cover to cover reading... What would a reader of it learn? It is in twelve chapters, ordered, after the first, chronologically, the breaks determined by key events such as exchange rate regime changes. There are also five appendices, and, absolutely essential to understanding, a list of acronyms – of which there are many."

"The chapters deal with the planning for and birth of the BIS; its organization; and then into rough waters, with 1931. The next three chapters cover the discussions after the collapse of the international gold standard; actions between the end of gold and the start of war; and wartime. Then of course comes Bretton Woods and its long aftermath –multilateral payments, convertibility, and the "Patching Up" (Toniolo's apt phrase) of the 1960s. Finally comes monetary union and the move of the BIS into being concerned with financial stability."

"There is something, then, for almost everyone with an interest in monetary or international financial, history. The book is plainly comprehensive. Is it good? Obviously, Toniolo's reputation leads one to expect so — but a check is always useful, and I first carried out that check by looking at chapter five, which is on a period on which I have worked fairly recently, and at chapter one, where the issue of defining cooperation is considered."

"As that strikes me as not altogether straightforward I wanted to see what Toniolo made of it...I learned much from the chapter on the BIS in wartime; I encountered material completely new to me in the account of how the BIS survived Bretton Woods; and, in chapter 10 started to achieve, I think, a grasp of the tangled and vague notion of convertibility. There was no chapter from which I did not learn something, and that holds even for chapter 12, which covers "Monetary Union and Financial Stability." Both of these topics, European monetary union, in particular the Werner plan, and the stability implications of Eurocurrency markets, are areas where I have been involved both as a researcher and as a worker on policy, and even here I learned — not only some fresh perspectives, but also facts new to me...We should all be grateful to Toniolo for by his efforts providing us with the material to address a large number of important questions, and for embedding that material in a useful and informative historical narrative."

Carl Teichrib contributed to an article or report entitled "Global Banking: The Bank for International Settlements" prepared by *The August Forecast and Review*, which was published on October 14, 2005. The article presented a comprehensive history of the creation of the BIS and a short biography of the founders and history of BIS up to 2005. Edward Jay Epstein wrote an article about the BIS in *Harpers* magazine in 1983. He described the BIS as the "most exclusive, secretive, and powerful supranational club in the world."

This photo was taken by Haydée Prado de Varona, who is the wife of this writer, during their visit to Basel, Switzerland on July 19, 2017. The building was constructed in 1977. It is an 18-story circular skyscraper that rises over the city of Basel, Switzerland. This is the main building of Bank for International Settlements and is called the Tower of Basel.

In spite of the books and many articles that have been published, the BIS is completely unknown by the vast majority of Americans and people around the world. On July 19, 2017, during this author's visit to the beautiful city of Basel, Switzerland, which is the location of BIS, he spoke to a well-informed tourist guide from that city and she had no idea of the role of international central bankers and their employees at the BIS.

This photo was taken by Haydée Prado de Varona, who is the wife of this writer, during their visit to Basel, Switzerland on July 19, 2017. This is another building with a round shape of the Bank for International Settlements.

This most powerful supranational bank has always wanted to keep a low profile. Even well-known authors who have written books describing the history of the operations of the Federal Reserve Bank as well as the powerful organizations that run the United States and the world, such as the Bilderberg Group, the Trilateral Commission, and the Council of Foreign Relations, do not mention the existence of the BIS. This is surprising as the owners and employees of the banking cartels, who own the central banks of almost all the Western nations, including the United States, are all involved with the BIS. This international bank is the central bank of all the central banks in the United States and Europe, as well as in other nations in the world.

The Hague Agreement of 1930 that created the Bank for International Settlements

On January 20, 1930, the governments of the United Kingdom, Germany, France, Belgium, Italy, Japan, and Switzerland signed a document that became known as the Hague Agreement. Article 1 of the Hague Convention or Agreement stated that "Switzerland undertakes to grant to the Bank for International Settlements, without delay, the following Constituent Charter having force of law: not to abrogate the Charter, not to amend or add to it, and not to sanction amendments to be Statutes of the Bank referred to in Paragraph 4 of the Charter or otherwise than in agreement with the other signatory governments."

Article 10 of the Hague Convention or Agreement stated that "the bank, its property and assets and all deposits and other funds entrusted to it shall be immune in time of peace and in time of war from any measure such as expropriation, requisition, seizure, confiscation, prohibition or restriction of gold or currency export or import, and any other similar measures." Thus, the powerful BIS was born as a result of this international treaty.

According to Adam Lebor, Gianni Toniolo with Piet Clement, and James C. Baker, authors of books regarding the history of the Bank for International Settlements, this supranational banking institution was created with unprecedented powers and privileges. The central bankers who created the BIS held politicians with contempt, the exception being if the politician was one of their own.

The BIS founders wanted to build a transnational financial system that could move large amounts of capital free from political or governmental control. The central bankers demanded and received incredible immunity from their own governments, free from any type of regulation, scrutiny, or accountability for the BIS directors and members as well as their employees.

The unprecedented immunity that was granted was the following:

• Diplomatic immunity for persons and what they carry with them, such as diplomatic pouches.
• Not being subjected to taxation on any transactions, including salaries paid to employees.
• Embassy-type immunity for all buildings and/or offices operated by the BIS.

- Freedom from immigration restrictions.
- Freedom to encrypt any and all communications of any sort.
- Freedom from any legal jurisdiction.
- Immunity from arrest or imprisonment and immunity from seizure of their personal baggage, except in flagrant cases of criminal offense.
- Immunity from jurisdiction, even after their mission has been accomplished, for acts carried out in the discharge of their duties, including words spoken and writings.
- Exemption for themselves, their spouses, and children from any immigration restrictions, from any formalities concerning the registration of aliens, and from any obligation relating to national service in Switzerland.
- The right to use codes in an official communications or receive or send documents or correspondence by means of couriers or diplomatic backs.

On February 10, 1987, the BIS and the Swiss Federal Counsel signed a "Headquarters Agreement" which confirmed the immunities previously granted to the BIS when it was created, as well as additional immunities. Article 2 stated that "the Bank buildings shall be inviolable... No agent of the Swiss public authorities may enter therein without the express consent of the Bank... The archives of the bank and, in general, all documents and any data media belonging to the Bank... shall be inviolable at all times and in all places. The Bank shall exercise supervision of police power over its premises."

Article 4 of the Headquarters Agreement stated the following: "The Bank shall enjoy immunity from criminal and administrative jurisdiction, except to the extent that such immunity is formerly waived in individual cases by the president, the general manager of the Bank, or their duly authorized representative. The assets of the Bank may be subject to measures of compulsory execution for enforcing monetary claims. On the other hand, all deposits entrusted to the Bank, all claims against the Bank and the shares issued by the Bank shall, without the prior agreement of the Bank, be immune from seizure or other measures of compulsory execution and the sequestration, particularly of attachment within the meaning of Swiss law." In essence, the 1987 Headquarters Agreement granted the BIS similar protections given to the headquarters of the United Nations, the International Monetary Fund, and diplomatic embassies.

On February 27, 1930, the governors of the central banks of Germany, Great Britain, France, Italy, and Belgian met with representatives from Japan and three American banks to establish the

Bank for International Settlements. Each nation's central bank purchased 16,000 shares. Since the Federal Reserve Bank was not permitted to own shares of the BIS for political reasons, three United States banks, the First National Bank of New York, J. P. Morgan, and the First National Bank of Chicago, created a consortium and each bank purchased 16,000 BIS shares. Thus, the United States representation at the BIS was three times as that of any other nation.

This international bank's initial share capital was set at 500 million Swiss francs. The owners of the BIS purchased 200,000 shares of 2,500 of gold francs. The governors of the founding central banks were ex-officio members of the board of directors and each could appoint a second director of the same nationality.

Many years later, on January 8, 2001, an Extraordinary General Meeting of the BIS approved a proposal that restricted ownership of the BIS shares to central banks. At the time, 13.7% of all shares were in private hands. The BIS set a price of $10,000 per share which was over twice the book value of $4,850. Some private owners of the BIS shares filed a lawsuit against the bank insisting that the shares were worth much more money than what was offered.

At the beginning, central bankers wanted to keep a very low profile and complete anonymity for their activities. The first headquarters of the BIS was an abandoned six-story hotel, the Grand et Savoy Hotel Universe, with an address above the adjacent Frey's Chocolate Shop, near the train station at Basel, Switzerland. No sign was placed at the door identifying the BIS.

In May 1977, however, the BIS moved to a more visible and efficient headquarters. The new building was an 18-story circular skyscraper that arises over the medieval city of Basel, Switzerland and soon it became known as the "Tower of Basel." The new building is completely air-conditioned and self-contained. It has a nuclear bomb shelter in the basement, a private hospital, and some 20 miles of subterranean archives. From the top floor of the Tower of Base there is a panoramic view of Germany, France, and Switzerland.

Wall Street bankers and American multinational corporations helped Germany prepare for Word War II

James Perloff explains in his book *The Shadows of Power* how members of the Council on Foreign Relations, banker Charles Dawes and businessman Owen Young, assisted Germany to recover economically. The Dawes Plan of 1924 asked for massive loans to Germany. Dr. Carroll Quigley said of this plan, "it is worthy of note that this system was set up by the international bankers and that the subsequent lending of other people's money to Germany was very profitable to these bankers." J.P. Morgan was involved as well.

Perloff stated the following: "Three German cartels in particular were beneficiaries of credit under the Dawes Plan. This trio became the industrial backbone of the Nazi war machine, and the financial backbone of Adolf Hitler's rise to power in Germany. All of this three cartels, the chemical enterprise I.G. Farber stands out. The Farber Company received significant assistance under the Dawes Plan, including a flotation of $30 million bonds from the Rockefeller's National City Bank."

A can of the deadly Zyklon B with granules and original signed documents detailing ordering of Zyklon B as "materials for Jewish resettlement" (Auschwitz Concentration Camp Museum.)

Perloff stated the following: "I.G. Farber grew to be the largest chemical concern in the world… This is entirely supported by statistics. In 1943, for example, Farben produced 100% of Germany's synthetic rubber, 100% of its lubricating oil, and 84% of its explosives. It even manufactured the deadly Zyklon B gas, used to exterminate human beings in Hitler's concentration camps… I.G. Farber also supplied 45% of the election funds use to bring the Nazis to power in 1933." After World War II, an investigation by the United States War Department it was noted that: "Without I.G. Farber's immense productive facilities, its intense research, and the vast international affiliations, Germany's key prosecution of the war would have been unthinkable and impossible."

Perloff pointed out the following: "What is particularly odious is that certain American companies did robust business with I.G. Farber, which hired CFR member Ivy Lee to handle its public relations in the United States. In 1939, on the eve of blitzkrieg the Rockefeller's Standard

Oil of New Jersey sold $20 million in aviation fuel to the firm. I.G. Farber even had an American subsidiary called American I.G."

"Among the directors of the latter were the ubiquitous Paul Warburg (CFR founder), Herman A. Metz (CFR founder), and Charles E. Mitchell, who joined the Council on Foreign Relations in 1923 and was a director of both the New York Federal Reserve Bank and National City Bank. There were also several Germans on the board of American I.G.; after the war, three of them were found guilty of war crimes at the Nuremberg trials. But none of the Americans were ever prosecuted."

It is very surprising to this writer how so many Jewish bankers aided Nazi Germany. The Jewish firm Kuhn, Loeb and Company was also involved. Another Jewish banker was Paul Warburg, who similarly to George Soros, a Hungarian Jew, helped the Nazis during World War II.

Antony C. Sutton wrote the book *Wall Street and the Rise of Hitler* in 1976.

Amazon describes Sutton's book as follows: "The contribution made by American capitalism to German war preparations can only be described as phenomenal. It was certainly crucial to German military capabilities.... Not only was an influential sector of American business aware of the nature of Nazism, but for its own purposes aided Nazism wherever possible (and profitable) and with full knowledge that the probable outcome would be war involving Europe and the United States."

"Penetrating a cloak of falsehood, deception, and duplicity, Professor Sutton reveals one of the most remarkable and under-reported facts of World War II that key Wall Street banks and American businesses supported Hitler's rise to power by financing and trading with Nazi Germany. Carefully tracing this closely guarded secret through original documents and eye-witness accounts, Sutton comes to the unsavory conclusion that the catastrophe of World War II was extremely profitable for a select group of financial insiders. He presents a thoroughly documented account of the role played by J.P. Morgan, T.W. Lamont, the Rockefeller interests, General Electric, Standard Oil, and the National City, Chase, and Manhattan banks, Kuhn, Loeb and Company, General Motors, Ford Motor Company, and scores of others in helping to prepare the bloodiest, most destructive war in history."

"This classic study, first published in 1976 and the third volume of a trilogy, is reproduced here in its original form. The other volumes in this trilogy are *Wall Street and the Bolshevik Revolution* and *Wall Street and FDR*."

Adam Lebor reported that in 1929 the multinational Rockefeller's Standard Oil entered into a "division of fields" arrangement with I.G. Farber, the German cartel. I.G. Farber retained supremacy in the field of chemicals, including in the United States, in exchange for giving its oil patents to the Standard Oil for use everywhere--except Germany. In 1938, Standard Oil sent the full specification of its processes for synthesizing Buna-- artificial rubber-- to I.G. Farber.

Later, I.G. Farber built a factory called I.G. Auschwitz, which was run by slave labor in the diabolical concentration camp at Auschwitz in Nazi-occupied Poland, using partially American scientific knowledge. In March 1942, six Standard Oil subsidiaries and three company officials were fined $5,000 each by a federal judge for violating antitrust laws. Assistant Attorney General Thurman Arnold accused Standard Oil of "treason" and of entering an "illegal conspiracy" to prevent the development and distribution of artificial rubber.

Lebor explained how World War II brought immense profits to the American car industry. Opel, General Motors' German division, produced the "Blitz" truck on which the Wehrmacht, as the Nazi military was called, invaded Poland. The German subsidiary of Ford Motor Company's built almost half of all the two-and three-ton trucks in Nazi Germany.

Lebor wrote the following: "There is a strong argument that without General Motors' and Ford's German subsidiaries the Nazis would not have been able to wage war. Hitler was certainly an enthusiastic supporter of the American motor industry's methods of mass production. He even kept a portrait of Henry Ford by his desk. In July 1938, Henry Ford was awarded the Grand Cross of the German Eagle, the highest honor Nazi Germany could bestow on a foreigner. The following month James Mooney, who ran General Motors' overseas operations, was also awarded a high Nazi honor… Numerous American business leaders traveled to Berlin to ingratiate themselves with the Nazis. Thomas Watson, the president of IBM, arrived at in 1937, to be decorated with the Merit Cross of the German Eagle… The following year, after the Nazi annexation of Austria, the SS used one of IBM's prototype computers, known as a Hollerith machine, to keep a record of Jewish properties… The historian Edwin Black argues that IBM's technology used for cataloging and identifying the Jews of Europe, was crucial for the organization of the Holocaust."

The Dulles brothers

John Foster Dulles was a powerful globalist who assisted Nazi Germany.

Dulles was born in Washington, D.C. on February 25, 1888 and died on May 24, 1959. He served as Secretary of State under Republican President Dwight D. Eisenhower from 1953 to 1959. Dulles was the grandson of former Secretary of State John Watson Foster and the nephew of Woodrow Wilson's Secretary of State Robert Lansing. Dulles was surrounded by members of the foreign affairs community from an early age.

During his adolescence, he spent a year in Paris before attending Princeton University. Dulles returned to Paris to attend the Paris Peace Conference of 1919 as part of the globalist Bernard Baruch's Reparations Commission and Economic Council.

During this time, Dulles formed strong opinions about the danger of holding Germany responsible for war reparations and he regretted the failure of President Woodrow Wilson to obtain the support of the Senate for the League of Nations. In 1932, European countries met in Lausanne, Switzerland and agreed to cancel the German reparations, except for one final payment.

Lebor wrote that John Foster Dulles and his brother Allen Dulles became partners at Sullivan and Cromwell, the most powerful law firm in the United States, if not the world. The law firm had its headquarters at 48 Wall Street in New York City. Allen Dulles ran Sullivan and Cromwell's office in Paris and knew the German BIS Director Hjalmar Schacht well.

Allen Dulles was a powerful globalist similar to his brother. While serving as CIA director during the Bay of Pigs invasion on April 17, 1961, he left Washington, D.C. Dulles was not available to persuade President John F. Kennedy to not cancel the Assault Brigade 2506 airstrikes to Cuba prior to the invasion as his agency had planned. Was his absence done deliberately so that the invasion would fail?

Allen Dulles was born on April 7, 1893 and died on January 29, 1969. He was a diplomat and lawyer who became the first civilian but third Director of Central Intelligence and its longest-serving director to date. As head of the Central Intelligence Agency during the early Cold War, he oversaw the 1954 Guatemalan coup d'état against the communist President Jacobo Arbenz, Operation Ajax (the overthrow of Iran's elected government), the Lockheed U-2 aircraft program, and the Bay of Pigs Invasion. Following the assassination of John F. Kennedy, Dulles was one of the members of the Warren Commission, which was a complete and shameful cover up. Between his stints at government service, Dulles was a corporate lawyer and partner at Sullivan and Cromwell.

Lebor said that during the 1930s John Foster Dulles assisted the Third Reich. Dulles was the director of the International Nickel Company (INKO), the largest producer of nickel in the world. In 1934, INKO signed a cartel agreement with I.G. Farber, exchanging supplies of nickel sources for licensing rights to the newly-patent and nickel refining process. Lebor pointed out that during the 1930s lawyer John Foster Dulles, as well as other American financiers and lawyers, ensured that "American money, commodities, and expertise flowed steadily into the Third Reich."

The mainstream media neglected to explain how American bankers and corporations had strong ties to Nazi Germany. The media has also ignored the fact that American bankers and corporations assisted Vladimir Lenin and the Bolsheviks overthrow Czar Nicholas II in Russia. Another chapter of this book documents how American bankers and John D. Rockefeller, the founder of the Standard Oil, assisted the communists in the Soviet Union to achieve and maintain power.

The shameful conduct of the Bank for International Settlements during World War II

Thomas McKittrick was president of the Bank for International Settlements during World War II. He served from 1940 to 1946.

During World War II the BIS continued operating from its headquarters in Basel, Switzerland. Adam Lebor explained that "during the war, the BIS became a de-facto arm of the German Reichsbank, accepting looted Nazi gold and carrying out foreign exchange deals for Nazi Germany." The alliance of the BIS with Germany was known in the United States and Great Britain. However, the need for the bank to keep functioning in order to maintain transnational financial operations was agreed by all the countries that fought each other during World War II.

Thomas Harrington McKittrick was born in 1889 and died in 1970. He was an American banker and president of the Bank for International Settlements during World War II whose close relationship with Hitler's Third Reich created a great deal of controversy. Lebor calls McKittrick "Hitler's banker."

McKittrick joined the National City Bank in 1916. Later, he assisted in opening a branch of the bank in Genoa. McKittrick was president of the Bank for International Settlements from 1940 to 1946, under the chairmanship of Otto Niemeyer and Ernst Weber. The BIS, which intended to facilitate effective monetary co-operation, declared its neutrality in World War II. After the war was declared in September 1939, it was no longer possible for representatives of Germany, France, or the United Kingdom to attend the BIS meetings. Due to the commencement of hostilities in France, only a few miles from the BIS headquarters in Basel, Switzerland, McKittrick was the only member of its assembly to attend the May 1940 meeting.

Thomas McKittrick was a family friend of another globalist Allen Dulles, a U.S. intelligence officer also based in Switzerland during World War II. Dulles later became a Director of the Central Intelligence Agency. Dulles was the CIA Director when he and other globalists in the Kennedy administration were responsible for the failure of brave Cuban patriots who fought at the Bay of Pigs in 1961 to liberate Cuba from communism.

During World War II, the BIS received gold as interest payments from the German Reichstag, which later investigations showed had been looted from the central banks of Belgium, the Netherlands and other nations conquered by Nazi Germany. From 1946 to 1954, McKittrick worked for the globalist Chase National Bank, becoming a senior vice president and director.

Lebor pointed out the following: "A few miles away, Nazi and Allied soldiers were fighting and dying. None of that mattered at the BIS. Board meetings were suspended, but relations between the BIS staff of the belligerent nations remained cordial, professional, and productive. Nationalities were irrelevant. The overriding loyalty was to international finance."

During the war years, an American, Thomas McKittrick, was president of the bank. A Frenchman, Roger Auboin, was the general manager and a German, Paul Hechler, was the assistant general manager and a member of the Nazi party. An Italian, Raffaelle Pilotti, was the Secretary-General; a Swedish, Per Jacobssen, was the Bank's economic advisor; and other employees were British.

McKittrick passed economic and financial intelligence to the Nazi Reichsbank. He also shared information on Nazi Germany with Allen Dulles.

Four of the five Nazi directors of the BIS were convicted of war crimes

Since the time that Adolf Hitler came to power in Germany in 1933 and to the end of World War II in 1945, five German members of the board of directors of the BIS were Nazis. After World War II four of them were convicted of war crimes. These BIS directors were the following:

Hjalmar Schacht was the architect of the economic recovery of Germany and served as President of Reichsbank until 1939. He was one of the four individuals who founded the BIS, as explained earlier. After the war, he was tried at Nuremberg but acquitted. In 1953, he founded a private banking house in Düsseldorf.

This picture of Hermann Schmitz was taken after his arrest by the U.S. Army.
He was sentenced to four years in prison at the Nuremberg Trials.

Hermann Schmitz was born on January 1, 1881 and died on October 8, 1960. He was a German industrialist and Nazi war criminal. In 1941, Hitler gave him a portrait of him with his autograph as a gift for his dedication to the aims of Nazi Germany. He was sentenced to four years in prison for war crimes and crimes against humanity through the plundering and spoliation of occupied territories.

Hermann Schmitz was the Chief Executive Officer of IG Farben from 1935 to 1945, a gigantic German chemical conglomerate that during the war built and ran a factory of synthetic rubber using prisoners as slave laborers at the concentration camp at Auschwitz. He was released in 1950 and went on to become member of the administrators' council of Deutsche Bank in Berlin, as well as the honorary president of Rheinische Stahlwerke AG.

Walther Funk was sentenced to life in prison at the Nuremberg Trials.

Walther Funk was born on August 18, 1890 and died on May 31, 1960. He was an economist and prominent Nazi official who joined the Nazi party in 1931. Funk replaced Hjalmar Schacht at the Reichsbank. Funk worked for the SS Chief Heinrich Himmler, who was one of the most powerful men in Nazi Germany and one of the people most directly responsible for the Holocaust.

Funk was tried and convicted as a major war criminal by the International Military Tribunal at Nuremberg and sentenced to life in prison. At the Nuremberg trials American Chief Prosecutor Jackson labeled Funk as "The Banker of Gold Teeth," referring to the practice of extracting gold teeth from Nazi concentration camp victims, and forwarding the teeth to the Reichsbank for melting down to yield bullion. Many other gold items were stolen from victims, such as jewelry, eyeglasses, and gold finger rings.

As Minister of Economics, Funk accelerated the pace of rearmament and, as Reichsbank president, banked for the SS the gold rings of Nazi concentration camp victims. Funk was held at Spandau Prison along with other senior Nazis. He was released on May 16, 1957 because of poor health. Walther Funk died three years later in Düsseldorf of diabetes.

Baron Kurt von Schröder was sentenced to three months in prison at the Nuremberg Trials.

Kurt Freiherr von Schröder was born on November 24, 1889 and died on November 4, 1966. He was a German nobleman, financier, and SS-Brigadeführer. Baron Kurt von Schröder was the owner of the J.H.Stein Bank, a bank that held the deposits of the Gestapo. After World War II Schröder was arrested and was tried by a German court for crimes against humanity. He was found guilty and was sentenced to three months' imprisonment.

Emil Puhl is standing on the left in the picture. He was sentenced to five years in prison at the Nuremberg Trials.

Emil Johann Rudolf Puhl was born on August 28, 1889 and died on March 30, 1962. Puhl was a Nazi and director and vice-president of Germany's Reichsbank during World War II. Similar to Walther Funk, Puhl sent gold stolen from countries occupied by the Nazis and gold stolen from their victims incarcerated in Nazi concentration camps to the Reichsbank . Much came from the victims of Operation Reinhard at Auschwitz, Majdanek, Treblinka, Bełżec, Chełmno, and Sobibór. After prisoners were mass murder by gas, their property was removed. Puhl was convicted of war crimes and sentenced to five-years imprisonment

During the Nuremberg trials that followed the end of World War II, 104 Germans were sentenced to death or to prison terms. Those who received terms in prison included four of the five German Nazi directors of the BIS. With the exception of Funk, to the other three were given very lenient sentences. These Nazis directors of the BIS deserved stronger punishment!

The proposal to liquidate the BIS during the Bretton Woods conference in 1944 was reversed in 1948

After the war during the Bretton Woods conference held in New Hampshire in July 1944, Norway proposed the liquidation of the BIS at the earliest possible moment for assisting Nazi

Germany to deposit the stolen gold from the occupied nations that it had conquered in the bank. The liquidation of the bank was supported by other European delegates as well as the United States delegates who included Soviet Spy Assistant Secretary of the Treasury Harry Dexter White and the Secretary of the Treasury Henry Morgenthau.

Soviet Spy Harry Dexter White (left) with socialist Fabian John Maynard Keynes at the Bretton Woods Conference.

However, the liquidation of the bank was never actually undertaken. In April 1945, the new United States President Harry S. Truman and the British government suspended the dissolution of the bank. The decision to liquidate the BIS was officially reversed in 1948.

How does the Bank of International Settlements operate today?

Jaime Carauna from Spain has been the BIS General Manager since April 1, 2009.

The BIS is a bank for all the central banks of the major nations in the world. According to the website of the Bank for International Settlements, the mission for this international bank is to serve central banks in their pursuit of monetary and financial stability, foster international cooperation in those areas, and act as a bank for central banks. The BIS pursues its mission by:

• Promoting discussion and facilitating collaboration among central banks.

• Supporting dialogue with other authorities that are responsible for promoting financial stability.

• Conducting research on policy issues confronting central banks and financial supervisory authorities.

• Acting as a prime counterparty for central banks in their financial transactions.

• Serving as an agent or trustee in connection with international financial operations.

The BIS is owned by 60 member central banks, representing countries from around the world that together make up about 95% of world GDP. Its head office is in Basel, Switzerland and it has two representative offices: in the Hong Kong Special Administrative Region of the People's Republic of China and in Mexico City.

Acting as the central bank, the BIS has sweeping powers to do things for its own benefit or to assist one of its member's central banks. Article 21 of the original BIS statute defines the day-to-day operations as follows:

• Buying and selling of gold coin or bullion for its own account or for the account of central banks;

• Holding gold for its own account under reserve in central banks;

• Accepting the supervision of gold for the account of central banks;

• Making advances to or borrowing from central banks against gold, bills of exchange, or other short-term obligations of prime liquidity or other approved the securities;

• Discounting, rediscounting, purchasing or selling with or without its endorsement deals of exchange, checks, and other short-term obligations of prime liquidity;

• Buying and selling foreign exchange for its own account or for the account of central banks;

• Buying and selling negotiable securities other than shares for its own account or for the account of central banks;

• Discounting for central banks bills taken from their portfolio and rediscounting with central banks bills taken from its portfolio;

- Opening and maintaining current or deposit accounts with central banks;

- Accepting deposits in connection with trustee agreements that may be made between the BIS and governments in connection with international settlements.

Organization and governance of the Bank for International Settlements

The bank currently employs 647 staff members from 54 countries. The three most important decision-making bodies within the bank are the general meeting of member's central banks, the board of directors, and the management of the bank. The BIS currently has 60 members in the central banks, all of which are entitled to be represented and to vote in the general meetings. However, voting power is proportionate to the number of the BIS shares issued in the country of each member represented at the meeting.

At present, the board of directors of the bank has 20 members. The board has six ex officio directors, made up of the governors of the central banks of Belgium, France, Germany, Italy, United Kingdom and the chairman of the Board of Governors of the Federal Reserve System. Each ex officio member may appoint another member of the same nationality. The rest of the board of directors is made up through the election of nine other governors from members of central banks. The governors of the central banks of Canada, China, Japan, Mexico, the Netherlands, Sweden, Switzerland, and the president of the European Central Bank are currently elected members of the board of directors.

The board of directors of the Bank for International Settlements is responsible for determining the strategies and policy directions for the bank, supervising the management, and fulfilling these specific tasks given by the bank's statutes. The board meets six times a year.

Edward Jay Epstein explained the major beliefs of the inner circle of the BIS. The members of the board of directors have the firm belief that central banks should act with complete independence of their own governments. Another belief is that politicians should not be trusted to decide the fate of the international monetary system. The powerful central bankers of the world share a preference for pragmatism and flexibility over ideology. The most important belief is that they cannot allow a central bank of a large country to fail for fear that it could jeopardize the entire international monetary system due to interconnectedness with the central banks of other nations. This is a result of globalization and interdependence.

History professor Carroll Quigley from Georgetown University wrote a book entitled *Tragedy and Hope: A History of the World in our Time* (1966). This professor was a mentor of President Bill Clinton. Professor Quigley was very familiar with how the international bankers operated in the world. He agreed with their goals. Professor Quigley wrote the following: "I know of the operations of this network because I have studied it for 20 years and was permitted for two years, in the early 1960s to examine its papers and secret records. I have no aversion to it or to most of its aims and have, for much of my life, been close to it and too many of its instruments… There does exist, and has existed for a generation, an international…network which operates, to some extent, in the way the radical Right believes the communist act. In fact, this network, which we may identify as the Round Table groups, has no aversion to cooperating with communists, or any other groups, and frequently does so."

Dr. Quigley described the international banking network in the following manner: "The powers of financial capitalism had another far-reaching aim, nothing less than to create a world system of financial control in private hands able to dominate the political system of each country and the economy of the world as a whole. This system was to be controlled in a feudalist fashion by the central banks of the world acting in concert, by secret agreements arrived at frequent private meetings and conferences. The apex of the system was to be the Bank for International Settlements in Basel, Switzerland; a private bank owned and controlled by the world's central banks which are private corporations. The key to their success was that the international bankers would control and manipulate the money system of a nation while letting it appear to be controlled by the government."

The founder of the most powerful banking dynasty in the world, Mayer Amschel Bauer, (who later adopted the name Rothschild), said in 1791, "Allow me to issue and control a nation's currency and I care not who makes its laws." Four of his five sons were sent to London, Paris, Vienna, and Naples to establish a banking system that would be outside government control. The eldest son stayed at Frankfurt, Germany where the first Rothschild bank had been established. Eventually, a privately-owned central bank was established in almost every country, including the United States in 1913. These banking cartels have the authority to print money in their respective countries and governments must borrow money to pay their debts and fund their operations from them. And of course, at the top of this network is the privately-owned BIS, the central bank of the central banks of the world.

Ellen Brown wrote an article entitled "The Tower of Basel: Secretive Plans for the Issuing of a Global Currency" which was published in *Global Research* on April 17, 2013. The reporter explained that the British newspaper The London *Telegraph* had an article entitled "The G-20 Moves the World a Step Closer to a Global Currency." The British newspaper said that the leaders of the G-20 nations have agreed to support a currency that was created by the International Monetary Fund called Special Drawing Rights or SDR.

The leaders of the G-20 nations have activated the power to create money and begin global quantitative easing, which is printing money out of thin air, not backed by gold or any other thing. The world is now a step closer to a global currency, backed by the global central banks that are running the monetary policy for all humanity. The London newspaper the *Telegraph*'s article stated that the financial institution that would do this would be the BIS.

There is no doubt that the BIS is moving the entire world to regional currencies and ultimately, a global currency. The global currency could be a successor to the SDR, and may be the reason why the BIS recently adopted the SDR as its primary reserve currency. Canada, Mexico, and the United States are members of the trade group called the North American Free Trade Association (NAFTA). The Trump administration is presently reviewing the NAFTA agreement. Globalist Gary Cohen, former president of Goldman Sachs, is the head of the National Council on Economics in the White House. He has recommended to President Donald Trump not to withdraw from NAFTA. The president during the presidential campaign had promised to quit NATFA. Apparently that is a promise that he will not fulfill.

It may be that soon a common currency will be used for these three North American nations. It might be called the amero, which will sound like the euro, or some other name such as the NAFTA dollar. The adoption of the common currency is a voluntary surrender of sovereignty and is a step towards a one-world government dominated by these powerful international bankers.

After World War II, Jean Monnet, a French internationalist, who helped found the League of Nations, had the idea of creating a European Union where nations would relinquish their national sovereignty as an economic necessity. The BIS came up with the idea of creating the euro, which eventually was adopted by 17 European countries. The removal of the sovereignty of European nations was presented as an economic necessity, rather than as a profound political process. The powerful globalist elite made up of international bankers, powerful industrialists, and owners of media, with the complicity of government officials, decided to create a one-world government under the United Nations, but controlled by them. Thus, the European Union was born.

The officials and technocrats from the BIS were most instrumental in the creation of the European Union and its currency, the euro. They also created the very powerful European Central Bank, a bank that is not accountable to any government or to the European Parliament despite controlling the monetary policy of 17 countries.

The BIS has done very well financially over the years. In 2012, the supranational bank had 355 metric tons of gold and an estimated value of $19 billion. By the end of March 2012, the BIS made a profit of $1.17 billion. Each year the bank makes over $1 billion in profits. The bank makes much of its profits from the fees and commissions that it charges to central banks for its services.

On June 25, 2017, the BIS reported its balance sheet in its Annual Report. The BIS included a balance sheet total of Special Drawing Rights (SDR) of 242.2 billion (U.S. $329.0 billion) and on March 31, 2017, a net profit of SDR 827.6 million (U.S. $1.124 billion). Special Drawing Rights is a basket of the following currencies: U.S. dollar 41.73%, Euro 30.93%, Renminbi (Chinese yuan) 10.92%, Japanese yen 8.33%, British pound 8.09%

World Bank headquarters is in Washington, D.C.

The International Monetary Fund (IMF) lends money to national governments when these countries have some type of fiscal or monetary crisis. The IMF raises money by receiving contributions from its 184 member nations. Thus, all of its funds are taxpayer's money. The World Bank also lends money and has 184 member nations. Within the World Bank are two separate institutions: The International Bank for Reconstruction and Development, which lends money to middle income, and poor countries that have good credit, and the International Development Association, which lends money to the poorest countries of the world.

The BIS, as the central bank to the other central banks, facilitates the movement of money and provides what is known as "bridge loans" to central banks while waiting for the funds of the IMF and/or the World Bank. For example, when Brazil in 1998 had a currency crisis because it could not pay the enormous accumulated interest on loans made over a protracted period of time, the IMF, the World Bank, and the United States bailed out Brazil with a $41.5 billion package. If that nation had not paid its creditors, the United States banks such as Citigroup, J.P. Morgan Chase, and Fleet Boston, would have lost an enormous amount of money. Thus, the real winners of rescuing the largest country in South America were the U.S. banks that had made risky loans.

The Secretariat of the IMF's new Financial Stability Board is located in Basel, Switzerland, and housed at the headquarters of the secretive Bank for International Settlements. The relationship between BIS and IMF is very close.

Conclusion

Adam Lebor has made very strong criticisms of the BIS. He said that this bank is an elitist, opaque, and anti-democratic institution which is out of step with the 21st century. The legal immunities of the supranational bank perpetuate the belief that the central bankers are unaccountable to everyday citizens and their own governments. The bank does not reveal the discussions that take place at their meetings with the central bankers of the world or its internal operations. The bank has no accountability or transparency in its operation.

Lebor wrote that the BIS should lose its legal inviolability. It is important that citizens around the world demand more transparency and accountability from the financial institutions that have power over their lives and that include the BIS. It is very important for Americans to pay attention to the operations of the BIS and the Federal Reserve Bank since America could very easily lose its sovereignty and be subjected to the desires and wishes of unelected and undemocratic central bankers of the world.

Chapter 23

The International Monetary Fund threatens our wealth

The International Monetary Fund (IMF) headquarters is in Washington, D. C. The IMF Managing Director Christine Lagarde said she would not mind moving it to Beijing, China.

On March 19, 2013, a date that will live in infamy among Cypriots, its government was forced by the "Troika," a triumvirate composed of a globalist banking elite from the International Monetary Fund (IMF), the European Central Bank (ECB), and the European Commission (EU) to confiscate bank deposits between 6.75% to 9.9%. Prior to that day Cypriots hurried to pull their money out of banks and ATMs before the government could finalize a plan to seize depositors' funds to satisfy euro zone leaders. However, many of them lost thousands of euros and suffered immensely.

This was outrageous confiscation of property that had set a very dangerous precedent to the entire Western world. Gone was the long-standing ECB's guarantee that bank accounts would be protected up to 100,000 euros per account. News of the seizure bank accounts in Cyprus sent shockwaves through European Union and beyond. Many worried Europeans were asking what other countries would suffer the same fate. What about the United States? It turns out that the perverse International Monetary Fund wants to take this tax on wealth measures worldwide.

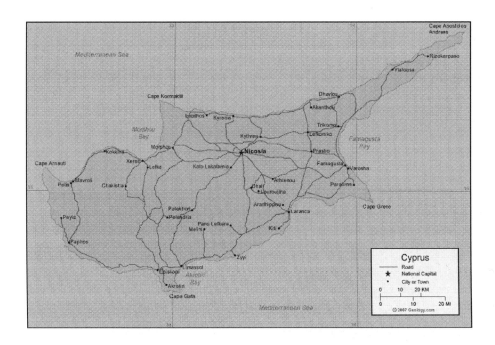

Cyprus is a small nation founded in 1960. It is part of the European Union and uses the euro as its currency. The Mediterranean island has 3,572 square miles and had a population of 1.14 million in 2013.

This enormous confiscation of bank accounts of depositors in the small island brought a great deal of pain to Cypriots. This unwise action is truly "Uncharted Territory." Only people from Cuba, Russia, China and other nations who lost their entire wealth due to communist regimes can truly understand how it feels to go to bed rich or with modest wealth and wake up completely poor. Once private property is not respected, it would always be at risk of further and more painful confiscations.

Rebecca Christie and Corina Ruhe wrote an article titled "Cyprus Bank Deposits to Be Taxed in $13 Billion Bailout" on March 16, 2013 which was published on *Bloomberg*. The reporters explained that finance ministers from the Eurozone agreed to an unprecedented tax on Cypriot bank deposits as officials unveiled a 10 billion-euro ($13 billion) rescue plan for the country. The theft of bank deposits in Cyprus raised about 5.8 billion euros.

The International Monetary Fund may contribute to the package and junior bondholders may also be recruited in a so-called bail-in, the ministers' statement said. The European Central Bank will use its existing facilities to make funds available to Cypriot banks as needed to counter potential bank runs. Similar to what is going on in Greece, ATMs in the country ran out of cash.

The IMF Managing Director Christine Lagarde is from France.

IMF Managing Director Christine Lagarde, who travelled to Brussels for the financial discussions, said "We believe that the proposal as outlined by Jeroen Dijsselbloem (President of the Eurogroup of the Council to the European Union) is actually sustainable." Corporate tax rates in Cyprus will rise to 12.5% to 10% as part of the deal, Dijsselbloem said.

Cyprus was forced to pledge to increase asset sales and implement budget cuts amounting to 4.5% of Gross Domestic Product (GDP). The arrangement called for the banking sector to shrink substantially by 2018.

The reporters pointed out that there were many skeptics. One of them was Luxembourg's Jean-Claude Juncker, who is currently President of the European Commission, said that imposing investor losses in Cyprus "risked reigniting the financial crisis that has so far pushed five of the euro zone's 17 members to seek aid." European Union Economic and Monetary Affairs Commissioner Olli Rehn stated the tax assessment is a strictly fiscal measure

At the talks, the ministers also agreed to give extra time to Ireland and Portugal to repay loans to the European Financial Stability Facility. The euro group, IMF and ECB will approve the details of the extensions and the Cyprus deal once technical details have been ironed out and national parliaments have acted as needed, the finance ministers said in a statement.

Meeting of the International Monetary Fund

William F. Jasper wrote an article on May 7, 2015 titled "IMF: The New Global Fed" which was published in the *New American* magazine. Jasper described the financial pain of having lifetime savings confiscated in Cyprus as follows: "It is robbery," said Maria Zembyla, from Nicosia. "People like us have been working for years, saving to pay for our children's studies and pensions and suddenly they steal a big share of this money." "You sit down after a lifetime of labor at 60, and find half of all you worked for has gone,"

Larnaca resident Panikos Demetrious told the *BBC*. "I thought I would be comfortable and a lot of the money could also have gone to my son," he said. Demetriou had 80,000 euros ($86,000) seized from his savings account. "This wasn't dirty Russian cash — it came from my solicitor after the sale of my house," he protested. "I went to sleep Friday as a rich man. I woke up a poor man. I lost all my money." Such was the lament of 65-year-old John Demetriou of the Cypriot fishing village of Leopetri.

Jasper explained that the stories of personal financial tragedy affected many. However, the Cyprus tragedy is set to go global, with the savings of virtually every person on the planet at risk.

Jasper wrote the following: "The Cypriot banking meltdown was but one in an on-going series of debacles that have continued to unfold since the start of the 2008 economic crisis, where in the United States many saw the values of their 401(k)s plummet and many lost their homes.

Globally, the crisis was brought on by governments wildly spending money they don't have and central banks manufacturing money out of thin air. The result was a massive bubble — and then, a massive mess when the bubble burst, as all bubbles inevitably do. Cleaning up the mess, we were told, required massive bailouts of the Too Big To Fail (TBTF) banks and financial institutions that had caused the crisis by engaging in unwise, unethical, and criminal conduct. Yes, bailouts were distasteful, but there was no other way to avoid systemic risk and financial collapse, we were told. But one bailout led to another and another — and so on."

To finance these on-going bailouts, the Federal Reserve Bank in the United States and the European central banks have printed $11 trillion out of thin air under the label of "quantitative easing" (QE). But instead of paying off the enormous debt, the irresponsible quantitative easing has piled $11 trillion more onto the already crushing debt load. Thus it has created another financial bubble that will, inevitably, burst, causing even greater devastation, chaos, and pain.

William F. Jasper pointed out the Cypriot experience presents a danger to the rest of the world. It was a cruel laboratory experiment that the global bankers and their kept politicians intend to replicate many times over in the coming months. Because taxpayers have become weary of, and rebellious against, more bailouts for the TBTF casino banks, the Cyprus gambit introduced a new form of theft, euphemistically called a "bail-in," which pays off the banksters with funds confiscated from bank customers, i.e., savers, rather than the taxpayers. The Cypriot bail-in was devised by the "Troika," a triumvirate composed of banking fraternity officials from the International Monetary Fund, the European Central Bank, and the European Commission.

The financial elite at the IMF, World Bank, and the central banks may now intend to repeat the Cyprus theft on a much grander scale. The "bail-in" (also disingenuously referred to as a "haircut," but more honestly described as an amputation or decapitation) is referred to officially in banking circles as a "capital levy." It is important to point out that plundering the savings of depositors through "capital levies" is but one of the outrageous criminal enterprises being planned.

The effort by former Congressman Ron Paul and his son Senator Rand Paul to audit the Federal Reserve, and to expose where (and to whom) the trillions of dollars it was creating were going, came too close for comfort. The Fed has successfully resisted any independent audits, but the TBTF banking elites have determined that they must speed up their long-range effort to empower a global institution with the Fed's capabilities — and more — all completely unaccountable and beyond the reach of Congress or any other national authorities. Hence the escalating campaign to "supersize" the IMF to assume the functions of a "Global Fed."

Supposedly, the super-sized IMF is just what the United States and other countries need to achieve economic stability and growth. But considering how wretchedly the Fed has managed the U.S. economy is it reasonable to expect that a global Fed would do any better? Yet that is exactly what the global financial elite claim!

Some Safety Net

Tharman Shanmugaratnam

William F. Jasper explained that on April 19, 2013, International Monetary Fund official Tharman Shanmugaratnam during an interview stated the following: "In the last crisis, the Fed and some other central banks had a system of swaps that was applied to only certain financial centers, but you can't leave it to an individual central bank to make those decisions. It has to be a global player, and the IMF is the only credible institution to perform that role."

Shanmugaratnam, who is both the finance minister and deputy prime minister of Singapore, has served for the past four years as chairman of the International Monetary and Financial Committee, the powerful policy steering committee of the IMF. He made the comments as officials from around the world gathered for the IMF's annual spring meetings in Washington, D.C.

"The Washington-based IMF needs to evolve into more of a 'system-wide policeman' that enforces global financial stability, rather than solely a lender to individual countries that run into trouble," said Shanmugaratnam, as reported by *Bloomberg News* in an April 19 story entitled "Fed Crisis-Liquidity Function Reviewed for Potential Use by IMF."

"IMF member nations are discussing how to expand the lender's mandate to include keeping markets liquid during a financial crisis, a role played by a group of major central banks led by the Federal Reserve in 2008," *Bloomberg* reported, noting that the IMF's main committee of central bank governors and finance ministers "is working on ways for the fund to provide a better financial 'safety net' during a crisis."

William F. Jasper pointed out that the "safety net" is of course supposedly intended for all of us, but that is not how it has worked in practice. Consider the Federal Reserve bailouts in the wake of the 2008 crisis that benefited the Wall Street elites at the expense of Main Street. But imagine how much greater the wealth transfer will be if the globalist banking elites are able to transform the IMF into their "supersized" global Federal Reserve, with massive transfusions of dollars from the American taxpayers, unparalleled powers for creating money out of nothing — and bailouts without end, to the usual privileged players.

The new "mandates" being proposed for the IMF are nothing short of astounding, and if the American people allow Congress to approve these powers for the IMF, we can expect nothing less than eventual total confiscation of all our treasure, as well as all our liberty. And yet, as monumental as the stakes are, and as imminent as this approaching danger now is, there is precious little coverage of it in either the corrupt Establishment-controlled "mainstream" or the "alternative" media.

Jasper explained the following: "It should come as no surprise to those who have been following these matters for any length of time that the chorus of Wall Street Insiders, think tanks, central bankers, academics, and media pundits calling for supersizing the IMF is receiving its primary direction from that premier brain trust of one-worldism, the Council on Foreign Relations (CFR). The effort received its launch in a November 13, 2008 op-ed in the CFR-dominated *Washington Post* entitled "Supersize the IMF. The author of that salvo was Sebastian Mallaby, the Paul A. Volcker senior fellow for international economics at the CFR."

"Mallaby's op-ed, which has been amplified by many similar appeals since, appeared on the eve of the new G-20 financial summit, which had just been expanded from its traditional G-7/G-8 to include a dozen new countries and the European Union. Mallaby asserted that government commitments to the IMF should be tripled — and if you take into account the vast growth of cross-border derivatives, an even larger expansion is needed." It also coincided with the White House changeover from Bush to Obama. Mallaby noted that the Obama team will soon have its hands on the controls. A bigger IMF should be on its agenda. This theme has been repeated with increasing frequency and urgency in various and sundry insider forums over the past several years, including successive G-8 and G-20 summits, the annual Jackson Hole confabs of world central bankers, and the annual gatherings of the World Economic Forum in Davos, Switzerland."

In 2009, at their summit in Toronto, Canada, the G-8- G-20 leaders issued a declaration stating that "our reform agenda rests on four pillars." "The first pillar," it said, "is a strong regulatory framework."

Mario Draghi, a former employee of Goldman Sachs, **is the President of the European Central Bank which is located in Frankfurt, Germany.**

Mario Draghi was born on September 3, 1947. He is an Italian economist who has served as President of the European Central Bank since November 2011. He has served as Chairman of the Financial Stability Board from 2009 to 2011 and Governor of the Bank of Italy from 2005 to 2011.

Draghi previously worked at Goldman Sachs from 2002 until 2005 before becoming the governor of the Bank of Italy in December 2005, where he served until October 2011. In 2014 Draghi was listed as the 8th most powerful person in the world by *Forbes*. In 2015 *Fortune* magazine ranked him as the world's second greatest leader.

Mark Carney, a former employee of Goldman Sachs, is the Governor of the Bank of England.

The Bank of England in its website posted the biography of Carney. It is as follows: "Mark Carney is Governor of the Bank of England and Chairman of the Monetary Policy Committee, Financial Policy Committee and the Prudential Regulation Committee. His appointment as Governor was approved by Her Majesty the Queen on 26 November 2012. The Governor joined the Bank on 1 July 2013."

"In addition to his duties as Governor of the Bank of England, he serves as Chairman of the Financial Stability Board (FSB), First Vice-Chair of the European Systemic Risk Board, a member of the Group of Thirty and the Foundation Board of the World Economic Forum. Mark Carney was born in Fort Smith, Northwest Territories, Canada in 1965. He received a bachelor's degree in Economics from Harvard University in 1988. He went on to receive a master's degree in Economics in 1993 and a doctorate in Economics in 1995, both from Oxford University."

After a thirteen-year career with Goldman Sachs in its London, Tokyo, New York and Toronto offices, Mark Carney was appointed Deputy Governor of the Bank of Canada in August 2003. In November 2004, he left the Bank of Canada to become Senior Associate Deputy Minister of Finance. He held this position until his appointment as Governor of the Bank of Canada on 1 February 2008. Mark Carney served as Governor of the Bank of Canada and Chairman of its Board of Directors until 1 June 2013."

Jasper said the following: "The key institution, thus far, in that strong regulatory framework is the Financial Stability Board (FSB), created in 2009. The initial chairman of the FSB was Mario Draghi, who was then governor of the Bank of Italy, but who has since been graduated to president of the European Central Bank (ECB). Draghi has been replaced as chairman at the FSB by Mark Carney, governor of the Bank of England. Its worthy of more than passing notice that Draghi and Carney share a common tie: They are both top alums of Goldman Sachs, the infamous TBTF banking house that has become known worldwide as the vampire squid. Before entering public service, Draghi was vice chairman and managing director of Goldman Sachs International. Carney served in many senior management capacities at the firm. Among other Goldman Sachs alums who have held major conflict-of-interest posts in national treasuries, central banks, and the IMF/World Bank are Robert Rubin, Henry Paulson, Stephen Friedman, and Robert Zoellick (all of whom are leading CFR members). Goldman Sachs has long been a top corporate member of the Council on Foreign Relations, occupying the elite Founders Circle of the CFR's eight biggest corporate contributors."

William F. Jasper explained the core reforms that the globalists insist must be adopted to avert global systemic risk:

1) The IMF must be given vast new global financial regulatory powers.

2) The IMF must be given huge new infusions of capital through member country "subscriptions."

3) The IMF must be encouraged to issue debt bonds to finance global loans.

4) The IMF must be "legitimized" by giving China and other emerging nations weighted votes in IMF policies.

Jasper pointed out that these connections paid off big-time when Goldman wanted access to subsidized Federal Reserve loans during the 2008 crisis, with the privileged firm benefiting from $782 billion in special loans through the Fed's Primary Dealer Credit Facility and the Term Securities Lending Facility.

Bank for International Settlements (BIS) is located in Basel, Switzerland.

Jasper explained that the Secretariat of the IMF's new Financial Stability Board is located in Basel, Switzerland, and housed at the headquarters of the secretive Bank for International Settlements (BIS). The BIS, of course, is composed of the topmost TBTF tier of "Bankers' Bankers," the plundering criminal class most responsible for the monetary policies that have produced the bubbles and busts that are wrecking our global financial system, destroying the middle classes, and transferring colossal sums and assets from the many to the few. So, the IMF's vaunted "regulatory framework" is, in reality, a prime example of giving the foxes the key to the chicken coop.

Radical Alternative Scheme

Jasper said that the IMF plan, however, goes beyond "mere" regulatory control. He explained the following: "The real agenda was laid out most boldly and explicitly, perhaps, in an essay for the CFR journal *Foreign Affairs* in the Fall of 1984. The article, entitled "A Monetary System for the Future," was authored by Harvard University Professor of International Economics Richard N. Cooper, a former chairman of the Boston branch of the Federal Reserve, and a long-time member (and former director) of the CFR, as well as a member of the elite Trilateral Commission and Aspen Institute."

Professor Cooper wrote in his famous *Foreign Affairs* proposal the following: "I suggest a radical alternative scheme for the next century: the creation of a common currency for all of the industrial democracies, with a common monetary policy and a joint Bank of Issue to determine that monetary policy. The currency of the Bank of Issue could be practically anything.... The key point is that monetary control — the issuance of currency and of reserve credit — would be in the hands of the new Bank of Issue, not in the hands of any national government.... [However] a single currency is possible only if there is in effect a single monetary policy, and a single authority issuing the currency and directing the monetary policy. How can independent states accomplish that? They need to turn over the determination of monetary policy to a supranational body.

Jasper wrote that monetary control continues to be the "key point" that the internationalists are obsessed with. They insist that nation states "need to turn over the determination of monetary policy to a supranational body" — a body over which they will exercise control. They have already succeeded on that score with the Eurozone nations that have turned over national monetary policy to the European Central Bank (ECB).

Zhou Xiaochuan is the governor of the People's Bank of China.

Zhou Xiaochuan was born on January 29, 1948. As governor of the People's Bank of China since December 2002, he has been in charge of the monetary policy of the People's Republic of China. He was reappointed to the same position in March 2013, making him the longest-serving central bank chief since the establishment of the People's Republic of China.

Jasper said Zhou Xiaochuan, governor of the People's Bank of China wrote a paper in March 2009 echoing Professor Cooper's proposal. Zhou Xiaochuan also want a new currency reserve system based on the IMF's Special Drawing Rights (SDRs), the IMF's basket of currencies, made up of the dollar, the euro, the Japanese yen, and the British pound. Until now, SDRs have been used only as accounting entries by international organizations, but recent proposals would have it transformed into a genuine currency for more general use. According to Zhou, the economic crisis of 2008-2009 exposed the "inherent vulnerabilities and systemic risks in the existing international monetary system," showing the need to "create an international reserve currency that is disconnected from individual nations and is able to remain stable in the long run."

Jasper wrote that the IMF issued a report in 2010 in favor of allowing it to print its own money to provide "international liquidity." According to Jasper the IMF report stated the following: "A global currency, bancor, issued by a global central bank would be designed as a stable store of value that is not tied exclusively to the conditions of any particular economy. The global central bank could serve as a lender of last resort, providing needed systemic liquidity in the event of adverse shocks and more automatically than at present."

Jasper pointed out the following: "These recent overtures for a global currency have brought the IMF full circle, to the subversive plans hatched by its original architects more than seven decades ago. It was John Maynard Keynes, the British economist and Fabian Socialist, who coined the term bancor for a world currency. Together with Soviet agent Harry Dexter White, Keynes was the guiding light of the United Nations Bretton Woods Monetary Conference that designed the IMF in 1944."

"This subversive duo understood very well the revolutionary nature of the project they were launching. In his famous treatise The Economic Consequences of the Peace, which he had written years before (in 1919), Keynes explained: By a continuous process of inflation, governments can confiscate, secretly and unobserved, an important part of the wealth of their citizens. By this method, they not only confiscate, but they confiscate arbitrarily; and while the process impoverishes many, it actually enriches some.... There is no subtler, no surer means of overturning the existing basis of society than to debauch the currency. The process engages all the hidden forces of economic law on the side of destruction, and does it in a manner which not one man in a million is able to diagnose."

Jasper wrote that Keynes' disciples — Cooper, Carney, Draghi, Rubin, Paulson, et al. — have been engaging "all the hidden forces of economic law on the side of destruction" with ever greater audacity. And while they are indeed impoverishing many, so too, are they enriching some — specifically, their fellow "bankster" associates.

Trillion-dollar "Firewall"

Jasper said that IMF Managing Director Christine Lagarde and her cohorts fully embrace the advice of French Revolutionist Georges Jacques Danton, who counselled, "Audacity, more audacity, always audacity." In a January 23, 2012 speech in Berlin to the German Council on Foreign Relations (GCFR), Lagarde declared: "We need a larger firewall." The dictionary defines "firewall" as a "wall or partition designed to inhibit or prevent the spread of fire." But the proposed "firewall" would actually give the IMF-TBTF arsonists more matches and gasoline.

Jasper pointed out that Lagarde warned "We need to act quickly or else we could easily slide into a 1930s moment," referring to the Great Depression. The members of GCFR to which she spoke, like its interlocking counterparts in the United States (CFR), Britain Royal Institute of International Affairs (RIIA), and other countries, represents the globalist elites of corporate, banking, political, and academic circles that are promoting convergence toward world government. They also represent the crony banks and corporations that have been first in line to receive IMF and ECB bailouts. Lagarde told the Germans that an additional $1 trillion in "financial firewalls" is urgently needed: $500 billion for the European Stability Mechanism (ESM) and a $500 billion for the IMF. Lagarde estimates that one trillion dollars will be needed to fight the crisis in the coming years.

Jasper said globalists always say "Global crises call for global solutions" —to justify expanding the powers and funding for the United Nations, World Trade Organization, World Bank, IMF, and other world government-promoting institutions. Creating a monopoly of economic and political power on a planetary scale is supposed to solve problems believed too big for national governments. Lagarde's IMF wants a global wealth tax or a "capital levy" — on all "positive net worth," meaning all savings, pensions, and home equity. IMF stated in its Fiscal Report released in October 2013 stated the following: "The sharp deterioration of the public finances in many countries has revived interest in a 'capital levy' — a one-time tax on private wealth — as an exceptional measure to restore debt sustainability."

Jasper stated the following: "Make no mistake, the IMF's proposed tax, which was given a test run in Cyprus, would apply to all private wealth on the planet. And it doesn't even contemplate balancing budgets, only bringing them down to "sustainable" levels — meaning levels that will allow government borrowing and spending to continue without interruption. The proposed capital levy would have to be implemented rapidly, before savers and investors could react and move their assets, or themselves, out of harm's way: The appeal is that such a tax, if it is implemented before avoidance is possible … [will not] distort behavior. How painful and con-fiscatory would the IMF's capital levy theft be? According to the IMF authors: "The tax rates needed to bring down public debt to precrisis levels are sizable: reducing debt ratios to end-2007 levels would require … a tax rate of about 10% on households with positive net worth."

"It is important to note that the "low" six-to-10-percent "capital levy" most frequently pro-posed for savings could — and almost certainly would — slide quickly upwards, if that camel's nose is ever allowed inside the tent. That is the way with virtually all taxes. Consider our own federal income tax. When it was enacted in 1913, most Americans paid zero or 1%, and the top tax rate was a mere 7% on incomes above $500,000 (which was more than $10 million in 2007 inflation-adjusted dollars)."

"The IMF report notes that previous attempts to install wealth taxes at the national level have largely failed because the wealthy could move. However, the IMF sees a global plan utilizing mutual governmental cooperation as being more likely to succeed because there will be fewer escape hatches. It stated the following: In principle, taxes on wealth … offer significant rev-enue potential at relatively low efficiency costs. Their past performance is far from encour-aging, but this could change as … stepped up international cooperation … reduces evasion opportunities."

China's Asian Infrastructure Investment Bank (AIIB)

Jasper asked how do the globalists expect to gain public and legislative support for such an outrageous scheme? Well, one ploy is to present a supersized IMF as the best alternative to China's rising economic threat. "Europeans defy US to join China-led development bank," de-clared the headline of a *Financial Times* story on March 16, 2015, about China's new Asian Infrastructure Investment Bank (AIIB). This bank was created by Communist China's President Xi Jinping, the AIIB has been presented in the establishment press as a dangerous challenge to the dollar, with President Obama, the IMF, and the World Bank as the unlikely champions of America's dwindling economic heft in this post-unipolar world.

Jasper stated the following: "As the AIIB was rolling out during March and traditional U.S. allies and trading partners (Britain, France, Germany, Italy, the European Union) were moving toward jumping on board, the Obama administration appeared to be making efforts to scuttle the moves in that direction. As it turns out, however, the deeper reality was far different from the surface appearances. The administration and its Wall Street allies were merely using the AIIB threat as a ploy to wheedle more money and power for the IMF and World Bank. Reuters reported on March 17, 2015 that Treasury Secretary Jacob J. "Jack" Lew (a CFR member) "warned the Republican-dominated Congress that China and other rising powers were challenging American leadership in global financial institutions, and he urged lawmakers to swiftly ratify stalled reform of the IMF. The AIIB was launched in Beijing last year to spur investment in Asia in transportation, energy, telecommunications and other infrastructure, the Reuters report noted. It was seen as a rival to the Western-dominated World Bank and the Asian Development Bank."

"International Monetary Fund chief Christine Lagarde has said the IMF would be delighted to co-operate with the China-led Asian Infrastructure Investment Bank (AIIB). She said there was "massive" room for IMF co-operation with the AIIB on infrastructure financing. Lagarde, speaking at the opening of the China Development Forum in Beijing, said she believed that the World Bank would co-operate with the AIIB. Lagarde suggested that the IMF headquarters may someday be moved from Washington, D.C., to Beijing. Lagarde made it clear at the time that she found the dictators of China's brutally repressive Communist regime more to her liking than the Congress, which she faults for obstructing the reforms that would further empower the IMF."

Jasper concluded his article by stating the following: "In truth, the IMF belongs in Beijing, where its totalitarian-minded officials would undoubtedly be more politically comfortable, and where it would not enjoy the protective camouflage of American sponsorship. We should happily send it there — after withdrawing our membership … and our money."

Conclusion

The infamy done against Cypriots by the globalist banking elite from the International Monetary Fund (IMF), the European Central Bank (ECB), and the European Commission (EU) to confiscate bank deposits that were protected by ECB was nothing more than the confiscation of private property or a tax on wealth. This was an outrageous confiscation of property that had set a very dangerous precedent to the entire Western world. Gone was the long-standing ECB's guarantee that bank accounts would be protected up to 100,000 euros per account.

News of the seizure bank accounts in Cyprus sent shockwaves through the world. What about other nations including the United States. It turns out that the perverse International Monetary Fund wants to take this tax on wealth measures worldwide. The IMF is demanding to be given vast new global financial regulatory powers as well as huge new infusions of capital through member country "subscriptions." Americans must fight the IMF's demands and Congress must never approve to give this globalist institution more power than it already has!

Chapter 24

President Trump's Son-in-law, Jared Kushner, Business Partners Include Goldman Sachs, other Banks, and George Soros

Jared Kushner is meeting with President Donald Trump in the Oval Office.

On May 3, 2017, Jean Eaglesham, Juliet Chung, and Lisa Schwartz wrote an article titled "Trump Adviser Kushner's Undisclosed Partners Include Goldman and Soros" which was published in the *Wall Street Journal*. The reporters said Jared Kushner, the president's son-in-law and his senior adviser, is currently in business with Goldman Sachs Group, Inc. and billionaires George Soros, and Peter Thiel, according to people familiar with securities filings. Jared Kushner cofounded and currently partly owns a real-estate tech startup called Cadre.

Eaglesham, Chung, and Schwartz pointed out that the international bank Goldman Sachs, George Soros, and Peter Thiel, as well as other billionaires' firms, also have stakes in the company. The company is based in a Manhattan building owned by the Kushner family's company, according to people familiar with Cadre. According to a *Wall Street Journal* review of securities and other filings, Cadre company is one of many interests—and ties to large financial institutions—that Mr. Kushner did not identify in his government financial-disclosure form. They said that properties and companies part-owned by Mr. Kushner include loans totaling at least $1 billion from more than 20 lenders and that he has also provided personal guarantees on more than $300 million of the debt.

The reporters said that Jamie Gorelick, a lawyer representing Jared Kushner, wrote in a statement that his stake in Cadre is housed in a company he owns, BFPS Ventures LLC. His ownership of BFPS is reported in his disclosure form, although it does not mention Cadre. Ms. Gorelick explained that the Cadre stake is described in a revised version of his disclosure form. She further added that Mr. Kushner has previously discussed his Cadre ownership with the Office of Government Ethics and that he has "resigned from Cadre's board, assigned his voting rights and reduced his ownership share." The reporters wrote that experts in ethics are concerned that Mr. Kushner's business connections could "jeopardize his impartiality in certain areas and that, absent disclosures, the public is in the dark about potential conflicts."

The reporters is stated the following: "President Trump's son-in-law Jared Kushner's has a great deal of responsibilities that range from working on a Middle East peace deal to making the federal government operate more efficiently. As a senior federal official, he is bound by ethics laws that require him to recuse himself from matters that would directly affect his financial interests. Ms. Gorelick, who was deputy attorney general in former President Bill Clinton's administration, said Mr. Kushner will "recuse consistent with government ethics rules."

"Jared Kushner co-founded Cadre in 2014 with his brother, Joshua Kushner, and Ryan Williams. Cadre markets properties to prospective investors, who can put their money into specific buildings or into an investment fund run by Cadre, which collects fees on each deal. To start the company, Cadre turned to a Goldman Sachs fund and a number of other investors. Among the investors were the venture-capital firms of Peter Thiel, Silicon Valley's most prominent supporter of the GOP president, and Vinod Khosla, a co-founder of Sun Microsystems Inc. Chinese entrepreneur David Yu, co-founder with Ali Baba Group Holding Ltd's Jack Ma of a Shanghai-based private-equity firm, hedge-fund manager Daniel Och and real-estate magnate Barry Sternlicht. Cadre also received a $250 million line of credit from the family of George Soros. Mr. Soros's family office is also an investor in Cadre."

George Soros made his investment in early 2015 before Donald Trump declared his presidential candidacy. Currently, Soros and his radical allies are funding over 170 communist and radical organizations that are trying to destroy the presidency of Donald Trump.

The reporters explained that Jared Kushner has received loans for properties he co-owns from many international banks. These include Bank of America Corp., Blackstone Group LP, Citigroup, Inc., UBS Group AG, Deutsche Bank, and Royal Bank of Scotland Group. Jared Kushner will recuse himself from matters involving these banks.

On May 15, 2017, Michael Warren wrote an article entitled "The Voice in His ear" which was published by the *Weekly Standard*. He explained that Jared Kushner has been called president Trump's "secret weapon," his "secretary of everything," the "super secretary of state," and, during the campaign, the "de facto campaign manager."

Warren said that Steven Bertoni, a writer for *Forbes* magazine, thought that Jared Kushner was Trump campaign's "savior." Steve Bannon, White House chief strategist, thinks that Kushner is a "globalist" and a "cuck." Kellyanne Conway, the president's counselor and former campaign manager, believes that Jared Kushner is an essential part of the team. Conway said the following: "Without Jared, Donald Trump would not be president. And with Jared, Donald Trump will be a more successful and transformative president."

Warren pointed out that to many individuals of Trump's base, Jared Kushner is "a suspect operator who has installed a gang of like-minded Goldman Sachs Democrats in the administration. And if the swamp isn't drained, it will be their fault." Warren stated the following: "Kushner may be all or none of those things, but what nobody in the White House or in the president's orbit would deny is that Trump trusts Jared Kushner above all. He is Trump's well-heeled, respectable avatar, the better angel of the president's nature. As the husband of Trump's daughter Ivanka, Kushner is practically unfireable. But his role isn't a case of reflexive nepotism—from Trump's perspective, Kushner's advice is valuable precisely because he's not going anywhere. Even the most steadfast of aides have their personal biases and agendas, but to Trump, Kushner has just one loyalty: to his father-in-law's and his family's legacy."

"More cynically, Kushner and his wife have more at stake—professionally, financially, socially, and perhaps even politically—in the success or failure of the Donald Trump administration than just about anyone besides the president himself. So far, the White House has Kushner's fingerprints all over it. He introduced Trump to Gary Cohn, the CEO of Goldman Sachs, and encouraged the incoming president to tap Cohn as the director of the National Economic Council—which Trump did. He cultivated speechwriter and nationalist ideologue Stephen Miller, working closely with Miller throughout the campaign and now in the White House to find Trump's voice. He elevated veteran White House aide (former Goldman Sachs banker) Dina Powell, a friend of his and Ivanka's, to a high-ranking position on the National Security Council staff."

Warren said that Jared Kushner and Steve Bannon believe of themselves as the true representatives of President Trump's vision for the country. They frequently clash on foreign policy, healthcare, and other issues. Kushner has won over the economic nationalist Bannon in the contest of who has the most influence on the president. For Steve Bannon, Jared Kushner and his crowd of Democrats are "the sort of cosmopolitan establishmentarians that Trump the populist decried in his winning campaign." Steve Bannon talks about the "deconstruction" of the administrative state, while Jared Kushner's goal is to transform government to work more efficiently. Warren said "don't ever take sides with anyone against the family—and that means Jared Kushner."

Roger Stone, a friend of President Donald Trump for over 40 years, recently said in an interview *InfoWars* that Jared Kushner was the White House's leaker. However, others have accused Steve Bannon of leaking information.

Conclusion

This writer was very surprised that Jared Kushner, whose grandparents were sent to Nazi concentration camps and some of his great aunts were killed in these camps during World War II, would do business with George Soros. Soros, a Jew, survived World War II in Budapest, Hungary during World War II by working with the Nazis in rounding up Hungarian Jews to send to concentration camps.

In the following chapter, it will be explained how Steve Bannon and Dr. Sebastian Gorka were fired from the White House. Many of the president's supporters were very surprise that these two nationalists were terminated while many globalists remain in the White House and the administration.

This writer believes Donald J. Trump is a patriot but like all previous presidents, including Ronald Reagan, he had to name some globalists to his administration. President Trump has hired an inferior number of globalists that all previous presidents.

Chapter 25

Were Steve Bannon and Sebastian Gorka fired or forced out from the White House by Globalists?

On August 18, 2017, White House Chief Strategist Steve Bannon was fired by the president. He was the chief architect of Donald Trump election victory and a champion of nationalism and anti-globalism. Bannon appears in the center of this photo to the right of Chief of Staff General John F. Kelly. On the same day that he was dismissed, *Breitbart News* announced that Bannon would return as its executive chairman. "White House Chief of Staff John Kelly and Steve Bannon have mutually agreed today would be Steve's last day," Sarah Huckabee Sanders, the White House press secretary, said in a statement. "We are grateful for his service and wish him the best," she added.

Who is Steve Bannon?

Stephen Kevin Bannon was born on November 27, 1953 in Norfolk, Virginia. According to *Wikipedia,* upon graduating from high school, Bannon attended Virginia Tech and was elected as president of the student government association. He graduated from Virginia Tech in 1976 with a bachelor's degree in urban planning. While serving as naval officer in the Pentagon, Bannon received a master's degree in national security studies from the School of Foreign Service at Georgetown University. In 1985, Bannon graduated from Harvard with a Master of Business Administration.

Service as naval officer

Bannon served in the Navy for seven years in the late 1970s and early 1980s, working on board of a destroyer in the Pacific. Later, he became a Special Assistant to the Chief of Naval Operations at the Pentagon. When he left the Navy, Bannon was a lieutenant.

In 1980, Bannon was deployed to the Persian Gulf to assist during the Iran hostage crisis. The failure of the mission changed his political world-view from largely apolitical to a strong supporter of President Ronald Reagan.

Bannon stated the following: "I wasn't political until I got into the service and saw how badly President Jimmy Carter f---ed things up. I became a huge Reagan admirer. Still am. But what turned me against the whole establishment was coming back from running companies in Asia in 2008 and seeing that Bush had f---ed up as badly as Carter. The whole country was a disaster."

Business career

Wikipedia explained that after his naval service, Bannon worked at Goldman Sachs as an investment banker in the Mergers and Acquisitions Department. In 1987, Bannon relocated from New York City to Los Angeles to assist Goldman Sachs to expand its presence in the entertainment industry. He stayed at this position with Goldman Sachs in Los Angeles for two years, leaving with the title of vice president.

In 1990, Bannon and several colleagues from Goldman Sachs launched Bannon & Co., a boutique investment bank specializing in media. In one of Bannon & Co. investment bank's transactions, the firm represented Westinghouse Electric that wanted to sell Castle Rock Entertainment. Bannon negotiated the sale of Castle Rock to *CNN*. Instead of a full adviser's fee, Bannon & Co. wisely accepted a financial stake in five television shows, including Seinfeld. He became wealthy. Bannon still receives cash residuals each time Seinfeld is aired. In 1998, Bannon sold Bannon & Co. to Société Générale.

Entertainment and media

Steve Bannon in 2010

According to *Wikipedia*, Bannon entered into the entertainment and media industry in the 1990s. He produced 18 films. In 2004, Bannon made a documentary about President Ronald Reagan titled "In the Face of Evil." While making the documentary, Bannon met writer Peter Schweizer and publisher Andrew *Breitbart*.

In 2007, Bannon wrote an eight-page outline for a new documentary called "Destroying the Great Satan: The Rise of Islamic Fascism in America." The outline stated that "although driven by the "best intentions," institutions such as the media, the Jewish community and government agencies were appeasing jihadists aiming to create an Islamic republic.

Bannon was executive chair and co-founder of the Government Accountability Institute, where he helped in the publication of *Breitbart News* senior editor-at-large Peter Schweizer's book *Clinton Cash*. Bannon also hosted a radio show (*Breitbart News* Daily) on the Sirius XM Patriot satellite radio channel.

Breitbart News

Wikipedia explained that Bannon was a founding member of the board of *Breitbart News*, an online conservative news, opinion, and commentary website. In March 2012, after the death of its founder Andrew *Breitbart*, Bannon became executive chair of *Breitbart News* LLC, the parent company of *Breitbart News*. Under Bannon, *Breitbart* adopted a nationalistic anti-globalist agenda. In 2016, Bannon declared the website "the platform for the alt-right". Bannon identifies himself as a conservative. Speaking about his role at *Breitbart*, Bannon said, "We think of ourselves as virulently anti-establishment, particularly 'anti-' the permanent political class."

Donald Trump's presidential campaign

On August 17, 2016, Bannon was appointed chief executive of the presidential campaign of Donald J. Trump. Bannon resigned from *Breitbart*, as well as the from Government Accountability Institute and Cambridge Analytica, to take the position.

On November 13, 2016, following Donald Trump election as president a few days earlier Bannon was appointed chief strategist and senior counselor to the President-elect. His appointment was denounced by the Muslim Brotherhood front group Council on American-Islamic Relations (CAIR) and the Marxist Southern Poverty Law Center as well as by Democrats and some establishment Republicans, many of whom opposed and still are opposing President Donald Trump's agenda.

Many conservatives, including Pamela Geller, Ben Shapiro, David Horowitz, Morton Klein, Bernard Marcus, Alan Dershowitz, and Rabbi Shmuley Boteach, as well as the Zionist Organization of America defended Bannon against the allegations of anti-Semitism. On November 15, 2016, a letter was sent to President-elect Trump signed by 169 Democratic House Representatives urging him to rescind his appointment of Bannon. The letter stated that appointing Bannon "sends a disturbing message about what kind of president Donald Trump wants to be", because his "ties to the White Nationalist movement have been well documented." Bannon has always denied being a white nationalist and claimed, rather, that he is an "economic nationalist."

In an interview with the *New York Times* in late November 2016, Present-elect Trump responded to the criticism over Brannon's appointment by stating the following: "I've known Steve Bannon a long time. If I thought he was a racist, or alt-right, or any of the things that we can, you know, the terms we can use, I wouldn't even think about hiring him."

The Trump administration

Breitbart editor Julia Hahn followed Bannon to the White House, where she was appointed as Bannon's aide, as well as Special Assistant to President Trump. Bannon, along with Steve Miller, was involved in the creation of the executive order, which resulted in restricted U.S. travel and immigration by individuals from seven Middle Eastern countries, suspension of these individuals from coming to the United States for 120 days, and indefinite suspension of the entry of Syrians to the United States.

Political views

Bannon's political views are described as anti-globalist nationalism and America First. Donald Trump described his agenda in similar terms during his campaign. Bannon describes himself as an economic nationalist. He rejects allegations that he is a white nationalist. He recently called white nationalists "losers," a "fringe element," and a "collection of clowns."

Bannon has advocated reductions in immigration and restrictions on free trade particularly with China and Mexico. He views trade agreements such as NAFTA as part of the New World Order and as being pushed by an elite of globalists who want a one-world government under the United Nations. Bannon also supports significantly increasing spending on infrastructure and he opposes government bailouts, describing them as "socialism for the very wealthy."

Bannon believes in reducing the size of the federal bureaucracy, declaring that he favored the "deconstruction of the administrative state." He was a strong opponent of the Paris Climate Agreement, which was being pushed by globalists in the Trump administration, including Gary Cohen, Jared Kushner and Ivanka Trump.

Bannon was successful in persuading President Trump to withdraw from Climate Agreement since withdrawing from it was one of Trump's campaign promises. He is skeptical of military intervention abroad.

The reasons why President Trump may have fired Steve Bannon

Steve Bannon clashed with the members of Goldman Sachs globalist wing in the White House and the cabinet. For months, Bannon was engaged in a battle with Jared Kushner and other senior White House officials who had Wall Street ties. Fighting the president's son-in-law and his daughter took courage but endangered Bannon's survival in the White House. However, it showed that Bannon is a man of principles. The globalists in the Trump administration and many of their allies in the Republican Establishment wanted to get rid of the nationalist Bannon and finally they succeeded.

Gary Cohn is the Chief Economic Advisor to President Donald J. Trump and Director of the National Economic Council. Previously, he was president and chief operating officer of Goldman Sachs from 2006 to 2017. Cohn is a Democrat and is thought to be one of the most influential voices in the Trump administration.

Cohn was being considered for replacing Janet Yellen when her term expires as Chair of the Board of Governors at the Federal Reserve. However, Cohen criticized unfairly the president's response to the violence in Charlottesville, Virginia. President Trump condemned the KKK and the Nazis as hate groups but also said that among the counter protesters that included the violent groups Antifa and Black Lives Matter also engaged in violence. Cohn unprecedented criticism of President Trump may have doomed his chances for the Fed Chair. The president was correct but received unfair criticisms from the left, some Republicans in Congress, and sadly by Gary Cohen and Secretary Rex Tillerson.

Goldman Sachs is an extremely powerful globalist investment bank. Former Goldman Sachs executives have occupied important cabinet and White House positions in both Republican and Democratic administration as well as in the central banks of other countries and the Bank for International Settlements which runs the world.

On August 18, 2017, Sarah Westwood wrote an article titled "There's a new sheriff in town: Inside Steve Bannon's ouster" which was published by the *Washington Examiner*. The reporter explained that many people close to Steve Bannon said that other top White House aides had clashed with the chief strategist for months and actively worked to undermine him. Bannon's allies frequently refer to those aides — a group that includes the Director of the National Economic Council and registered Democrat Gary Cohn; Deputy National Security Adviser Cairo-born Dina Habib Powell; Senior adviser Jared Kushner, Donald Trump's son-in- law; and Senior adviser Ivanka Trump — as the "West Wing Democrats" or "globalists." All of them have strong ties to Wall Street and to the Democratic Party.

Senior adviser Jared Kushner is Donald Trump's son-in-law.

Sources inside and outside the White House described Steve Bannon's firing as the inevitable result of his enemies' efforts to get rid of him. This was made easier by the dismissal last month of Bannon closest ally, former chief of staff Reince Priebus.

Cairo-born Dina Habib Powell is the current Deputy National Security Advisor for Strategy to President Donald Trump. She appears to the left of the picture with Hillary and Huma Abedin.

Powell is also an Assistant to the President and Senior Counselor for Economic Initiatives. Previously, Powell was a managing director and partner at Goldman Sachs and president of its non-profit subsidiary, the Goldman Sachs Foundation. Powell is a friend of Ivanka Trump and is considered to be her mentor. Powell is a friend of Hillary Clinton, Huma Abedin, and Valery Jarrett. When Powell was the head of the Goldman Sachs Foundation, she worked with the very corrupt Clinton Foundation.

Westwood stated the following: "President Trump's decision to remove Steve Bannon, his chief strategist, came after a period of internal and external pressure to part ways with the controversial figure, and it was no coincidence that the move happened just a few weeks into the tenure of chief of staff John Kelly, White House aides and allies said. And while some cited Kelly's arrival to the West Wing as the catalyst for Bannon's exit, others said the opposition Bannon faced internally persuaded the president to dismiss him…The official suggested Bannon had a good working relationship with Kelly, noting it was Bannon's advocacy that helped Kelly land the nomination to become secretary of Homeland Security."

The reporter explained that a senior White House official told the *Washington Examiner* the following: "I would say it is very unlikely that this decision was taken weeks ago, as has been reported. This was also not going to be a unilateral decision made by the chief of staff, but a decision that was taken by the president based upon those within the White House pressurizing the president to fire him." She said that Bannon's conservative allies expressed fear that in the absence of Bannon, "the remaining senior staffers would not pursue proposals — like the border wall or decreased involvement in international conflicts — that Bannon championed during his tenure." "This becomes a Democratic White House to us," one Bannon ally said of the impending personnel change.

Westwood pointed out that staffers in the White House suggested, both before and after Bannon's departure became public, that the onetime *Breitbart* chief, who is now returning to the his previous position, could do more damage outside the White House than within it. But others said General John Kelly and Steve Bannon "operated on completely different wavelengths, as the former prefers structure and order and the latter sometimes worked outside the chain of command Kelly is hoping to build in the West Wing."

The reporter wrote that individuals close to the White House said that General John Kelly's alignment with national security adviser General H.R. McMaster contributed to Bannon's dismissal. Westwood stated the following: "Bannon and McMaster fought openly in recent weeks over what people close to the White House have described as long-simmering ideological tensions. While McMaster has pushed for increased troop levels in Afghanistan and has led the president away from tearing up the Iran nuclear agreement, Bannon has encouraged Trump to disentangle the U.S. from international conflicts and has long fought to void the Iran deal."

"McMaster recently sought and obtained from Kelly permission to fire a national security aide considered close to Bannon in a move that increased friction between the two men. A source close to the White House suggested Bannon may not be the last aide to go in a West Wing shake-up that has already seen the departures of press secretary Sean Spicer, communications director Anthony Scaramucci, chief of staff Reince Priebus and press aide Michael Short. Kelly was said to be reviewing the portfolios of the existing staff in an effort to streamline operations and formalize roles."

Bannon returns to *Breitbart News* and the White House fears he might go on the attack

Westwood said that one individual close to Bannon said that the former White House strategist would likely turn up his website's heat on the administration in areas where he believes the president has been straying from his campaign platform. On his last day at the White House, Bannon told Joshua Green, an author who wrote a recent book about him, that he plans to "go to war" for Trump against his enemies outside the White House.

Bannon said to the *Weekly Standard* the following: "The Trump presidency that we fought for, and won, is over. We still have a huge movement, and we will make something of this Trump presidency. But that presidency is over. It'll be something else. And there'll be all kinds of fights, and there'll be good days and bad days, but that presidency is over. The Republican establishment has no interest in Trump's success on this. They're not populists, they're nationalists, they had no interest in his program. Zero."

 Bannon recognized that his frustration with the Republican establishment was part of the reasons he left the White House. He ridiculed the "half-hearted attempt" at replacing ObamaCare and found the malaise on infrastructure discouraging. Bannon predicted that the tax cuts would be the "standard Republican version." He said he was excited to return to *Breitbart News* and fuel the populist-nationalist movement forward. "I feel jacked up," he stated. "Now I'm free. I've got my hands back on my weapons. Someone said, 'it's Bannon the Barbarian.' I am definitely going to crush the opposition."

The *New York Times* reported that Bannon clarified to the newspaper, which is the voice of the globalist Council on Foreign Relations, that he did not mean that the Trump's agenda was over. Instead, he said he was referring to his direct work with Donald J. Trump from the end of the campaign to the first stages of his presidency.

Bannon told *Bloomberg* that he will be "going to war" on President Trump's behalf as he will continue pushing the populist message with the political and corporate establishment. Bannon stated the following: "If there's any confusion out there, led me clear it up: I'm leaving the White House and going to war for Trump against his opponents-on Capitol Hill, in the media, and in corporate America."

On February 20, 2017, President Donald J. Trump appointed General H.R. McMaster Director of the White House Security Council following the resignation of General Michael T. Flynn on February 13. General McMaster indicated that he "intends to remain on active duty while he serves as national security adviser."

Steve Bannon is joining Republican donor Robert Mercer, Co-CEO of the investment management company Renaissance Technology, and his daughter, Rebekah, in a new business, possibly a television channel. *Breitbart News*, which was founded in 2007, has been highly critical of White House National Security Adviser General H.R. McMaster recently. General McMaster was accused of belonging to an organization that had links to George Soros and of secretly briefing him. Soros and other Destroy Trump associates are funding over 170 communists and radical organizations which are trying to undermine the president and, if possible, drive him from office.

General McMaster was also denounced by *Breitbart News* for giving Susan Rice security clearance and saying that she did not illegally unmasked any Trump's associates. The president had said earlier that she needed to be investigated for the possible unmasking of his associates which is a felony. General McMaster was also accused of being hostile to Israel.

Westwood concluded her article by stating the following: "His exit turns control of the West Wing fully over to Kelly, a relative centrist. The chief strategist position was created when Trump, during the transition, struggled to choose between Priebus and Bannon for his chief of staff, so the strategist post became a way to give Bannon equal influence in the White House without placing the polarizing figure in the storied chief of staff role, where he would have to deal with Republican congressional leaders he had sharply criticized while at *Breitbart.*" "There's a new sheriff in town," the person said of General Kelly.

Should the president fire or transfer General McMaster from the White House?

General H.R. McMaster is the Director of the White House Security Council.

On August 4, 2017, Alex Newman wrote an article titled "Globalist McMaster Purges Trump Loyalists, Protects Obamaites" which was published in the *New American* website. The reporter explained that General H.R. McMaster has attended Bilderberg Group meetings (the president sent him to the June 2017 Bilderberg meeting held in Virginia) and is a member of the globalist swamp known as the Council on Foreign Relations. Newman said that General McMaster is currently dismissing key President Trump loyalists within the administration who are trying to protect the president and implement his "America First" agenda, according to multiple sources and reports. He pointed out that one White House official who was recently fired for just highlighting in a report the unholy alliance against the president by Islamists and globalists.

Newman stated the following: "McMaster is said to be protecting and elevating radical Obama appointees dedicated to globalism, neoconservativism, and the infamous swamp that Trump promised to drain. Indeed, McMaster sent a letter to Susan Rice, Obama's extreme national security adviser, waiving legal requirements and promising her continued access to classified information — a month after the start of a congressional investigation into her involvement in lawlessly unmasking the identities of Americans whose communications were intercepted. Much of McMaster's scheming has been happening without Trump's knowledge, inside sources and reports said. But now, with scandal swirling around the national security adviser, Trump is reportedly thinking of replacing McMaster and sending him off to Afghanistan. And among Trump's supporters, a movement of sorts aimed at getting McMaster and other establishment globalists fired is gathering steam, with multiple hash tags calling for McMaster's ouster spreading across social media."

Newman explained that National Security Council Director for Strategic Planning Rich Higgins was terminated for outlining the powerful forces working to subvert President Trump and their strategy. Higgins wrote a seven-page memo describing what was and still is happening. Higgins said that the "Maoist insurgency model" was being used by subversive forces, both in and out of government, to destroy President Trump's "America First" agenda that Americans voted for in massive numbers. Higgins, who was also fired, is an ally of anti-globalist White House strategist Steve Bannon and other anti-establishment forces in the administration.

Rich Higgins pointed out that globalists, bankers, deep state officials, and Islamists are all involved in trying to undermine the president. Higgins stated the following: "Through the campaign, candidate Trump tapped into a deep vein of concern among many citizens that America is at risk and slipping away. Globalists and Islamists recognize that for their visions to succeed, America, both as an ideal and as a national and political identity, must be destroyed.... Islamists ally with cultural Marxists because, as far back as the 1980s, they properly assessed that the left has a strong chance of reducing Western civilization to its benefit. Because the left is aligned with Islamist organizations at local, national and international levels, recognition should be given to the fact that they seamlessly interoperate through coordinated synchronized interactive narratives. These attack narratives are pervasive, full spectrum and institutionalized at all levels. They operate in social media, television, and the 24-hour news cycle in all media and are entrenched at the upper levels of the bureaucracies."

Newman said that for writing this memo Higgins was fired by General McMaster, apparently without President Trump's knowledge. But he was not the only one. Another recent victim of the globalist-led purge was Ezra Cohen-Watnick, the National Security Council's senior director, and Senior Middle East Director, Derek Harvey. Both of them were General Flynn's appointees. Yet another, Adam Lovinger, had his security clearance pulled by McMaster for attending a bar mitzvah in Israel, forcing him to leave his post.

Newman said that General McMaster has a list of more senior officials of the Trump administration that he intends to fire in the coming weeks. "They're taking out people who were chosen to best implement the president's policy that he articulated during the campaign," a source said, with at least four more pro-Trump senior National Security Council officials said to be in the crosshairs.

Newman stated the following: "Other sources said the reason for the developments was that McMaster has a different agenda than Trump does. Among other issues, the swamp creatures backed by McMaster have supported the unconstitutional United Nations Paris Accord on climate, more war in Syria, Obama's globalist and unconstitutional Iran deal, and more, while Trump loyalists have supported America First policies that reject those schemes. Lieutenant General McMaster appears to be a firmly committed globalist and a willing tool of the establishment. As The *New American* has been reporting since his appointment in February, McMaster has a solid globalist pedigree dating back more than a decade. Perhaps the most damning evidence of his globalist worldview and subservience to the establishment's anti-American agenda is his membership in the Council on Foreign Relations (CFR). Despite its roster of powerful members, the CFR pushes an ultra-fringe agenda that virtually no mainstream American would support if they understood it."

Newman wrote that 10 years ago General McMaster joined the globalist-minded International Institute for Strategic Studies (IISS) in London as a "senior research associate." According to the organization itself, his mandate was to "conduct research to identify opportunities for improved multi-national cooperation and political-military integration in the areas of counterinsurgency, counter-terrorism, and state building." In short, his job was to find ways to advance globalism and what globalists often refer to openly as the "New World Order."

Newman wrote that 10 years ago General McMaster joined the globalist-minded International Institute for Strategic Studies (IISS) in London as a "senior research associate." According to the organization itself, his mandate was to "conduct research to identify opportunities for improved multi-national cooperation and political-military integration in the areas of counterinsurgency, counter-terrorism, and state building." In short, his job was to find ways to advance globalism and what globalists often refer to openly as the "New World Order."

The Arundel House in London is the headquarters of the International Institute for Strategic Studies. The globalist institute is a British research think tank in the area of international affairs.

Newman concluded his article by saying the following: "Unfortunately, as The *New American* has documented extensively, McMaster is not the only establishment-backed globalist swamp creature haunting the administration and seemingly betraying the American people who voted for Trump. In fact, **there are a number of CFR members and Bilderberg attendees burrowed into strategic positions all across the administration.** If Trump truly hopes to Make America Great Again, he will have to begin with a purge of globalists and establishment operatives. Considering the on-going purge of Trump's most loyal people by McMaster, the national security advisor might be a good place to begin draining the swamp — before the swamp manages to drain Trump."

The *Washington Post*, which is part of the Destroy Trump corrupt mainstream media, reported on August 19, 2017, that the decision to fire Bannon came from General Kelly. It came three weeks after General Kelly was named Chief of Staff was given extraordinary power to overhaul the West Wing staff in an effort to stop the infighting among officials and leaks to the news media.

Stephen Miller is serving as President Trump's senior advisor for policy and speechwriter.

Stephen Miller worked previously as the communications director for then-Republican Alabama Senator and current Attorney General Jeff Sessions. He also served as a press secretary to Republican Representatives Michele Bachmann and John Shadegg. Miller is one of President Trump's chief speechwriter. He has been a key adviser since the presidential campaign and the early days of Donald Trump's presidency. Together with Steve Bannon, Miller was chief architect of President Trump's executive order restricting immigration from several Middle Eastern countries.

It is believed that Stephen Miller, President Trump's top policy adviser and speechwriter, will continue serving in the White House. His views on immigration policy and radical Islam, among other things, are similar to the ones held by Steve Bannon. Although Miller is viewed as the natural heir of Bannon's status as the in-house nationalist, he has made efforts to build bridges with Jared Kushner and other globalist officials.

The Destroy Trump *New York Times* reported on August 19, 2017 that Christopher Ruddy, the chief executive of Newsmax Media and a friend of President Trump, stated the following: "I think it's going to be good for both Steve and for the president. The president has a major hurdle in the fall, I think, in getting legislation passed." Ruddy cited several legislators who had told the White House "that they had a real problem with Steve because of *Breitbart*, and *Breitbart*'s been a thorn in the side for a lot of congressional Republicans."

The *New York Times* indicated that President Trump's first year in office has been plagued by departures of many White House officials. Among those dismissed or who resigned were Anthony Scaramucci and Michael Dubke, both of whom served as communications director; Michael T. Flynn, the president's first national security adviser; Sean Spicer, the press secretary; and Reince Priebus, who served as chief of staff before General Kelly. On August 19,

Carl Icahn, a billionaire investor who was advising President Trump on regulatory issues, announced that he was stepping down from that role. On that same day, A.R. Bernard, a pastor on the president's Evangelical Advisory Board, quit, citing a "deepening conflict in values between myself and the administration."

The *New York Times* said the following: "By dismissing Mr. Bannon, the president loses the most visible avatar of the nationalist agenda that propelled him to victory. Contentious and difficult, Mr. Bannon was nonetheless a driving force behind the president's most high-profile policies: imposing a ban on travelers from several majority-Muslim countries; shrinking the federal bureaucracy; shedding regulations; and rethinking trade policies by aggressively confronting China and other countries… Mr. Bannon had become increasingly critical of Mr. Trump, according to a person close to both men, complaining that the president lacked the political skills and discipline to avoid a succession of self-inflicted public relations disasters. But ultimately, he viewed the president as losing sight of what propelled Mr. Trump to the White House. There were different interpretations of how Mr. Bannon left his job, which had been long anticipated in Washington. One White House official, who would not be named discussing the president's thinking, said Mr. Trump has wanted to remove Mr. Bannon since he ousted Mr. Priebus three weeks ago. Since then, Mr. Kelly has been evaluating Mr. Bannon's status, according to the official. But a person close to Mr. Bannon insisted that the parting of ways was his idea, and that he had submitted his resignation to the president on August 7, to be announced at the start of this week, timed to his one-year anniversary of working for Mr. Trump."

President Trump thanked Bannon for his service in the campaign and the White House

It is believed that the dismissal of Steve Bannon could hurt the president with his conservative anti-globalist and nationalistic populist base. Republican Congressman Steve King from Iowa, who is close to Steve Bannon, said that President Trump's base could revolt. Representative King stated in an interview the following: "With Steve Bannon gone, what's left of the conservative core in the West Wing? Who's going to carry out the Trump agenda?"

Steve Bannon recently said that he talks frequently with President Trump. Bannon is deeply concerned about the Republican establishment which Donald Trump criticized during the presidential campaign. On September 10, 2017, Bannon told Charlie Rose in Sunday 60 Minutes that "The Republican establishment is trying to nullify the 2016 election." He added, "That's a brutal fact we have to face."

Dr. Sebastian Gorka resigned or was forced to leave the White House

Sebastian Gorka was hired as a Deputy Assistant to President Donald J. Trump in January 2017 and left in August 2017.

Sebastian Lukács Gorka was born in 1970 in the United Kingdom to Hungarian parents. He lived in Hungary from 1992 to 2008, and in 2012 became a naturalized American citizen. Gorka has written for a variety of publications, is considered politically conservative. While he served the Trump administration, Gorka gave a series of interviews with the media in which he defended the administration's positions on national security and foreign policy as well as President Trump's public statements.

On August 25, 2017, Sebastian Gorka left his position in the White House. *CNN* reported on August 26, 2017, that Gorka's role outside of television appearances was unclear. He did not play a major policymaking role, according to administration officials. One White House official said Gorka submitted his resignation to Chief of Staff General John Kelly. The official said "it had become clear to Gorka that he would not be allowed to have a meaningful role going forward." Several White House officials have told *CNN* Gorka was forced out of the administration. Read MoreBut a separate White House official disputed that he resigned. Most White House staffers came to see the departure of the previous week of Chief Strategist Steve Bannon as a sign that Gorka's days were numbered. *CNN* explained that Gorka's work for Donald Trump goes back as far as 2015. According to Federal Election Commission filings showed that Gorka was paid $8,000 that October to be a policy consultant for the Trump campaign. Gorka also was "a member of the White House's Strategic Initiatives Group, which he described as a focal point for task forces collaborating with people outside government."

Dr. Sebastian Gorka, who since January has served as deputy assistant to President Donald Trump, resigned from the White House administration on Friday evening, saying, "it is clear to me that forces that do not support the MAGA promise are – for now – ascendant within the White House."

Breitbart News published a full copy of Dr. Sebastian Gorka's resignation letter. It says as follows:

Dear Mr. President,

"It has been my high honor to serve in the White House as one of your Deputy Assistants and Strategists. In the last thirty years our great nation, and especially our political, media, and educational elites, have strayed so far from the principles of our Republic's Founding that we faced a grim and godless future.

Your victory last November was truly a "Hail Mary pass" on the way to re-establishing America upon the eternal values enshrined in our Constitution and Declaration of Independence. It is, therefore, all the more difficult for me to tender my resignation with this letter. Your presidency will prove to be one of the most significant events in modern American politics. November the 8th was the result of decades during which the political and media elites felt that they knew better than the people who elect them into office. They do not, and the MAGA platform allowed their voices finally to be heard.

Regrettably, outside of yourself, the individuals who most embodied and represented the policies that will "Make America Great Again," have been internally countered, systematically removed, or undermined in recent months. This was made patently obvious as I read the text of your speech on Afghanistan this week. The fact that those who drafted and approved the speech removed any mention of "radical Islam" or "radical Islamic terrorism" proves that a crucial element of your presidential campaign has been lost.

Just as worrying, when discussing our future actions in the region, the speech listed operational objectives without ever defining the strategic victory conditions we are fighting for. This omission should seriously disturb any national security professional, and any American who is unsatisfied with the last 16 years of disastrous policy decisions which have led to thousands of Americans killed and trillions of taxpayer dollars spent in ways that have not brought security or victory.

America is an incredibly resilient nation, the greatest on God's Earth. If it were not so, we could not have survived through the unbelievably divisive years of the Obama Administration, nor witness your message to roundly defeat a candidate who significantly outspent you and had the Fake news Industrial Complex 100% on her side. Nevertheless, given recent events, it is clear to me that forces that do not support the MAGA promise are – for now – ascendant within the White House. As a result, the best and most effective way I can support you, Mr. President, is from outside the People's House.

Millions of Americans believe in the vision of Making America Great Again. They will help eventually rebalance this unfortunate temporary reality. Despite the historically unprecedented and scandalous treatment you have received at the hands of those within the Establishment and mainstream media who perennially see America as the problem and who wish to re-engineer our nation in their own ideological image, I know you will stay the course for the sake of all America's citizens. When we first met in your offices in New York, in the Summer of 2015, it was instantly clear that you love the Republic and will never give up once you have committed yourself to victory. When it comes to our vital National Security interests, your leadership guarantees that radical Islamic terrorism will be obliterated, that the threat of a nuclear Iran will be neutralized, and that the hegemonic ambitions of Communist China will be robustly countered.

I and like-minded compatriots will be working on the outside to support you and your official team as we return America to its rightful and glorious place as the shining "city upon a hill."

God Bless America.

In Gratitude,

Sebastian Gorka

Conclusion

Time will tell if the dismissal of Steve Bannon and Dr. Sebastian Gorka leaving the White House was a mistake. One thing is certain, the globalist wing in the White House is strong and influential. Those individuals, such as this writer, who worked hard to elect the patriot Donald J. Trump as president hope that he does not lose sight of what propelled him to the White House. It is very troubling to see so many globalists working in the White House and in the cabinet! However, this writer believes President Trump is a patriot and has had to include globalists in his administration.

Chapter 26

The leaders of the New Muslim Marxists Democratic Party

President Barack Hussein Obama

With the assistance of the globalist elite during the eight years in power Barack Obama transformed the Democratic Party from a center left to an extreme radical left and pro-Muslim Brotherhood party. Obama appointed many socialists, communists, and Islamic radicals to important positions in his administration. Muslim Brotherhood operatives became advisers to the White House and assisted Obama in changing his foreign policy and recommending him other Islamic radicals for positions in his administration.

Obama named many Muslim Brotherhood operatives as advisers to the FBI, CIA, Pentagon, and Department of Homeland Security to purge the training manuals used by these agencies of any valid criticism of the Qur'an and Islam. Obama's foreign policy in the Middle East assisted the Muslim Brotherhood to come to power in Egypt and al-Qaida-linked groups to advance in Libya and Syria. Obama and Hillary Clinton sent illegally tons of weapons from Libya to Turkey to Syria and most of them fell into the hands of the al-Qaida-linked Al Nusra Front and the Islamic States. As a result of the radicalization of the Democratic Party, former president

Barack Obama is now the leader of the new Muslim Marxist Democratic Party, as Ambassador Armando Valladares has called it.

During the 2016 presidential campaign, the very corrupt Hillary Clinton with ties to communists and Islamic radicals competed with the communist Senator from Vermont Bernie Sanders for the Democratic Party nomination. Clinton won the nomination after cheating during the primaries with the assistance of the Democratic National Committee.

Hillary Clinton ran a terrible campaign and her many scandals were exposed. Nevertheless, as the candidate of the New World Order globalist elite, she received millions in donation from Wall Street and the support of the biased New World Order-controlled mainstream complicit media. Only two newspapers endorsed Donald Trump and the majority of the fake polls showed Hillary Clinton as the next presidency. After the unexpected victory of Donald J. Trump on November 8, 2016, Obama, his communist allies foundations and organizations, paid criminals, and useful idiots began a civil war against him.

Obama is the leader of the so-called Deep State/Anonymous Network and has created a "Shadow Government." He is waging a civil war or a silent coup against President Donald J. Trump. Obama wants to oust President Trump from the presidency either by forcing his resignation or through his impeachment. Obama and his radical allies are providing the biased complicit mainstream media false stories pounding the idea that President Trump and the officials in his administration are corrupt, incompetent, and treasonous.

On March 7, 2017, Daniel Greenfield, a journalist at the Freedom Center, wrote an article titled "Obamagate: Exposing the Obama Deep State" which was published in the website *FrontPageMag.com*. The reporter explained that soon after Donald J. Trump obtained the GOP nomination for president, President Obama's officials filed a wiretapping request. Obama targeted Trump for destruction from the very beginning when it was clear he would be the nominee.

As candidate, when Donald Trump was on the verge of winning, Obama's officials did it again and filed another wiretapping request. After he won the presidential election in November 2016, Barack Obama and his officials, who are still serving in the federal government, are doing everything they can to bring Donald Trump down. Greenfield said that Obama's third term has begun and our Republic is in danger.

Daniel Greenfield stated the following: "One is the elected President of the United States. The other is the Anti-President who commands a vast network that encompasses the organizers of Organizing for Action (OFA), the official infrastructure of the Democratic National Committee (DNC) and Obama Anonymous Network, a Shadow Government of loyalists embedded in key positions across the government…And that the Obama Anonymous Network of staffers embedded in the government was the real threat. Since then, Obama's Kalorama mansion has become a Shadow White House." Greenfield wrote that the Obama Anonymous Network is doing everything it can to bring down an elected government. Valerie Jarrett has moved into the Shadow White House to help Obama in planning operations against Trump.

Obama's most important people in his civil war against President Donald J. Trump

There are three key individuals who represent the new Muslim Marxist Democratic Party. They are Valerie Jarrett, Tom Perez, and Keith Ellison.

Valerie Jarrett

Valerie Jarrett, who was born in Shiraz, Iran, is a red diaper baby whose relatives were Marxists. She married the son of the Chicago communist journalist Vernon Jarrett, who worked closely with Obama's mentor, Frank Marshall Davis. Valerie Jarrett was and continuous to be the most influential adviser to both Barack and Michelle Obama. In 1991, Jarrett served as deputy chief of staff for Chicago Mayor Richard Daley and she hired Michelle Robinson, who was then engaged to Barack Obama.

Jarrett served as the Senior Advisor to President Barack Obama and Assistant to the President for Public Engagement and Intergovernmental Affairs in the Obama administration from January 20, 2009 to January 20, 2017. Valerie Jarrett has moved into Barack Obama's Kalorama mansion in Washington, D.C., which has become the "Shadow White House Government" to plot operations against President Donald J. Trump.

Tom Perez

Marxist Tom Perez is the Chair of the Democratic National Committee.

Thomas Edward "Tom" Perez was elected Chair of the Democratic National Committee on February 25, 2017. Tom Perez was the Secretary of Labor from 2013 to 2017. Prior to that position, Perez served as the Assistant Attorney General for the Civil Rights Division of the Department of Justice under the corrupt Attorney General Eric Holder. He supported Holder in all his violations of the Constitution that eventually led Congress to declare Holder in Contempt of Congress for refusing to turn documents.

The election of the new chairman of the Democratic National Committee Party was fierce. It looked that Muslim Brotherhood-connected Congressman Keith Ellison was likely to win, but there was an internal protest from Jewish Democrats who threatened to leave the party if the anti-Semitic Ellison was elected. The majority of 447 delegates voted for Perez who received 235 votes.

Ellison received 200 votes. Only a few delegates voted for neither candidate knowing that their ideologies were unacceptable to them. After being elected, Perez named Congressman Keith Ellison, an Islamic radical, as deputy chair. Ellison had run against him with the support of the communist Senator Bernie Sanders.

Keith Ellison

Islamic radical Keith Ellison is the Deputy Chair of the Democratic National Committee.

Keith Ellison was elected to the House of Representatives in 2007 in Minnesota and reelected since that time. Ellison was the first Muslim to be elected to Congress. And, along with André Carson of Indiana, is one of two Muslims now serving in Congress. Ellison is a co-chair of the Marxist Congressional Progressive Caucus and a Chief Deputy Whip.

In November 2016, progressive groups and United States senators, including the Marxist Bernie Sanders of Vermont, supported Ellison for chair of the Democratic National Committee. On February 25, 2017, minutes after defeating him on the second ballot, newly elected Chairman Tom Perez motioned for Ellison to be elected his Deputy Chair, which was approved by a unanimous voice vote of DNC members.

Ellison has an anti-Semitism past, which he has not genuinely repudiated. More troubling is Congressman Ellison close association with the Muslim Brotherhood front organization the Council on American-Islamic Relations (CAIR) and the co-founder, Nihad Awad, who has publicly supported Islamic terrorism.

Ambassador Armando Valladares named the Democratic Party the new Muslim Marxist Party

Armando Valladares explained that the Democratic Party has become a Muslim Marxist Party.

Armando Valladares, was born on May 30, 1937, is a Cuban poet, diplomat, and human rights activist. In 1960, he was arrested by the Cuban bloody regime for denouncing Fidel Castro's rapid march to communism. Amnesty International named Valladares a prisoner of conscience.

Following his release in 1982, he wrote a book, *Against All Hope* (2001), detailing his imprisonment and torture at the hands of the Cuban government. *Against All Hope* is Armando Valladares' account of over twenty years in Fidel Castro's tropical gulag. Valladares suffered endless days of violence, putrid food, and squalid living conditions, while listening to Castro's firing squads eliminating "counter revolutionaries" in the courtyard below his cell.

Valladares survived by praying and by writing poetry. The publication of his poetry in Europe brought his case to the attention of international figures such as French President Francois Mitterrand and to human rights organizations whose constant pressure on the Castro regime finally led to his release. He was appointed by President Ronald Reagan to serve as the United States Ambassador to the United Nations Commission on Human Rights.

Ambassador Armando Valladares wrote an article titled "The New Muslim Marxist Democratic Party" which was published in English by the *Interamerican Institute for Democracy* website on April 17, 2017, and in Spanish in the website Nuevo Acción on April 4, 2017. Ambassador Valladares explained that when John F. Kennedy was elected in 1960, the Democratic Party was a party that respected the Constitution, the laws, and values that made America a great nation.

The ambassador stated the following: "Its members were patriotic and proud of their history. They valued decency, respected institutions and when the country was in danger, Americans united above parties and looked ahead together because they were identified by the Christian values upon which the United States was founded. Since the election of Bill Clinton and his wife, the Democratic Party began to disintegrate morally, perhaps contaminated by the most immoral couple that had occupied the White House. Only the name remains of that party. Values beyond freedom, totalitarian and anti-American ideologies have taken hold of it and the goal is the destruction of this Nation."

Who is Tom Perez?

Tom Perez was director of the extreme radical organization Casa de Maryland (Maryland House) for seven years. During his tenure, Perez cooperated with a large network of communist organizations. Ambassador Valladares said that Perez assisted these extreme radical groups in their work by organizing conferences and all kinds of activities offering them financial support for their subversive activities against the United States.

Ambassador Valladares stated the following: "The Casa received $1.5 million from Venezuelan dictator Hugo Chávez. It also received donations from CITGO then owned by the Venezuelan dictatorship and a member of CASA. Soros, the Hungarian who has sworn to destroy the United States, is also a donor to CASA. Other affiliates of this Maryland House led by Tom Perez are the FMLN, the Salvadoran communist guerrillas, the Communist Party of USA (CPUSA), the Maras Salvatrucha (MS-13) who offered $50,000 dollars to anyone who would murder an ICE policeman while Tom Perez was director. Another "affiliate" is ACORN, that Democratic organization that instructed illegals to commit fraud and vote in the elections. Its director, the Democrat, Bertha Lewis proposed socialism for the United States."

The former Ambassador to the United Nations Commission on Human Rights said Perez is a Marxist who led the Casa de Maryland, a communist organization. This extreme radical organization had a budget of $31 million in 2007. The Casa de Maryland supported a vast network of communist national and international organizations, all of them enemy of America and in favor of the destruction of the nation. The chart below illustrates the dozens of communist labor unions and organizations supported by the Casa de Maryland:

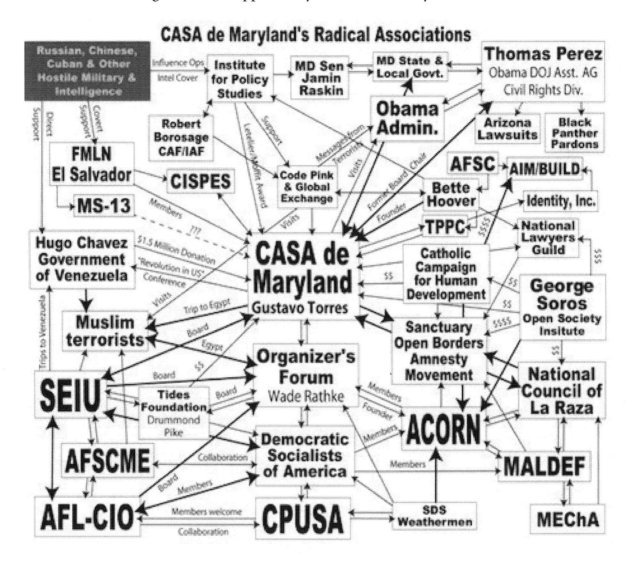

Even more dangerous, Ambassador Valladares said is that the CASA de Maryland maintains ties with the intelligence services of Cuba, China, Russia, and Iran and with some 50 other left-wing Marxist and anti-US organizations. He does not understand how it is possible for an organization such as the Casa de Maryland not to be investigated by FBI since it is a center of subversion against the national security of the United States.

Ambassador Valladares said that the terrorist organization Muslim Brotherhood belongs to the Casa de Maryland as does the Code Pink/Global Exchange, which offered $600,000 to the terrorists who fought against the U.S. Marines in Fallujah, Iraq. Two other communist groups that were founders of the Casa are the Committee of Solidarity which citizens of El Salvador

(CISPES) founded and are directed by Salvadoran communist leaders. The other one is the American Friends Service Committee (AFSC), which is communist organization that wants the unilateral disarmament of the United States

The communist organization Casa de Maryland headquarters is a building
with a 20,000 square foot that houses more than 250 employees.

Who is Congressman Keith Ellison?

Ambassador Valladares explained that the Islamic radical Congressman Keith Ellison rejects the bible and swore on the Qur'an. This Islamic holy book dictates the life and customs of Muslims. For example, it supports the death penalty for homosexuals who sometimes are thrown from the top of buildings, beating women to discipline them, etc. As a Muslim, Ellison believes in the Shariah Law and stated that he does not respect or believe in the American Constitution because its wording was inspired by the bible.

The ambassador pointed out that Ellison belonged to the Nation of Islam and that he helped Louis Farrakhan, organize the 1995 Million Man March (Obama and his preacher, Jeremiah Wright, also worked closely with Farrakhan and both participated in the March). Ellison was linked to terrorist groups such as the Muslim Brotherhood. Anti-Jewish at its best, one of his most controversial accusations was to blame President George W. Bush of having ordered the downing of the Twin Towers in conspiracy with the Jews. In 2007, Ellison compared President Bush to Hitler.

Ambassador Valladares wrote that for many years Ellison organized fundraisings for the terrorist Sara Jane Olson, member of the communist movement Symbiotic Liberation Army. This was the communist group which kidnapped Patricia Hearst. Sara Jean Olson was arrested in 1999 on charges of bombing two police cars. Ellison defended this communist terrorist and in a statement to Pioneer Press, Ellison stated that the arrest of Olson was for political reasons and, that her beliefs were the same of his. Thus, Ellison declared himself a supporter of communist terrorist.

Joanne Chesimard, also known as Assata Shakur, a murderer wanted by the FBI escaped to Cuba and was given sanctuary in by the bloody communist regime.

Ellison defended Joanne Chesimard, also known as Assata Shakur, who murdered a police officer and is currently fighting for the extradition in Cuba, the ambassador said. The defense of terrorists has been a constant of this Deputy Chair of the Democratic National Committee.

The ambassador denounced the two individuals chosen to lead the Democratic Party at the Democratic Party National Committee. He explained that both of them are enemies of the United States, whose goal throughout their lives has been to destroy the free market economy of America and Christian society and turn it into a Marxist nation.

Ambassador Valladares stated the following: "The two leaders of the Democratic National Committee are racist, anti-Semitic, despicable candidates, who ignore the Constitution and history of America. Both of them have been and are allies of all the terrorist movements in the world, with whom they have shared the hatred for the United States and its laws. They complement each other in their frustrations and hatred of the bible, lovers of foreign doctrines, and of all the subversive movements they have wished to sweep away with this American society… Debauchery, ideological mob, terrorists, communists, radical Muslims and all the scum of the country whose goal is to destroy it, joined the ranks of the Party, with the complicit silence of the leaders and they took possession of it. The result of this entire plan was seen in this last election to elect those who will lead the New Democratic-Marxist-Muslim Party."

The Democratic Party wants single-payer socialist health care system

Many Democrats in Congress have endorsed the single-payer health bill proposed by the communist Senator Bernie Sanders on September 13, 2017. Among the radical supporters of this socialist health care system are several Democratic senators considering running for president in 2020: Elizabeth Warren of Massachusetts, Corey Booker of New Jersey, Kirsten Gillibrand of New York, and Kamela Harris of California. In the House of Representatives, 117 radical Democrats are co-sponsoring a bill by radical leftist Congressman John Conyers of Michigan that would provide individuals of all ages free Medicare.

Sanders is also sponsoring the College for All Act which also is being supported by Warren, Harris, Gillibrand and other radicals. Dylan Matthews wrote in Vox the following: "Over time, some issues become so widely accepted within the party as to be a de facto requirement for anyone aspiring to lead it…And the way things are going, soon no Democratic leader will be able to oppose single payer." Very soon, the Communist Party USA could merge into the increasing extreme radical Democratic Party!

Never mind that the cost of a single-payer system will be astronomical and the fact that socialize medicine has not work in other nations, Never mind that free college for all cannot be afforded and will increase the federal debt to the sky. Democrats in Congress continue to turn their party into a Marxist one with the support of the globalist elite of the New World Order. Increased centralization of the already centralized federal government is the globalist objective since they exercise a great control the government. Perhaps, the death panels would come back as the costs of socialized medicine will so great that the sick elderly would not be treated sent home to die. Rationing care for the rest will be in effect.

On September 18, 2018, White House Press Secretary Sarah Huckabee Sanders said, "I think the president, as well as the majority of the country, knows that the single-payer system that the Democrats are proposing is a horrible idea. Previously, President Trump tweeted on September 14, 2017, "Bernie Sanders is pushing hard for a single payer health care plan, a curse on the U.S. and its people." However, millions of millennials and others voted for the communist Sanders in the Democratic primaries. They loved all the free things that Sanders promised: free college, free health care, and so forth.

Who is Marxist Senator Bernie Sanders?

Marxist Senator Bernie Sanders is an Independent from Vermont
who ran for president in 2016 on the Democratic Party.

Senator Bernie Sanders in spite of his communist background surged around the country drew misinformed crowds that were the envy of other candidates during the 2016 presidential campaign. Senator Sander's presidential campaign attracted thousands young volunteers who were taught that socialism was better that a market-based capitalism in schools and colleges. The campaign by Sanders was a great success for a Vermont senator with Marxist political roots, no experience in national politics and little establishment backing.

On April 30, 2015, socialist-Marxist Senator Bernie Sanders announced he was running for president. Senator Sanders in an address on the Capitol lawn, stated, "I don't believe that the men and women who defended American democracy fought to create a situation where billionaires own the political process." Radical leftist Senator Elizabeth Warren, Democrat from Massachusetts, a darling of socialist democrats, praised Sanders for entering the presidential race.

Senator Sanders told the *Associated Press* on April 29, 2015 that he would propose "very specific proposals" to increase taxes on the wealthy and corporations and offer tuition-free higher education at public universities. He also stated his support for more effective regulation of Wall Street and opposition to free trade agreements and the Keystone XL pipeline. Sanders said he would work to reverse the growing income inequality.

The communist senator from Vermont stated the following: "What we have seen is that while the average person is working longer hours for lower wages, we have seen a huge increase in income and wealth inequality, which is now reaching obscene levels. This is a rigged economy, which works for the rich and the powerful, and is not working for ordinary Americans … You know, this country just does not belong to a handful of billionaires."

Sanders wants a political revolution and shakeup of the United States

Presidential candidate Senator Bernie Sanders said he hopes to lead a "political revolution" for working families and against money in politics in his bid for the White House. In a May 3, 2015 interview with *ABC*'s This Week, George Stephanopoulos, Senator Sanders stated the following: "I think I'm the only candidate who's prepared to take on the billionaire class. We need a political revolution in this country involving millions of people who are prepared to stand up and say, enough is enough, and I want to help lead that effort."

When asked whether the United States was ready to elect an avowed socialist, Sanders said: "Well, so long as we know what democratic socialism is. And if we know that in countries, in Scandinavia, like Denmark, Norway, Sweden, they are very democratic countries, obviously. The voter turnout is a lot higher than it is in the United States. In those countries, healthcare is a right of all the people. And in those countries, college education, graduate school is free. In those countries, retirement benefits, childcare are stronger than United States of America. And in those countries, by and large, government works for ordinary people and the middle class, rather than, as in the case right now in our country, for the billionaire class."

What Sanders did not explain was that in those countries the people are taxed over 50% of their income. Do Americans want to have that extremely federal high tax rate? Do Americans want to elect another Marxist to the White House?

The ideology of Bernie Sanders

Bernie Sanders was born on September 8, 1941 in Brooklyn, New York, the son of Dorothy and Eli Sanders. In 1971, Sanders became a candidate for the Senate for the radical anti-Vietnam war Liberty Union Party and receive 2% of the vote. He ran as a candidate for the Liberty Union three more times, earning 6% of the vote before finally giving up. He included in his platform the nationalization of all United States banks, public ownership of all utilities, and the establishment of a worker-controlled government. He declared himself to be a socialist.

After several unsuccessful runs for senator, Sanders was elected mayor of Burlington, Vermont's largest city, in 1981 with the majority of 10 votes. He was re-elected to three more two-year terms as mayor. Mayor Sanders hung a Soviet flag in his office in Burlington, in honor of the city's Soviet sister city, Yaroslavl. In 1985, Mayor Sanders celebrated the sixth anniversary of the Sandinista victory in Managua, Nicaragua with the communist dictator Daniel Ortega.

In 1990, Sanders was elected to Congress, as a socialist, on the third party ticket. At the time, Bernie Sanders was a member of leftist Jesse Jackson's National Rainbow Coalition. He served in Congress for 16 years before being elected to the Senate in 2006. Six years later he was re-elected to the Senate.

As an independent politician since 1979, Sanders is associated with the Vermont Progressive Party and he was a member of Liberty Union party from 1971 to 1979. Although Sanders runs for office as an independent, he caucuses with the Democratic Party and is counted as a Democrat for purposes of committee assignments.

When he arriving Congress in 1991, Sanders co-founded the extreme radical Congressional Progressive Caucus, and served as chairman during its first eight years. At the beginning the website of the Congressional Progressive Caucus played the song of the Communist International song. Later it was removed to hide from the public the Marxist ideology of its members.

Senator Barack Obama campaigned for Sanders in Vermont when he ran for the Senate since both of them shared the same Marxist ideology.

Sanders communist and socialist connections

Trevor Loudon in his book *The Enemies Within: Communist, Socialist and Progressive in the United States Congress* (2013) pointed out Bernie Sanders communist and socialist connections. Trevor Loudon wrote that Sanders received the support of journalist I.F. Stone in 1988, a former secret Communist Party USA member and a Soviet agent in a letter endorsing Sanders's congressional campaign. Stone wrote the following: "Sanders is and on apologetics socialist... He has travel to Nicaragua to speak out against Reagan administration's war and to establish a sister city relationship between Burlington and Managua, Nicaragua. More recently, he went to the Soviet Union to set up a sister city program with Yaroslavl. While socialism has a long and proud history America, extending back to the utopian experiments of the early 1800s, it has been a long time since we've had a socialist voice in Congress."

Loudon explained that Sanders participated in the 1989 U.S. Peace Council national conference together with many communists who were followers of the agenda set by the Communist Party USA and the Soviet-controlled World Peace Council. Communist Mike Bayer supported strongly Sanders's campaign for the Senate. Bernie Sanders has been a close ally of the Democratic Socialists of America (DSA) and has been a regular speaker at their conferences and the organization is a major fundraising for his campaigns.

Loudon wrote that Sanders has also been supported by the radical Council for a Livable World. The Council website explaining 2012 when it endorse Sanders for reelection to the Senate the following: "Bernie, as is universally known, as the perfect record on the Council for a Livable World's voting scorecard on key national security issues... He opposed authorization for war in Iraq went in the House and supported measures in both the Senate and the House to withdraw troop... He enthusiastically endorsed the New STAR treaty and will post all Republican attempts to cripple the agreement... He is committed to the elimination of weapons of mass destruction, opposes preemptive wars and works hard on these issues."

Basically this radical Council is praising Sanders for weakening our national defense, as President Barack Obama has been doing since became president. Both Sanders and Obama have made the United States a weaker superpower and endangered our national security.

Bernie Sanders has been a part of the socialist movement since his college days. Loudon pointed out that Sanders joined the Young People's Socialist League, the youth wing of the Socialist party USA during the time he was a student at the University of Chicago., The Congress of Racial Equality and the Student Peace Union. He also worked for the communist-led United Packing House Workers Union.

Bernie Sanders is a communist.

Paul Sperry, a visiting Hoover Institution media fellow and author of many books, wrote an article titled "Don't be Fooled by Bernie Sanders- he's a Diehard Communist" which was published in the *New York Post* on January 16, 2016.

Sperry explained that as the self-described socialist Senator Bernie Sanders looks more like a serious contender for the nomination for president of the Democratic Party, the liberal media elite have suddenly stopped calling him socialist. He is now cleaned up as a "progressive" or "pragmatist." However, Sanders is not even a socialist. He is a communist. In order to mainstreaming Sanders requires whitewashing his radical pro-communist past. It will not be easy to do. If Senator Sanders were nominated for a Cabinet post, he would never pass an FBI background check. There would be too many subversive red flags popping up in his file. Sanders was a communist collaborator during the height of the Cold War.

We need to remember that there was another Marxist who would not pass an FBI or CIA background check. His name is Barack Hussein Obama. And he ended in the White House being the boss of the FBI and the CIA!

Rewind to 1964

Sperry pointed out that while Sanders was attending the University of Chicago, he joined the Young People's Socialist League, the youth wing of the Socialist Party USA. He also organized for a communist front, the United Packinghouse Workers Union, which at the time was under investigation by the House Committee on Un-American Activities. After graduating with a with a bachelor of arts in political science in 1964, Sanders moved to Vermont, where he headed the American People's History Society, an organ for Marxist propaganda.

Sperry explained that Sanders produced a glowing documentary on the life of socialist revolutionary Eugene Debs, who was jailed for espionage during the Red Scare and hailed by the Bolsheviks as "America's greatest Marxist." This subversive Marxist hero of Sanders, was denounced even by liberal Democrats as a "traitor," attacked "the barons of Wall Street" and hailed the "triumphant" Bolshevik revolution in Russia.

Eugene Victor "Gene" Debs (November 5, 1855 – October 20, 1926) was an American union leader, one of the founding members of the Industrial Workers of the World (IWW or the Wobblies). He ran five times for president as the candidate of the Socialist Party of America. Through his presidential candidacies, as well as his work with labor movements, Debs eventually became one of the best-known socialist living in the United States. Debs was convicted under the Espionage Act of 1917 and sentenced to a term of 10 years. Republican President Warren G. Harding commuted his sentence in December 1921.

Eugene Debs stated the following: "Those Russian comrades of ours have made greater sacrifices, have suffered more, and have shed more heroic blood than any like number of men and women anywhere on Earth. They have laid the foundation of the first real democracy that ever drew the breath of life in this world." In a 1918 speech in Canton, Ohio, Debs reaffirmed his solidarity with Vladimir Lenin and Leon Trotsky, despite clear evidence of their destruction of Russia and the tens of thousands of people they killed.

Young people are excited by the presidential campaign of Bernie Sanders.
Senator Sanders still hangs a portrait of Eugene Debs on the wall in his Senate office.

Sperry said that in the early 1970s, Bernie Sanders helped found the Liberty Union Party, which called for the nationalization of all U.S. banks and the public takeover of all private utility companies. After failed runs for Congress, Sanders in 1981 managed to get elected mayor of Burlington, Vermont, where he restricted property rights for landlords, set price controls and raised property taxes to pay for communal land trusts. Local small businesses distributed fliers complaining their new mayor "does not believe in free enterprise." Sanders took several "goodwill" trips not only to the Union of Soviet Socialist Republics (USSR), but also to Cuba and Nicaragua, where the Soviets were trying to expand their influence in the Western Hemisphere. In 1985, Sanders traveled to Managua, Nicaragua to celebrate the rise to power of the Marxist-Leninist Sandinista government. He called it a "heroic revolution." Undermining anti-communist U.S. policy, Sanders denounced the Reagan administration's backing of the Contra rebels in a letter to the Sandinistas.

Sperry wrote that Sanders lobbied the White House to stop the assistance to the anti-communists Contras and even tried to broker a peace deal. He adopted Managua as a sister city and invited Sandinista leader Daniel Ortega to visit the United States. He exalted Ortega as "an impressive guy," while attacking President Reagan. Sanders stated in 1985 that "The Sandinista government has more support among the Nicaraguan people — substantially more support — than Ronald Reagan has among the American people." Bernie Sanders also adopted a Soviet sister city outside Moscow and honeymooned with his second wife in the USSR. He put up a Soviet flag in his office, shocking even the Birkenstock-wearing local liberals. At the time, the Soviet Union was on the march around the world, and threatening the U.S. with nuclear annihilation.

Communist Sanders will definitely implement real change and, if elected president, he will continue Obama's rapid road to radically change our beloved country into a communist society.

Sperry said that in 1989 as the West was on the verge of winning the Cold War, Sanders addressed the national conference of the U.S. Peace Council — a known front for the Communist Party USA, whose members swore an oath not only to the Soviet Union but to "the triumph of Soviet power in the U.S." Currently, Sanders wants to bring what he admired in the USSR, Cuba, Nicaragua and other communist states to America. As it has been explained earlier, Sanders proposed to completely nationalizing our health care system and putting private health insurance and drug companies "out of business." He also wants to break up "big banks" and control the energy industry, while providing "free" college tuition, a "living wage" and guaranteed homeownership and jobs through massive public works projects. Price tag: $18 trillion.

Sperry stated the following: "Who will pay for it all? You will. Sanders plans to not only soak the rich with a 90 percent-plus tax rate, while charging Wall Street a "speculation tax," but hit every American with a "global-warming tax." Of course, even that wouldn't cover the cost of his communist schemes; a President Sanders would eventually soak the middle class he claims to champion. From each according to his ability, to each according to his need, right? Former mayoral advisers from Burlington defend their old boss. They note that Sanders was never a member of the Communist Party and deny he was even a small-c communist, even while acknowledging he named their city softball squad the People's Republic of Burlington and the town's minor league baseball team the Vermont Reds."

The Comrade from Vermont, Bernie Sanders, named his city softball squad the "People's Republic of Burlington" and the town's minor league baseball team, the "Vermont Reds."

Sperry concluded his article by stating the following: "What about those communist sister cities he adopted? Sanders and his Sandinistas are all still pining for what Debs called the Greater Revolution yet to come. What's revolting is how this hardcore commie's campaign has gotten this far. With his ascendancy in both Iowa and New Hampshire, Sanders is no longer just a fool; he's now a dangerous fool. While it may be hard to hate the old codger, it's easy — and virtuous — to hate his un-American ideas. They should be swept into the dustbin with the rest of communist history."

Sanders wants to provide free college tuition, single-payer socialist health care, Medicare for all, increased benefits for Social Security, increased infrastructure spending, create free leave paid for workers, bolster private pension funds, one million government jobs for youth

Senator Sanders announced two new bills — the "College for All Act" and its companion, "The Inclusive Prosperity Act of 2015 — that would eliminate undergraduate tuition at all public colleges and universities. This sounds great until one sees the astronomical cost of this idea. It is estimated that such a plan would cost taxpayers more than $70 billion a year and more $750 billion over the next decade. College tuition rises every year in double digits.

Laura Meckler wrote an article entitled "Price Tag of Bernie Sanders's Proposals: $18 Trillion" which was published in The *Wall Street Journal* on September 15, 2015. She explained that Senator Bernie Sanders is proposing many new federal government programs to fight poverty and income inequality that amount to at least $18 trillion in new spending over a decade. His proposals would amount to the largest peacetime expansion of government in modern America. According to a study by The *Wall Street Journal*, the immense cost of his plans alarms conservatives as well as many Democrats.

Meckler explained that the socialist agenda of Senator Sanders includes an estimated $15 trillion for a government-run health-care program that covers every American, plus large sums to rebuild roads and bridges, expand Social Security and make tuition free at public colleges. To pay for it, Sanders has so far detailed tax increases that could bring in as much as $6.5 trillion over 10 years, according to his staff. His "single-payer" proposed health plan, now in Congress, would be funded in part through a new payroll tax on employers and workers. Warren Gunnels, his policy director, stated that the programs would address an array of problems. Gunnels stated "Sen. Sanders's agenda does cost money, if you look at the problems that are out there, it's very reasonable."

Meckler pointed out that Sanders calls himself a democratic socialist. He has long stood to the left of the Democratic Party. Meckler wrote that Sanders' proposed program would increase the total federal spending by about one-third—to a projected $18 trillion or so over 10 years. For many years, government spending has equaled about 20% of gross domestic product annually; Sanders' proposals would increase that to about 30% in their first year. As a share of the economy, that would represent a bigger increase in government spending than the New Deal or Great Society and is surpassed in modern history only by the World War II military buildup.

This writer is convinced that such proposals are irresponsible and are pure Marxist populism. Sanders' plans promises are very similar to those made by Chavistas in Venezuela, the communist Podemos Party in Spain, and other Marxist political parties around the world. One has to look at the massive poverty in Cuba, Venezuela, North Korea and the countries in Europe that implemented generous social benefits that were economic unsustainable and now are almost bankrupt with very high unemployment.

Meckler explained that Sanders most expensive proposal is his plan to extend Medicare to all Americans. He is proposing a $1 trillion to repair roads, bridges and airports. He wants programs would provide youth jobs and prevent cuts to private pension plans. Sanders would raise an additional $1.2 trillion in Social Security taxes in order to increase benefits and pay those already promised for 50 years. Sanders said that he also would propose an expansion of federal support for child care and preschool, though he hasn't said how much those programs would cost, and they aren't included in this total.

Conclusion

Many economists say higher government spending would hurt long-term economic growth and the proposals by Sanders would stunt it altogether. They believe that the tax increases required to pay for the Sanders program would be "massively catastrophic" and destroy the free enterprise system. This writer believes that one thing is certain. And that is that the federal debt would continue to increase dramatically should another Marxist, such as Sanders and Warren, would be elected president. Such a Marxist president would raise taxes enormously to pay for his free tuition and other parts of his plans and severely damage the economy.

It is a sign of the times we are living in that a self-declared socialist-Marxist Bernie Sanders did so well in the Democratic Party primary elections and at the polls. Many young people who have graduated or are still in college have been influenced or brainwashed by socialist or Marxist secondary teachers and college professors. A poll taken by students recently the majority found the word "socialism" positive and "capitalism" negative.

If a Democratic Party Marxist were to be elected president or if his/her agenda were to be implemented in the nation, the United States would be bankrupt very soon. How can a nation with more than $20 trillion federal debt, as well as the unfunded federal mandates, the debt of the 50 states and territories and the counties and the cities, that brings the real debt of the United States to approximately $150 trillion adopt Sanders' proposed programs that would increase the total federal spending by about one-third—to a projected $18 trillion or so over 10 years? Sanders and other radicals in the Democratic Party will try hard to radically restructure our beloved country into a communist society.

It is very revolting to this writer, who was imprisoned in Cuba during two terrible years for trying to overthrow the communist regime in Cuba at the Bay of Pigs in 1961, to see how the once center left Democratic Party has become a Muslim Marxist Party. It is absolute madness!

It is very sad and dangerous that the once center left Democratic Party was radicalized tremendously by Obama and has turned into a Muslim Marxist Party. It is politicians, such as the Marxist Senators Elizabeth Warren of Massachusetts and Bernie Sanders of Vermont, who have gained influence over Democratic Party. There are millions of Democrats who are unaware of the extreme radical ideology of their leaders. The mainstream media has done an excellent job in concealing how radicalized the Democratic Party has become and the mainstream media has covered up the backgrounds of their leaders. Hopefully, patriotic members of the Democratic Party will wake up and rescue their party before it is too late or abandon it if it cannot be changed.

The election of Donald J. Trump was the victory of a battle but the war continuous. The Trump administration needs to identify the massive numbers of communist and Islamic radicals of the Deep State which are embedded in the federal government and fire them and indict and prosecute those who have committed crimes. It also needs to investigate George Soros and the many other foundations and organizations that are paying criminals to engage in violence. If Obama is involved, then he needs to be prosecuted.

The FBI needs to investigate the Casa of Maryland, other communist organizations, and the many Muslim Brotherhood fronts in America and issue indictments. America does not need to tolerate subversion and Fifth columnists in its mist. As this writer has stated, President Trump needs to quickly drain the swamp or these subversive elements in the swamp will defeat him as he is trying to make America Safe and Great again. President Trump needs to go on offense, not defense in order to survive and save America from communism and Islamic radicalism.

Chapter 27

The response of the United States to the attacks on its diplomats

In this picture Obama and his family attended a baseball game in Havana with the bloody tyrant Raúl Castro and other high-ranking communists while never complaining of the beatings and arrests made on peaceful opponents of the brutal regime before, during, and after his visit.

President Barack Obama's failed and disastrous Cuban policy was instigated by globalists belonging to the Council on Foreign Relations, Trilateral Commission, and the Bilderberg Group. Obama gave the mass murdering regime in Cuba a series of shameful unilateral concession with no "Quid Pro Quo" or something in return. The U.S. embassy in Havana, Cuba was reopened in the summer of 2015 as part of former President Obama's shameful détente with the Cuban bloody regime. In spite of all these concessions given to the Cuban communist regime by Obama, in the summer or the fall of 2016 the regime tolerated or participated in deliberate sonic and ultrasonic attacks on American and Canadian diplomats and their families in Havana which caused hearing, cognitive, visual, balance, sleep, and other health problems. Obama covered up the severe injuries inflicted to Americans in Havana in order to protect his "legacy" of normalizing relations with the oppressive regime.

These outrageous attacks happened inside the homes provided by the regime to diplomats and at multiple hotels in Havana. These sonic attacks may have also happened inside the embassy itself. The Department of State under Secretary Rex Tillerson has not reported these injuries on a timely manner. Why the delay in informing the America people of the diabolical incidents against American and Canadian diplomats in Cuba?

General John Kelly was appointed Secretary of Homeland Security on January 20, 2017, by President Trump. On July 28, 2017, he was appointed to replace Reince Priebus as White House Chief of Staff, taking office on July 31, 2017.

On October 12, 2017, White House Chief of Staff General John Kelly said that "We believe that the Cuban government could stop the attacks on our diplomats." On October 16, 2017, President Trump stated at the White House, "I do believe Cuba is resposible." If that is correct why not break diplomatic relations with such a terrorist bloody regime?

The United States responded to the injuries sustained by its diplomats in Havana

On October 3, 2017, the United States ordered the expulsion of 15 Cuban diplomats within seven days from Washington, D.C. The United States announced the withdrawal of 60% of the approximately 50 embassy staff in Havana. Washington warned American travelers not to visit the island, and stop the processing of visas for Cuban travelers to the United States indefinitely. Later, the U.S embassy in Havana said that it would resume issuing unification family visas.

On September 29, 2017, President Donald Trump expressed outrage at the injuries of diplomats at the U.S. embassy. The president said that in Cuba "they did some very bad things" that hurt American diplomats, but he did not state who he might meant by "they."

Secretary of State Rex Tillerson's expulsion of the Cuban diplomats was praised by Republican Senator Marco Rubio from Florida who had previously criticized the State Department's earlier response to the incidents.

"No one should be fooled by the Castro regime's claim it knows nothing about how these harmful attacks are occurring or who perpetrated them," Senator Rubio said. He believes that Cuban dictator Raul Castro's regime is hiding information that might explain mysterious attacks on American officials in Havana. Senator Rubio had previously said the following: "All nations have an obligation to ensure the protection of diplomatic representatives in their countries. Cuba is failing miserably and proving how misguided and dangerous the Obama administration's decisions were."

Senator Marco Rubio calls for oversight hearing into the State Department's response to the attacks and the victims' complaints

On October 10, 2017, Susan Crabtree wrote an article titled "State Department Mum on Timeline of Attacks on Diplomats in Cuba" which was published in the *Washington Free Beacon* website. The reporter said that the "State Department has repeatedly declined to provide a specific timeline of when officials first became aware of mysterious attacks on U.S. diplomats in Cuba—even after a new accusation from a victim that U.S. officials ignored his complaints."

Republican Senator Marco Rubio from Florida said that he will hold an oversight hearing into the State Department's response to the attacks and the victims' complaints. A *CBS News* report quoting an anonymous victim of the attack who charged senior embassy leadership and top State Department officials with having "ignored for months complaints by U.S. diplomats who were suffering from memory loss and other ailments related to the attacks."

Crabtree pointed out that the *CBS News* report is "fueling new questions on when the attacks began and who at the State Department allegedly ignored them and whether the Obama administration was trying to downplay or suppress public knowledge about the attacks in order to protect the administration's historic diplomatic and commercial thaw with Cuba."

Crabtree stated the following: "The State Department has said the attacks began late in 2016 when the Obama administration was still running the agency, but it so far has refused to indicate whether the initial complaints occurred during the Obama or Trump administration and which officials knew about the initial complaints and how much they knew. Several sources have told the *Free Beacon* that the initial complaints about the attacks from U.S. diplomats in Havana occurred months earlier in the summer of 2016. A State Department spokesperson last week declined to provide a hard timeline about when the first complaints occurred. The spokesperson did not respond to follow-up questions about the timeline."

The Department of State spokesperson told the *Washington Free Beacon* in an emailed statement the following: "We became aware of the incidents over a period of several months, stretching from the end of 2016 and into this year. The incidents appear to have occurred sporadically, with long lulls in between. It took time for those who experienced an incident to report it. It took time to realize that the experience had potentially impacted their health and then to verify that. It took further time yet to realize that multiple people had experienced things that might be connected. Once we realized that there was a pattern to the incidents and their impact on the health of our personnel, we began an aggressive investigation."

Crabtree explained that critics of the State Department's handling of the attacks say the response provides little clarity on the actual timeline. Those that fault the State Department "suspect because any strange diplomatic experience, not to mention one that impacted diplomats' health, in Havana would have immediately set off alarm bells throughout the State Department." Foreign policy experts and former State Department officials say that the State Department "must be more forthcoming about exactly when complaints first surfaced about the health issues in Cuba and how the U.S. government responded."

José Cárdenas, a former State Department official during the George W. Bush administration who now consults on Latin America issues, stated the following: "The American people have every right to understand everything that happened to our diplomats serving abroad. We need an explicit timeline of when the State Department first learned of these reports of the health attacks. We need to know who knew and when they knew it because there's going to be a lot of suspicion that perhaps information was covered up in order to protect President Obama's normalization process."

On September 29, 2017, Nora Gámez Torres wrote an article titled "U.S. suspends all visas for Cubans, withdraws most staff from embassy in Havana" which was published by the *Miami Herald*. The reporter said that "Cuban Americans trying to have their relatives join them from the island will not be able to do so — at least for the time being." She added that "It is not known how long the suspension of the visa reunification program will last." As it was stated earlier, the visa reunification program will continue but the exact date has not been announced.

Secretary of State Rex W. Tillerson has delayed reporting on the acoustic attacks against American diplomats in Havana and no timeline of the attacks have been given.
Was there a cover up by the Department of State?

Secretary of State Rex W. Tillerson said that in the fall of 2016 American diplomats had been attacked with covert sonar weapons. U.S. diplomats began suffering unexplained loss of hearing and memory problems. Two Cuban diplomats were expelled from Washington, D.C. in May 2017, yet the news of their expulsion and the illnesses of U.S. diplomats suffered in the fall of 2016 were not revealed until August 2017, months after it had occurred. Why were these events not reported earlier? On August 11, 2017, Secretary of State Rex W. Tillerson said the illnesses were a result of "health attacks," and added, "We've not been able to determine who's to blame."

Gámez Torres explained that the Department of State has issued a new alert warning Americans not to travel to the island because of the attacks. This writer believes that if it is dangerous for American citizens and permanent residents to visit the island, America needs to stop all travel to Cuba.

The Seal of the Department of State

On September 29, 2017, Secretary of State Rex Tillerson made the following statements regarding U.S. government personnel in Cuba: "Over the past several months, 21 U.S. Embassy employees have suffered a variety of injuries from attacks of an unknown nature (now the number has been raised to 22). The affected individuals have exhibited a range of physical symptoms, including ear complaints, hearing loss, dizziness, headache, fatigue, cognitive issues, and difficulty sleeping. Investigators have been unable to determine who is responsible or what is causing these attacks."

"On September 29, the Department ordered the departure of non-emergency personnel assigned to the U.S. Embassy in Havana, as well as all family members. Until the Government of Cuba can ensure the safety of our diplomats in Cuba, our Embassy will be reduced to emergency personnel in order to minimize the number of diplomats at risk of exposure to harm."

"In conjunction with the ordered departure of our diplomatic personnel, the Department has issued a Travel Warning advising U.S. citizens to avoid travel to Cuba and informing them of our decision to draw down our diplomatic staff. We have no reports that private U.S. citizens have been affected, but the attacks are known to have occurred in U.S. diplomatic residences and hotels frequented by U.S. citizens. The Department does not have definitive answers on the cause or source of the attacks and is unable to recommend a means to mitigate exposure."

"The decision to reduce our diplomatic presence in Havana was made to ensure the safety of our personnel. We maintain diplomatic relations with Cuba, and our work in Cuba continues to be guided by the national security and foreign policy interests of the United States."

"Cuba has told us it will continue to investigate these attacks and we will continue to cooperate with them in this effort. The health, safety, and well-being of our Embassy community is our greatest concern. We will continue to aggressively investigate these attacks until the matter is resolved."

But why has the Department of States waited so long to take this measure to protect American diplomats and their families? If diplomats were attacked in their homes as well as in Cuban hotels, why is the Department of State not informing Americans regarding the wives and children of the diplomats who may also have been severely injured? How would Americans react at the news of an American diplomat's child with a brain injury? Will Americans demand a complete break in diplomatic relations with the mass murdering bloody regime in Havana? Is this another cover up?

Hotel Capri in Havana, which is located steps from the famous Havana's Malecon, was one of the two hotels where American diplomats were injured by a sonic or ultrasonic device attack. The other one was Hotel Nacional.

Why are Americans not being informed of the names of the other hotels where sonic or ultrasonic attacks took place against Americans? American tourists may be staying or stayed in the hotels that are being or were subjected to acoustic attacks.

The famous Hotel Nacional has been added to the list of hotels where the American officials have said Americans should not stay due to previous sonic or ultrasonic attacks.

Gámez Torres pointed out that "the State Department announced the suspension of visas for Cubans without having finalized the details on how the U.S. embassy in Havana will handle this situation." The reporter said that another official said "that perhaps Cubans could apply for visas in third countries without explaining how the procedure would work."

Senator Rubio wants the United States to expel Cuban diplomats from Washington

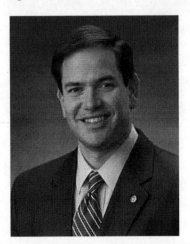

|Republican Senator Marco Rubio from Florida

Republican Florida Senator Marco Rubio criticized the administration for not going further. "Shameful that the State Department withdraws most staff from the U.S. Embassy in Cuba but [Raúl] Castro can keep as many as he wants in U.S.," the Florida senator tweeted.

On September 29, 2017, Susan Crabtree wrote an article titled "Rubio Renews Call for Trump Administration to Expel Cubans from the U.S." which was published in the website of the

Washington Free Beacon. The reporter said that Senator Marco Rubio is calling on the Trump administration to expel Cuban diplomats from the United States. On September 29, 2017, the Republican Florida Senator Marco Rubio questioned the logic of continuing to allow Cuban diplomats to stay in the United States but reducing the staff at the U.S. embassy in Havana to emergency-only staff. Senator Rubio tweeted for the second time, "So Castro regime allows attacks on Americans forcing us to drawdown to keep them safe but he gets to keep about the same # of people here?"

Crabtree said that the measure effectively reverses many aspects of President Barack Obama's policy of normalizing relations with Cuba, but Secretary Tillerson "tried to downplay the decision's impact on diplomatic and commercial ties between the two countries." An American official earlier told reporters that "for the foreseeable future, any bilateral meetings between U.S. and Cuban officials would take place on American soil, not Cuban."

Susan Crabtree stated the following: "Speculation in the foreign-policy community has focused on the possibility of Russia or another third party as the likely perpetrators but Cuba experts say the Castro regime monitors Americans so closely on the island that it's impossible they would not know about or have some complicity with such activity. The fact that some of the attacks targeted at least one U.S. diplomat staying in a hotel and happened as recently as August led to the State Department's decision to issue the travel warning to all Americans." The U.S. official said, "The fact that some of these attacks have occurred at hotels where American citizens could be at, and we have no way of advising American citizens how we can mitigate these attacks, we felt we must warn them not to travel to Cuba."

Crabtree pointed out that while U.S. officials said Cuba is still cooperating with the investigation, they stressed that "the probe has produced little usable information that could help protect Americans staying there." The government official said, "We don't know the means or the methods or how these attacks are being carried out," noting that it appears that U.S. embassy personnel are most at risk. "But we cannot rule out given the nature of these attacks that the American public traveling to Cuba might be at risk as well," the official added.

Crabtree concluded her article by stating the following: "Washington's foreign-policy community was bracing for the move. Two sources familiar with the State Department's deliberations told the *Washington Free Beacon* over the last two days that State was putting the final touches on a new sanctions package that would go beyond reducing staffs at both embassies and that an announcement could come early. One source said the State Department had to overcome strong bureaucratic resistance among supporters of Obama's rapprochement to take the dramatic step of reducing staff at the U.S. embassy in Havana to emergency personnel only."

Cuban communist official Josefina Vidal, who is the Director General for the U.S. Affairs Division in the Ministry of Foreign Affairs, told the Cuban press that "We consider that the decision announced by the State Department is hasty and will affect bilateral relations, in particular, cooperation on issues of mutual interest and exchanges of a different nature between the two countries." She added that Cuba wants "to continue an active cooperation between the authorities of the two countries, for the full clarification of these facts, for which a more efficient US involvement will be essential."

Josefina Vidal has been Director General for the U.S. Affairs Division in the Ministry of Foreign Affairs since 2013. In August 2017, it was reported that Vidal had travelled to Moscow in late July for talks with Russian Deputy Foreign Minister Sergei Ryabkov and the Cuban Ambassador in Moscow Emilio Lozada Garcia. Why did Vidal travel to Moscow? Did Cuba allow the Russians to attack American diplomats? Is Cuba asking for Moscow's help to deal with this crisis?

Cuban-American Congressman Carlos Curbelo from South Florida said he wants the government to do more "to hold the Cuban dictatorship accountable" but added that "changes in visa policies should focus on denying entry to the United States to Cuban government officials and those who through their actions buttress the dictatorship — not everyday Cubans attempting to visit their families."

There are 21 confirmed cases of affected persons, not 25 as originally reported, said Gámez Torres, and she stated the following: "Another State Department source said that the attacks did not occur at the U.S. embassy. American authorities believe the attacks occurred at diplomats' homes — all leased from Cuban government — and in the Hotel Capri in Havana. In the press conference Friday, the high-ranking State Department official said he was unaware of any attack on U.S citizens who were not diplomatic staff. But the significance of the attacks and the fact that they occurred in at least one hotel prompted the government to issue the travel alert to protect Americans. Diplomatic personnel who suffered attacks at hotels were temporary staff at the embassy, he said."

This writer thinks that if American diplomats were attacked and injured in their homes, family members also are also likely to have been injured. "Not been aware," as the American official said, is not acceptable!

Cuban Foreign Minister Bruno Rodriguez met recently with Secretary Tillerson in Washington.

Cuban regime Foreign Minister Bruno Rodriguez in a speech at the United Nations once again denied any Cuban responsibility and said that the Cuban government complies with its obligations to protect all diplomats on the island. Cuba has a very long history of harassing and subjecting to oppressive surveillance American diplomats in Havana.

Secretary Tillerson and Cuban Foreign Minister Bruno Rodríguez met recently in Washington, D.C. According to a State Department statement, Secretary Tillerson "conveyed the seriousness of the situation and underscored the Cuban authorities' obligations to protect Embassy staff and their families under the Vienna Convention."

The meeting was requested by the Cuban government

Gámez Torres stated the following: "From the outset, the Cuban government has denied responsibility in the attacks and allowed entry to the FBI to the island to investigate. But remarks by Rodriguez, considered a conservative in government, did not appear to alleviate the crisis. According to a previous statement by the Cuban Ministry of Foreign Relations, Rodríguez told Tillerson that according to the preliminary results obtained by the Cuban authorities in their investigation, which has taken into account data provided by the U.S. authorities, there is as yet no evidence of the causes and origin of health conditions reported by U.S. diplomats. The Cuban foreign minister also complained about what he called the unjustified decision of the U.S. government to expel two Cuban diplomats from Washington and added it would be unfortunate to politicize a case of this nature and to make hasty and unsupported decisions on inconclusive evidence and investigative results." The U.S. actions are sure to damage the ties between America and Cuba that only recently began putting their hostility behind.

This photo shows the Cuban embassy in Washington, D.C. The Trump administration expelled two Cuban diplomats from Washington, D.C. in May 2017 because Cuba had failed in its obligation to keep American diplomats safe. Strangely, Americans were not informed until several weeks later. Why?

Conclusion

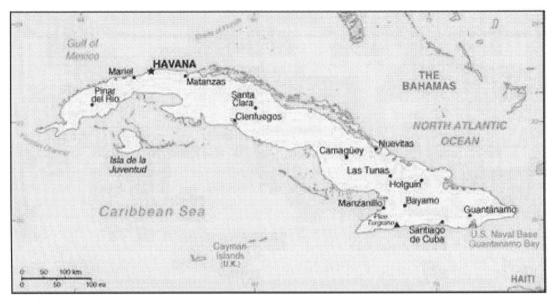

Map of Cuba showing the location of its capital, Havana, where up to 21 American diplomats and some Canadian diplomats were injured with sonic or ultrasonic weapons. American cruise ships visit many cities in Cuba, including Havana, Santiago de Cuba, and Cienfuegos, which bring millions to the members of the communist Mafia who runs Cuba. Over 200,000 cruise ship passengers will visit Cuba in 2017. How would these cruise ship passengers traveling to Cuba will be affected by the travel warning from the Department of State? And those who go to Cuba by air or private boats?

It is disconcerting to this writer why America has tolerated so much abuse from the mass murdering Cuban totalitarian regime for almost 60 years. Cuban thugs tortured and killed American pilots in Hanoi and Havana during the Viet Nam War. Cuban pilots flew Migs against American aircraft and a Cuban engineer brigade called Girón operated in the Ho Chi Ming Trail during that war. Cuba has sent tons of drugs to America over the years and Cuban intelligence agents have committed fraud in the billions of dollars against Medicare, Medicaid, and private companies. Cuban spies have penetrated the Departments of Defense and State, as well as the CIA. Cuba has been and continuous to be a center of world-wide terrorism.

Cuba has an Occupation Army in Venezuela led by generals and assisted by its intelligence services. Venezuela sends financial help to Iran's militia Hezbollah. Venezuela sends uranium to Iran, its close ally.

The fates of their communist regimes are interrelated. Venezuela and Cuba are national security threats to the United States and both are close allies of Russia and China. Venezuela and

Cuba are strong allies and both nations assist Islamic terrorist groups. There is a Hamas office in Havana.

Even now the United States has taken pains not to accuse Havana of perpetrating the sonic and ultrasonic attacks. Nothing in Cuba occurs without the permission of the late tyrant Fidel Castro and later his equally brutal brother dictator Raúl Castro. This writer agrees with the five prominent Republican senators who told Secretary Tillerson that "Cuba's neglect of its duty to protect our diplomats and their families cannot go unchallenged." This writer agrees with Senator Rubio that the United States should expel all Cuban diplomats from Washington, D.C. and that he needs to hold a hearing on the Department of State timely response to the attacks.

The FBI must conclude quickly its investigation to determine if the Castro regime was responsible for the 50 attacks on American diplomats. If it is determined that the Cuban regime was involved or tolerated a third country to attack American diplomats, then the Trump administration will need to consider all of the recommendations outlined by this writer which include breaking diplomatic relations with the brutal regime and implement regime change strategies. America should not tolerate such abuse to at least 21 of its diplomats and their families.

Today in Cuba there is more repression, beatings of peaceful opponents, and arbitrary arrests than before the restoration of United States diplomatic relations with the communist regime by President Obama. President Trump has severely criticized the enormous abuses of human and civil rights by the Castro regime. Upholding the Helms-Burton Law is crucial. Restating the important parts of the Helms-Burton Law is necessary and President Trump did it in his speech in Miami. The president stated the following: "We will not lift sanctions on the Cuban regime until all political prisoners are free, freedoms of assembly and expression are respected, all political parties are legalized and free and internationally supervised elections are scheduled."

If such a courageous regime change policy is implemented successfully by President Donald J. Trump, he would go down in history as the Liberator of two mass murdering communist regimes that have brought much suffering to their people and other nations in the world.

Chapter 28

The United States will withdraw from UNESCO

On October 12, 2017, the Department of State announced that the United States will withdraw from United Nations Educational, Scientific, and Cultural Organization (UNESCO) on December 31, 2018 citing bias on Israel as one of the reasons. The decision could be revisited. Why?

Farnaz Fassihi wrote an article titled "U.S. to Exit UNESCO, Citing Bias on Israel" which was published in the *Wall Street Journal* on October 13, 2017. The reporter wrote that the State Department said that the United States will withdraw from UNESCO, a move that could further strain relations between the Trump administration and the United Nations. The State Department said the decision to leave UNESCO "was not taken lightly" and reflects American concerns over the need for overhauls in the United Nations, as well as its "continuing anti-Israel bias." The withdrawal will take effect at the end of the year.

President Ronald Reagan withdrew from UNESCO in 1980 because it said the organization had become politicized. The United States rejoined in 2003. However, since 2011, it has withheld funds to UNESCO amounting to $542.67 million because of its decision to confer membership to the Palestinian territories. Israeli Prime Minister Benjamin Netanyahu said his country was also preparing to exit UNESCO "in parallel with the United States."

Nimrata "Nikki" Haley was born on January 20, 1972. She was named United States Ambassador to the United Nations. Previously, she served as governor of South Carolina from January 2011 to January 2017. Before her tenure as governor, Haley was a member of the South Carolina House of Representatives

Fassihi explained that after arriving at the United Nations, U.S. Ambassador Nikki Haley has criticized what she has called a bias against Israel both in the Security Council and at various U.N. agencies. She has said that the United States is reviewing its commitment to the U.N.'s Human Rights Council, citing concerns coming from issues related to Israel, Iran, and Venezuela and warning that the U.S. would withdraw from the Human Rights Council without changes. In July 2017, UNESCO designated the Old City of Hebron and Tomb of the Patriarchs as Palestinian heritage sites despite diplomatic efforts by Israel and political pressure from the U.S. to stop the designation. Ambassador Nikki Haley said that "The United States will continue to evaluate all agencies within the United Nations system through the same lens."

The U.S. has withheld nearly $550 million in funds to Unesco since 2011 because of its decision to confer membership on the Palestinian territories.

António Manuel de Oliveira Guterres was born on April 30, 1949. He is a Portuguese politician and diplomat who is serving as Secretary-General of the United Nations. He was the United Nations High Commissioner for Refugees between 2005 and 2015. Guterres was the Prime Minister of Portugal from 1995 to 2002 and Secretary-General of the Socialist Party from 1992 to 2002. He served as President of the Socialist International from 1999 to 2005. Like all previous Secretary-General of the United Nations, Guterres is a far left socialist politician.Notes: Data as of Oct. 5; Amounts due in € are reported using the constant rate of $1 = €0.869

United Nations Source: Unesco

Officials, including Secretary-General António Guterres, said they regretted the Trump administration's withdrawal from UNESCO. The communist Director General of UNESCO, Irina Bokova, expressed "profound regret" at the U.S. decision, calling it a loss for the U.N. family.

Fassihi pointed out that since Donald J. Trump became president, diplomats and U.N. officials have been concerned over U.S. disengagement from the world body and its pursuit of a more "America first" agenda in its diplomacy, rather than multilateralism. In his speech at the General Assembly in September 2017, President Trump praised the U.N.'s potential but said the organization needs widespread reforms to be effective. Fassihi stated the following: "The U.S. withdrawal from UNESCO continues a pattern of Washington reviewing and suspending international commitments and partnerships. The United States withdrew from the Trans-Pacific Partnership trade deal and the Paris climate agreement."

The *Wall Street Journal* wrote an editorial titled "America out of UNESCO" saying that the U.S. should not finance the anti-Israel U.N. agency. The editorial stated the following:

"The Trump Administration isn't known for public-relations savvy, and October 12 surprise announcement that the U.S. is withdrawing from the United Nations' main cultural agency is a case in point. The decision was still the right one. State Department spokeswoman Heather Nauert said the U.S. will leave the Paris-based U.N. Educational, Scientific and Cultural Organization, or UNESCO, on December 31 and become a non-member observer. She cited concerns with mounting arrears, the need for fundamental reform and continuing anti-Israel bias. Israeli Prime Minister Benjamin Netanyahu called the decision "courageous and ethical" on Twitter and said his country will also quit."

"For decades UNESCO has been a political agency masquerading as a cultural institution. The Soviets ran its education programs and its anti-American bent continues. UNESCO's current chief, Irina Bokova, is a Bulgarian with a Communist past who ran for U.N. Secretary-General with the backing of Vladimir Putin."

"In 2011 Ms. Bokova let the Palestinian Authority join UNESCO as a member state, triggering a U.S. law that prevents U.S. funding for any U.N. body that accepts a Palestinian state. UNESCO claims the U.S. now owes about $550 million in missed payments."

"In July UNESCO declared Israel's Tomb of the Patriarchs and other areas as Palestinian heritage sites, an act of political incitement. As U.N. Ambassador Nikki Haley explained Thursday, the agency has engaged in a long line of foolish actions, which includes keeping Syrian dictator Bashar al-Assad on a UNESCO human rights committee even after his murderous crackdown on peaceful protestors. Ms. Haley also wants to reform U.N. peacekeeping and has warned the U.S. may withdraw from the Human Rights Council absent reform. The UNESCO withdrawal is a good first step."

President Obama tried unsuccessfully to restore funding to UNESCO

On December 14, 2015, Adam Kredo wrote an article entitled "Obama Administration Moves to Restore Funding for Anti-Israel U.N. Organization" which was published in the website the *Washington Free Beacon.* Kredo pointed out that even though the funding for UNESCO was cut after accepting the "state of Palestine" as member nation, the Obama administration wanted to restore taxpayer's funding for this United Nations organization that has long been accused of having an anti-Israel bias, according to State Department funding requests obtained by the *Washington Free Beacon.*

The funding for this U.N. agency was cut in 2011 after UNESCO accepted Palestine as a member nation, an action that violated U.S. law barring the funding of any U.N. group that skirts the peace process by prematurely admitting Palestine as a full member nation. Kredo explained that the funding of around $80 million annually was cutoff. This brought "UNESCO to the brink of financial collapse and sparked further consideration of actions deemed by critics to be anti-Israel in nature."

Incredibly, but not surprisingly, given Obama's hatred for Israel and his ties to the Muslim Brotherhood, the State Department requested for a funding waiver in the 2016 appropriations bill that would allow the U.S. government to restart yearly payments of $76 million to UNESCO. The Obama administration also sought authority to give the organization up to $160 million to help erase outstanding debts. All various efforts by President Obama to restore funding to UNESCO were defeated in Congress.

UNESCO's anti-Israel bias was once again demonstrated when the U.N. agency tried to reclassify Jerusalem's Western Wall as a Muslim holy site. The U.S. was able to stop that move. Kredo wrote that the letter to the Senate by the State Department stated that "denying U.S. funds is weakening our role at UNESCO" and has "hampered our ability to safeguard both U.S. and Israeli interests."

Republican Mark Kirk served as Senator from Illinois from 2010 to 2017. On November 8, 2016, he was defeated in his bid for re-election by Democrat Tammy Duckworth.

Republican Senator Marco Rubio from Florida and Republican Senator Mark Kirk from Illinois stated the following in a letter to the members of Congress: "The proposed language would undermine over two decades of U.S. policy against funding U.N. organizations that admit the Palestine Liberation Organization (PLO) or other non-state actors as members. The proposed language also creates a deeply troubling precedent to other U.N. organizations, which seek to follow UNESCO's example and grant membership to non-state actors, may be encouraged to do so believing that the United States would eventually create another exception for them and restore withheld U.S. funding."

Republican Congresswoman Ileana Ros Lehtinen from South Florida also denounce the Obama administration's effort to restart funding for UNESCO. She said the following: "Secretary John Kerry has been pressuring the Israeli government to relent in its opposition to U.S. funding for UNESCO. It's a shame Secretary Kerry isn't using the full weight of his office to hold the Palestinian government accountable for their incitement violence and continued efforts to delegitimize and isolate the Jewish state at the U.N., while pursuing unilateral state recognition." Ros-Lehtinen pointed that U.S. law mandates that the administration continue withholding funding for UNESCO."

Communist Irina Georgieva Bokova, with the support of Barack Obama and Vladimir Putin, unsuccessfully tried to become Secretary General of the United Nations

Bulgarian communist Irina Georgieva Bokova, UNESCO head, tried unsuccessfully to become the United Nation's Secretary General in 2017. Georgieva Bokova was born on July 12, 1952.

On October 15, 2009, the General Conference elected Irina Bokova of Bulgaria as the tenth Director-General of the United Nations Educational, Scientific, and Cultural Organization (UNESCO). Bokova is the first woman and first Eastern European to be appointed head of UNESCO. In addition to her native language, she speaks English, French, Spanish, and Russian. She is married and has two grown children who live and work in the United States.

Bokova served for two terms in the Bulgarian parliament under the Bulgarian Socialist Party. She was appointed in 1996 as minister of Foreign Affairs and served one year in that post in the cabinet of Prime Minister Zhan Videnov. Later, she served as Bulgaria's ambassador to France and Monaco, Permanent Delegate of Bulgaria to UNESCO, and personal representative of the Bulgaria's president to the Organisation Internationale de la Francophonie from 2005 to 2009.

Irina Bokova is the daughter of the communist-era politician Georgi Bokov, editor-in-chief of *Rabotnichesko Delo*, the official newspaper and organ of the Bulgarian Communist Party.

Bokova graduated from the Moscow State Institute of International Relations. She was a member of the Bulgarian communist party until 1990.

Bokova's selection as head of UNESCO was criticized by many due to her past as a daughter of a member of the totalitarian communist elite. Bulgarian-born German writer Iliya Troyanov criticized Bokova's selection as Director-General of UNESCO in the German newspaper *Frankfurter Allgemeine Zeitung,* calling it "a scandal," in light of the communist past of Bokova's father as well as her own Communist Party affiliation. On the other hand, the *New York Times,* the voice of the Council of Foreign Relations (which is the invisible government of the United States), published an article supporting her nomination on the grounds that "She played an active role in Bulgaria's political transformation from Soviet satellite to European Union member." This, of course, is false!

Putin and Obama wanted Irina Bokova to head the United Nations. In June 2014, the Bulgarian government nominated Irina Bokova to be the official candidate of the country for Secretary General of the United Nations. Former President Obama and Russian dictator Vladimir Putin supported her since both of them share the same Marxist ideology and desire to create a planetary government where all nations would lose their constitutions, laws, courts, armies, and sovereignty. The UN bureaucrats would follow orders from the globalist elite who are members of the Council of Foreign Relations (CFR), the Bilderberg Group (BG), and the Trilateral Commission (TC). The powerful individuals belonging to these three globalist elite groups would be the masters and the rest of the people of the world would be slaves.

Alex Newman, a respected foreign correspondent of *New American* magazine and director of the anti-Communist organization *Bear Witness Central* (this writer is South Florida director of *Bear Witness Central*), wrote an article titled "Bulgarian Communist Is Now Frontrunner to Lead UN" which was published in *New American* on May 15, 2015. Newman explained that with the approval from the Obama administration, Bulgarian Communist Party operative Irina Bokova is reportedly the "frontrunner" to become the next secretary-general of the United

Nations. This radical woman, "whose communist roots run deep, is being promoted to lead the United Nations by the Western globalist establishment and totalitarian Third World regimes — even though she has close ties with Russia". The corrupt mainstream press is covering up her past and her communist views. However, Bokova's candidacy should be very troubling to all supporters of freedom and liberty, Judeo-Christian values, national sovereignty, capitalism, and free market economy. As already stated she did not become U.N. secretary-general.

Newman pointed out that the newspaper *Financial Times*, a well-represented publication at the Bilderberg Group meetings, published an article stating that the Bulgarian communist is well suited for the job. It said the following: "She certainly ticks many of the right boxes: heavy-weight U.N. experience, educated in Washington and Moscow, and a fluent French speaker to boot (without noting that her education in Moscow was at the mass-murdering Soviet regime's State Institute of International Relations). She is said to be acceptable to the U.S. and has been nominated by her own government, one of the few in the region that maintains cordial relations with Russia. Newman stated that the article explained the following: "The growing demands from emerging countries of the Global South for a U.N. that reflects twenty-first century realities adds a new factor to an already complex equation. The **old order is dying but a new one** has scarcely been conceived. Whoever ends up being tasked with responsibility for managing that change will need considerable skill to ensure that the UN is still capable of contributing to a peaceful, rules-based world order."

Alex Newman, an expert on the New World Order and the diabolical United Nations, said the following: "The scandal-plagued UNESCO organization, which is **seeking to become the global education establishment** and has **developed a World Core Curriculum to indoctrinate all of humanity**, was such a hot-bed of communists, criminals, dictators, Islamists, mass-murderers, and anti-American radicals that President Ronald Reagan withdrew U.S. membership in it." Bokova recently declared in an interview with state-run Russian media that "UNESCO was founded to promote the principles of humanism," without noting that humanism is fundamentally incompatible with Christianity and that it is, in fact, a direct assault on it.

On July 1, 2015, the United Nations Human Rights Council passed a resolution in Geneva, Switzerland calling the nations of the world to "monitor" and "regulate" non-government education. The resolution requests that nations throughout the world, which mostly are run by oppressive dictators, start to eliminate educational freedom under the guise of human rights. The UN resolution approved by the Human Rights Council to control all forms of private education violates the United Nations' Universal Declaration of Human Rights, which states in Article 26 that "parents have a prior right to choose the kind of education that shall be given to the children." Why is Pope Francis failing to complain about this arbitrary totalitarian resolution in Geneva by the dictator-dominated Human Rights Council since, if implemented, would negatively affect Catholic-run schools worldwide?

Newman pointed out that Bokova (similar to Obama) is also what is known as a "red-diaper baby" — a child born to devoted communist parents. Estimates suggest that the brutal Bulgarian dictatorship assassinated somewhere between 100,000 and 250,000 people — dissidents, Christians, and others. The real numbers could be even higher. Political science Professor Emeritus R.J. Rummel of the University of Hawaii put the death toll by the Bulgarian communists at around 222,000. Many more were ruthlessly tortured and persecuted.

Newman wrote that in spite of those atrocities, Bokova was an enthusiastic youth member of the Bulgarian Communist Party, later becoming an adult member and even serving in various capacities within the brutal dictatorship. Bokova continued with the Communist Party after it changed its name to the Bulgarian Socialist Party (BSP) following the apparent collapse of the communist terror regime. Newman said that, as *New American* writer and senior editor William F. Jasper explained, the name change of the Communist Party was primarily so "the communists could not only continue running Bulgaria as newly branded 'socialists,' but also benefit from the aid, loans, and investments being handed out by the United States and the European Union." The communists are still in charge today in that Eastern European nation that has close ties with Vladimir Putin's Russia.

Newman stated the following: "Bokova continues her involvement in the re-branded Communist Party, which is now part of the global tyranny-promoting Socialist International network. The alliance of communist and socialist political parties around the world regularly meets to demand global government, planetary socialism, and more. Recently, their annual Congress was hosted by the African National Congress-South African Communist Party regime, which has been linked by the world's top expert on genocide to promoting the extermination of an entire nation. In fact, its leader regularly sings songs, in public and in front of his military, advocating genocide against the embattled Afrikaner minority."

Newman pointed out that Rossen Vassilev, who served at the Bulgarian Mission to the United Nations in New York City from January 1980 until his defection to the West in July 1988, said that "Beneath Bokova unassuming exterior, she was a tough and loyal Communist apparatchik." It was explained that Bokova's stay in New York was cut short after the State Department rejected for nearly two years "the accreditation of her journalist-husband, Liubomir Kolarov, most likely because of his known association with Communist Bulgaria's spy agency, the DS."

Newman said "that those communists and criminals, most of whom were never punished for their crimes and murders after the alleged collapse of the Communist Eastern bloc, were the ones who nominated Bokova to lead UNESCO, and now, as secretary general of the United Nations. The *New York Times* has **emerged as a top cheerleader** for Bokova's aspirations."

Newman concluded his excellent article by stating the following: "The communist's bid is being celebrated as an opportunity to give Third World autocrats a bigger voice in global government as humanity is prepared for what globalists refer to as their **new, multi-polar world order.** However, with the globalist establishment on both sides of the manufactured East vs. West divide cheering for Bokova to lead the U.N., the scandalous effort may finally be enough to force the U.S. Congress to put its foot down. Americans should demand that the U.S. government completely withdraw from and defund the U.N. — and having an actual communist in charge might just serve as the catalyst to do that. For the sake of liberty, prosperity, and common sense, it is time for the U.N. to be relegated to ash heap of history."

Socialist United Nations Secretary-General Ban Ki Moon and UN Educational, Scientific, and Cultural Organization (UNESCO) Chief Irina Bokova, a long time Communist Party operative, appeared together at a meeting.

Alex Newman wrote an article called "U.N. and UNESCO Bosses to Join Communist Tyrants at Victory Day" which was published in *New American* on April 28, 2015.

Newman explained that Ban Ki Moon and Irina Bokova celebrated "Victory Day" in Moscow, Russia with Vladimir Putin. Russia invited the brutal North Korean dictator Kim Jong Un and the presidents of the Eurasian Union regimes. An estimated 100 Communist Chinese troops and even a contingent of Indian forces as well as thousands of Russian soldiers participated in the festivities. Western leaders did not participate in the celebration, citing, among other concerns, events in Ukraine.

This writer believes that Ban Ki Moon and Irina Bokova did not care at all about the Russian invasion and annexation of Ukraine's Crimean Peninsula and the continuing military aggression of Russia in Eastern Ukraine. This writer thinks that it was shameful for the current Secretary-General of the United Nations Ban Ki Moon and Irina Bokova to participate in Russia's 70th anniversary Victory Day festivity in Red Square.

Newman pointed out that this year's victory celebration, in what the Soviet regime called the "Great Patriotic War," was the largest ever. It involved approximately 16,000 Russian troops, 200 armored military vehicles, and 150 military planes and helicopters, according to news reports. A number of Putin's newest and most advanced military armaments were on display, covered in hammers and sickles, to show off the Russia's growing, modernized, and better equipped military. A total of 26 or more presidents and dictators, mostly from former Soviet puppet states, attended.

Newman said that last year Ban attended a G-77 plus Communist China summit in Bolivia pushing for what more than 130 governments and dictatorships called a "New World Order to Live Well." He stated the following: "Applauding the assembled rulers and their demands — global socialism, essentially — the UN chief declared: All countries need to act on these priorities, individually and collectively. That is how he understood the New World Order, he told the summit. Putin and Beijing, close allies, have both long been promoting what they call a multi-polar New World Order."

Newman explained that the victory of the brutal Soviet Union regime and its Western allies over Nazi Germany allowed Soviet bloody tyrant Joseph Stalin, one of the most savage dictators in human history, to enslave the peoples of Eastern Europe. President Franklin Roosevelt approved at Yalta the abandonment of the nations of Eastern Europe to the tyranny of the Soviet Union. The role of the USSR in defeating the Nazis was due in large part to massive U.S. military aid provided to the bloody dictator Joseph Stalin. Newman wrote that "The fruits of that alleged foreign policy blunder, of course, included millions more innocents murdered and enslaved, along with the eventual emergence of the Cold War."

Alex Newman ended his article by stating the following: "With U.S.-funded UN leaders brazenly consorting with some of the world's most brutal communist tyrants in Putin's communist-themed Victory Day celebration, Americans have yet another reason, as if more were needed, to demand a full U.S. government withdrawal from the dictator-dominated global organization. Under the Reagan administration, the U.S. has already withdrawn from UNESCO once over its anti-American extremism. Now, Obama's Education Secretary calls it a global partner of the administration in its cradle-to-career education reform machinations. It is past time to pull out of UNESCO and the entire planetary outfit once and for all." Achim Steiner, United Nations Under-Secretary General and United Nations Environmental Programme (UNEP) Executive Director, stated the following at the Rio+20 Conference: "World leaders and governments have today agreed that a transition to a green economy, backed by strong social provisions, offers a key pathway towards a sustainable 21st century." Dick Morris and Eileen McGann in their book, Here Come the Black Helicopters!: UN Global Governance and the Loss of Freedom (2012), described the statement by Steiner as a new form of global extortion and the first major step in "a global scheme to redistribute resources from the First World nations, whose industry and hard work has created them, to Third World dictators who can stash the money in Swiss bank accounts." The plan is for developed nations, which do not include China or India, to have a major transfer of wealth using the environment as an excuse.

The United Nations General Assembly elected Steiner Executive Director of the United Nations Environment Programme in 2006 for a four-year term. His mandate has been extended twice and will end in June 2016.

Achim Steiner, United Nations Under-Secretary General and United Nations Environmental Programme (UNEP) Executive Director, stated the following at the Rio+20 Conference: "World leaders and governments have today agreed that a transition to a green economy, backed by strong social provisions, offers a key pathway towards a sustainable 21st century." Dick Morris and Eileen McGann in their book, *Here Come the Black Helicopters!: UN Global Governance and the Loss of Freedom* (2012), described the statement by Steiner as a new form of global extortion and the first major step in "a global scheme to redistribute resources from the First World nations, whose industry and hard work has created them, to Third World dictators who can stash the money in Swiss bank accounts." The plan is for developed nations, which do not include China or India, to have a major transfer of wealth using the environment as an excuse.

Maurice Strong was involved in the Stockholm conference in 1971 that led to the establishment of the United Nations Environment Programme the following year. Strong organized the United Nations Conference on Environment and Development, known as the Earth Summit that was held in Rio de Janeiro, Brazil in June 1992. Maurice Strong, David Rockefeller, and other powerful individuals became members of the Club of Rome.

Maurice Strong

Isn't the only hope for the planet that the industrialized civilisations collapse? Isn't it our responsibility to bring that about?

- MAURICE STRONG

Secretary-General 1972 UN Conference on the Human Environment
First Executive Director of the UN Environment Programme (UNEP)
Secretary-General 1992 UN Earth Summit

The criminal Maurice Strong is a socialist who served as Undersecretary General of the United Nations. He is the so-called godfather of the environmental movement. Strong lived towards the end of his life in Beijing, China, where he taught at Chinese universities and advised the totalitarian Chinese regime. He died on November 25, 2015.

In 2005, Strong became involved in the investigation of the Oil-for-Food scandal of the United Nations. It was discovered that Strong, while working for the Secretary-General of the United

Nations Kofi Annan, had endorsed a check to himself for $988,885. Although he was not indicted, he resigned to his U.N. post. He then moved to Beijing, China, where he teaches at Chinese universities and advices the Chinese government. Should Maurice Strong and his socialist and communist friends at the United Nations and throughout the world be trusted?

In his illustrative and alarming article, Snyder explained that the U.N.'s sustainable development program is being given an entirely new name and the scope of its agenda is being broadened dramatically. The following is what **the official United Nations website** stated:

"The United Nations is now in the process of defining Sustainable Development Goals as part **a new sustainable development agenda** that must finish the job and leave no one behind. **This agenda, to be launched at the Sustainable Development Summit in September 2015**, is currently being discussed at the UN General Assembly, where Member States and civil society are making contributions to the agenda."

Snyder said that the core document for the 2030 Agenda was finalized. The following comes from the preamble of this document:

"This Agenda is a plan of action for people, planet and prosperity. It also seeks to strengthen universal peace in larger freedom. We recognize that eradicating poverty in all its forms and dimensions, including extreme poverty, is the greatest global challenge and an indispensable requirement for sustainable development.

All countries and all stakeholders, acting in collaborative partnership, will implement this plan. We are resolved to free the human race from the tyranny of poverty and want and to heal and secure our planet. We are determined to take the bold and transformative steps which are urgently needed to shift the world onto a sustainable and resilient path. As we embark on this collective journey, we pledge that no one will be left behind.

The 17 Sustainable Development Goals and 169 targets which we are announcing today demonstrate the scale and ambition of this new universal Agenda. They seek to build on the Millennium Development Goals and complete what these did not achieve. They seek to realize the human rights of all and to achieve gender equality and the empowerment of all women and girls. **They are integrated and indivisible and balance the three dimensions of sustainable development: the economic, social and environmental."**

Snyder pointed out the 2030 Agenda is not just a plan to fight climate change; this is literally a blueprint for transforming global society.

The following are 17 specific goals:

Goal 1 End poverty in all its forms everywhere

Goal 2 End hunger, achieve food security and improved nutrition and promote sustainable agriculture

Goal 3 Ensure healthy lives and promote well-being for all at all ages

Goal 4 Ensure inclusive and equitable quality education and promote lifelong learning opportunities for all

Goal 5 Achieve gender equality and empower all women and girls

Goal 6 Ensure availability and sustainable management of water and sanitation for all

Goal 7 Ensure access to affordable, reliable, sustainable and modern energy for all

Goal 8 Promote sustained, inclusive and sustainable economic growth, full and productive employment and decent work for all

Goal 9 Build resilient infrastructure, promote inclusive and sustainable industrialization and foster innovation

Goal 10 Reduce inequality within and among countries

Goal 11 Make cities and human settlements inclusive, safe, resilient and sustainable

Goal 12 Ensure sustainable consumption and production patterns

Goal 13 Take urgent action to combat climate change and its impacts

Goal 14 Conserve and sustainably use the oceans, seas and marine resources for sustainable development

Goal 15 Protect, restore and promote sustainable use of terrestrial ecosystems, sustainably manage forests, combat desertification, and halt and reverse land degradation and halt biodiversity loss

Goal 16 Promote peaceful and inclusive societies for sustainable development, provide access to justice for all and build effective, accountable and inclusive institutions at all levels

Goal 17 Strengthen the means of implementation and revitalize the global partnership for sustainable development

Snyder expressed his approval of many of those goals. After all, who would not want to "end poverty" or "halt biodiversity loss"? He stated the following: "But as you read through that list, ask yourself what forms of human activity would be excluded from it. The globalists want to use sustainable development as an excuse to micromanage the lives of every man, woman and child on the entire globe. We are told that individual liberty and freedom are "dangerous because when everyone just runs around doing whatever they want it is bad for the planet. For example, one of the goals of the sustainable development crowd is to push the human population into giant "megacities" (China is building a megacity of over 200 million people) and to allow nature to recapture much of what has already been settled by humanity."

Snyder wrote that an article written **by Dave Hodges presented** the following map, which comes **from America 2050** as one example of what the globalists want to do. It shows how the United States may look like in a few decades if the globalists have their way.

Snyder concluded his article by stating the following: "And of course this is just the tip of the iceberg. Eventually, the globalists want to fundamentally transform virtually everything about our society. This includes our economy, our government, our entertainment, our social interactions, our families and even our religious beliefs. So don't let all of the nice language fool you. This new universal Agenda is far, far more dangerous than Agenda 21 ever was, and it is a giant step forward into a **one-world system governed by bureaucratic control freaks.**"

President Trump decertifies Iran Nuclear Deal

On October 13, 2017, President Donald Trump declined to certify Iran's compliance with the 2015 nuclear agreement. Obama's Iran deal violated the Constitution since the Senate did not approved it with the 2/3 vote as required. Obama took the poorly-negotiated agreement to the United Nations first for approval as globalists wanted. He then asked Congress to approve it with a simple majority. The Iran deal was a treaty and needed the 2/3 vote in the Senate. The president also designated Iran Revolutionary Guard as a terrorist group and called for more sanctions.

Conclusion

This writer believes that the United States was correct in withdrawing from UNESCO since this U.N. agency is anti-Israeli and anti-capitalist. However, this writer would have liked an immediately withdrawal and not to wait until the end of 2018. Sadly, the United States, European Union, and Russia signed a treaty respecting the territorial integrity of Ukraine when that nation was asked to return all of its nuclear weapons as well as many of its conventional weapons to Russia.

The most powerful world elite made up of financial and banking interests and their political allies want the United States to surrender its sovereignty, wealth, liberty, and Constitutional Republic in the name of a phony environmental manufactured threat. But now the globalist elite and their servants, the bureaucrats from the United Nations, have created 2030 Agenda, a diabolical plan for an all-encompassing planetary government. In addition to addressing climate change, this agenda also includes ambitious goals in other areas such as economics, health, energy, education, agriculture, gender equality, and others.

This perverse global initiative is being billed as a **new universal agenda** for humanity. Some previous U.S. presidents, some globalists' politicians from both parties, and former President Barack Obama want to eventually move our country to the control of the United Nations by signing treaties that are against this country´s national interest. The future of the United States and its individual freedoms are in great danger! We must resist any and all attempts to take away our sovereignty and our liberty!

Goal 10, which is to reduce inequality within and among countries, is clearly a call to take the wealth of rich countries, such as the United States, and give it to the dictators of the world, such as the Castro brothers in Cuba, Putin in Russia, Jinping in China, and Islamic regimes, so that our national security would be enormously endangered. Additionally, it calls, as Obama constantly calls, for redistribution of wealth in the nation and the implementation of a socialist or communist regime. The other goals of the 2030 Agenda for sustainable development will micromanage the lives of every man, woman, and child on the entire globe.

Americans must demand complete U.S. government withdrawal from the United Nations, which is a dictator-dominated global organization backed by the globalist elite who want to enslave all. One should educate Americans and those in Congress, who are not part of the New World Order, so that they can fight arduously to stop the evil globalist elite who wants to take freedom and liberty away and destroy the U.S. Constitutional Republic.

Chapter 29

Stopping the globalists of the New World Order

The most powerful members of the globalist elite, which is made up of financial and banking interests and their political allies, want the United States to surrender its sovereignty, liberty, wealth, Constitution, and laws in the name of a phony environmental or other manufactured threat. Some previous U.S. presidents, including former president Barack Obama and some globalist politicians from both parties want to eventually move the United States to the control of the United Nations by signing treaties that are against the national interest of this country.

Not every individual who belongs to one of the three main powerful organizations of the New World Order is part of the Insider conspiracy. In fact, some of these individuals, who have later quit one of these organizations, have denounced the New World agenda. Others may have joined these groups to advance their careers in multinational corporations, international banks, the military, academia, or government. The diabolical members of the globalist elite who are running these organizations work in a circle within a circle. Often, they invite individuals to join these groups to disguise and confuse. These individuals are kept in the periphery and do not participate in the decision-making process of the organization.

The members of the globalist elite, who choose Obama in 2008 and 2012, selected Hillary Clinton as their candidate for the presidential election of 2016. All the newspapers in the nation, except for two, endorsed Hillary Clinton and tens of millions were donated to her campaign by Wall Street bankers. However Donald J. Trump won with a nationalist, anti-globalist, and

America First campaign. As previously stated, President Trump has named some globalists to the White House and to his cabinet.

John F. McManus wrote a book titled *America and the United Nations* (2013) where he argued for America's withdrawal from the United Nations. McManus compared the Declaration of Independence of July 4, 1776 and the Constitution of 1787 to the United Nations Charter and concluded that America's system of government is incompatible with the U.N. Charter and its push for a global government.

McManus explained that the Declaration of Independence thundered that "Men…are endowed by their Creator with certain unalienable Rights." After affirming that there is a God who grants rights to mankind and no government can take those rights away, the Declaration of Independence defines the purpose of government by declaring that is "to secure these Rights, Governments are instituted among Men, deriving their just powers from the Consent of the Governed." And what are those rights? They are "Life, Liberty, and the Pursuit of Happiness." And included in those rights was the right to own property. The Agenda 21 and Agenda 2030 of United Nations are an immense thereat to the right to own property.

McManus pointed out that the Constitution set up a government of limited powers for the federal government and to protect those God-giving powers, the Founding Fathers even added a Bill of Rights to ensure that government could not cancel what God has given.

McManus then said that that Article 8 of the U.N. Charter says that men's rights are granted "by the constitution or by law" and not by God. Therefore, what a government grants rights by some law is a government that can cancel them. He stated the following: "We conclude that governmental systems created by the U.S. and the U.N. cannot exist side-by-side. One will eventually triumph and the other will completely disappear. Contrasting the founding documents of our nation and those of the U.N. provides reason enough for withdrawal. But through examinations of other features of the world body provide more reasons."

On July 28, 1945, the Charter of the United Nations was approved by the Senate with vote of 89 in favor and 2 opposed. McManus explained that the senators never asked the following important questions: "Would membership in the U.N. lead to diluting, even abandoning, national independence? Would the world organization meddle in a nation's domestic affairs? Was there any possibility that the U.N. would have the authorization to use American forces in struggles not properly sanction by Congress? Would a powerful United Nations misuse its authority"?

Sadly, the United Nations has misused its authority and meddle continuously in America's affairs by demanding that the nation approve a series of treaties that would end or limit its sovereignty by taking away the Constitution, courts, laws, wealth, armed forces, internet, and so forth of the United States and other nations in the world. These actions have been fully explained in this book. This writer is in agreement with John F. McManus and many in Congress that the United States should quit the dictators' club that is the very corrupt United Nations. The General Assembly is an anti-Western and anti-Israel gathering of mostly Third World nations run by despots.

This writer believes that President Donald J. Trump is a patriot who wants to improve the economy, create jobs, and protect the national security of the United States. The president certainly is not part of the Insiders conspiracy. The members of the globalist elite are extremely powerful and President Trump may have to compromise at times with these individuals in order to survive. Obviously, if Hillary Clinton would have been elected president, it would have been the end of the United States as it is known today.

It is important to remember that a battle was won but not the war. There are continuous and daily attacks against President Trump by the New World Order-dominated mainstream media, which is aided by government officials of the so-called Deep State. The Deep State is well embedded in the federal government including intelligence agencies. It is an open question whether President Trump would be able to drain the Deep State of the swamp or the creatures of the swamp will take him out.

There are many ways how ordinary U.S. citizens can fight and try to stop or delay the agenda of the New World Order. One way is to share the information that is found in this book, The New World Order Threatens America and the World, or other books that have been mentioned by this writer in his book, with friends and family. Joining organizations such as the John Birch Society is another way to learn about communism and the Insider conspiracy to create a planetary government. Using social media is an effective way of sharing information on the Insider conspiracy.

Another way is to write new members of Congress to pass a law to withdraw from the United Nations or severely cut the American contributions to that corrupt entity, as President Trump promised during his campaign. In February 2011, 177 members of the House of Representatives voted to stop paying dues to the United Nations. This is considered by United Nations officials and supporters as essentially withdrawing America from membership in that international organization. Without American support, the United Nations cannot endure.

Such a withdrawal from the United Nations would certainly end any possibility that the world body would rule the American people or trample with U.S. sovereignty and liberty. The most terrible wars in modern history have been waged while the League of Nations and the United Nations have been in existence. Interestingly, from 1918 until today many leaders in several nations have insisted that more power should be given to these world bodies that want to create a global government.

On September 18, 2017, President Donald J. Trump participated in the "Reforming the United Nations: Management, Security, and Development" meeting during the United Nations General Assembly in New York City.

On September 18, 2017, President Donald J. Trump addressed the United Nations for the first time during a meeting called **Reforming the United Nations: Management, Security, and Development."** He praised the socialist Secretary General of the United Nations Antonio Guterres for sharing his vision of reforming the U.N. The president called on the United Nations Secretary General to slash the international body's burdensome bureaucracy and overhaul the "outdated" organization to better serve its member nations.

President Donald J. Trump stated the following: "I applaud the Secretary General for laying out a vision to reform the United Nations so that it better serves the people we all represent. We support your efforts to look across the entire system, and to find ways the United Nations can be better at development, management, peace, and security."

"In recent years, the United Nations has not reached its full potential because of bureaucracy and mismanagement. While the United Nations on a regular budget has increased by 140% and its staff has more than doubled since 2000, we are not seeing the results in-line with this investment. We seek a United Nations that regains the trust of people around the world. In order to achieve this, the United Nations must hold every level of management accountable, protect whistle-blowers, and focus on results rather than process."

"We must ensure that no one and no member state shoulders a disproportionate share of the burden; that's militarily or financially. We also ask that every peacekeeping mission have clearly defined goals and metrics for evaluating success."

The following day, President Trump gave a speech at the United Nations General Assembly. The president laid out his foreign policy which is rooted in his view of nationalism, sovereignty, and America First. He called for more burden sharing and cooperation among nations in the fight against Islamic terrorism, Iran's adherence to the nuclear accord, and the nuclear threat of North Korea.

Obviously, the president is not withdrawing America from the corrupt international organization. This writer hopes that the criticism of the U.N. by the president follows with a drastic cut in the U.S. funding for that world body.

President Thomas Jefferson

President Thomas Jefferson said the following: "My reading of history convinces me that most bad government results from too much government ... I predict future happiness for Americans if they can prevent the government from wasting the labors of the people under the pretense of taking care of them." Thus President Jefferson argued against a centralized and powerful federal government.

The future of the United States and individual freedoms granted to Americans by the Bill of Right and the Constitution are in great danger! Americans must resist any and all attempts to take away their sovereignty and liberty. Americans must also pray to God and ask that this evil globalist elite and their organizations do not succeed in enslaving them.